Understanding
The Dollar Crisis

UNDERSTANDING THE DOLLAR CRISIS

by

Percy L. Greaves, Jr.

With a foreword by
Professor Ludwig von Mises

The Ludwig von Mises Institute
Auburn, Alabama
2007

The Mises Institute would like to thank
Bettina Bien Greaves for her kind permission
to reprint this book.

To
Ludwig von Mises
whose contributions may yet
save our civilization

Table Of Contents

Foreword by Ludwig von Mises xi
Author's Preface xv

PART ONE

   I.   What Is Economics? 1
  II.   The Role of Value in Human Action 27
 III.   How Prices Are Determined 65
 IV.   The Effect Of Wage Rate Interventions 105

PART TWO

   V.   The Theory Of Money 141
  VI.   The Cause Of The 1929 Depression 175
 VII.   The Evolution Of The Present World Monetary
         Crisis 233

Index of Persons Cited 297
Index of Subjects 299

List Of Tables

Number	Subject	Page
I	Production Process (Assuming five processes)	35
II	Production Process, Interest Included (Assuming five processes)	38
III	Marginal Utility Scales	43
IV	Value Scale for Use of Six Bags of Grain	45
V	Simple Barter	72
VI	More Complex Barter	73
VII	Isolated Exchange	77
VIII	One-sided Competition Among Buyers	78
IX	One-sided Competition Among Sellers	80
X	Bilateral Competition (Problem Posed)	82
XI	Bilateral Competition (First Part of Problem Answered)	84
XII	Bilateral Competition (Second Part of Problem Answered)	87
XIII	Effect of Union Policies on Investment in and Operation of Steamship	124
XIV	Gold-Silver Ratios, 1792-1874	150
XV	Liberty Loans, 1917-1919	195
XVI	World War I Monetary Tableau, 1914-1920	196
XVII	Post-War Depression, 1920-1923	200
XVIII	Monetary Expansion, 1922-1924	202
XIX	Effects of Helping England, 1924-1927	208
XX	Average Annual Rate of Change, 1922-1927	223
XXI	Collateral Loan Data, 1922-1932	224
XXII	Development of the Crisis, 1927-1929	228
XXIII	Deflation, 1928-1933	236
XXIV	New Deal Pump Priming, 1933-1938	240
XXV	Unemployment and Production, 1933-1942	244
XXVI	World War II Monetary Tableau, 1938-1945	248
XXVII	Post War — Marshall Plan, 1945-1950	250
XXVIII	Korea and 1952	258
XXIX	Eisenhower Administration, 1953-1960	263
XXX	Some Key Monetary Data, 1953-1960	264
XXXI	Yearly Changes, 1961-1968	267
XXXII	Democratic Administrations, 1961-1968	269
XXXIII	Ownership of U.S. Government Debt, 1953-1968	270
XXXIV	U.S. Government Debt — Yearly Changes, 1961-1968	273

Foreword

The seven lectures that Professor Percy L. Greaves, Jr., delivered in June 1969 before the *Centro de Estudios sobre la Libertad* in Buenos Aires deal with the fundamental economic problems; they are about "human life," about "the ideas that motivate human beings," about "the most important and interesting drama of all — human action."

To us, mortal human beings as we are, the universe appears as consisting of two different fields or regions: the field of events human action is able to influence to some extent and the field of events that are beyond the reach of any human action. The line that separates these two regions from one another is not rigidly fixed forever. We know that in the course of history man has acquired the knowledge and the power to achieve things that to earlier generations had appeared as simply impossible. But we know also that certain things can never and will never be achieved by any human action, that man can and will never become omnipotent.

The history of mankind appears to us as the history of the progressive expansion of man's knowledge of what we call the laws that determine the course of all changes going on in the universe. But we do not affirm or assume or believe that this expansion of our knowledge will give to man one day something that could be called omniscience.

Man tries to learn as much as he can learn about the operation of the powers and factors that determine the mutual relations between the various elements that constitute the world, and he tries to employ this knowledge in attempts to influence the course of affairs. Man acts; that means, he tries to bring about definite effects. He aims at ends chosen. He is not, like the inanimate things and like the non-human animals, merely a puppet of the forces that have produced him and determine his environment. His endeavors to attain definite ends chosen are a factor cooperating in the emergence of the future states of world affairs.

II

The historical evolution of mankind's economic cooperation, which culminated in attempts — by and large successful — at establishing a world-embracing system of the division of labor and the international exchange of commodities and services, gave to the metal gold the function of a generally employed medium of exchange. It is idle to raise the question of what would have happened if such a thing as gold had not been available for use as a generally employed medium of exchange.

The gold standard made the marvelous evolution of modern capitalism technically possible. It led to the establishment of the modern methods of banking. But the businessmen who had developed them lacked the intellectual power to resist successfully the attacks upon the operation of the monetary and banking principles, the strict observance of which is absolutely necessary to make the system work and to prevent its catastrophic breakdown. If the determination of the quantity of money — the generally employed medium of exchange transactions — were subject to actions on the part of any individuals or groups of individuals whose material interests would be affected by changes in the purchasing power of the monetary unit, the system would not have been able to avoid a complete collapse. Neither inflation nor deflation is a policy that can last.

The eminence of the gold standard consists in the fact that geological conditions strictly limit the amount of gold available. This has up to now made the operation of a gold currency system possible.

III

These seven lectures are not merely a substitute for a textbook on economics. They are much more. They are an attempt to analyze and to explain the meaning and the effects of the various systems, methods, and measures of economic policies.

Ludwig von Mises

September 16, 1970

Author's Preface

The author of these lectures, born in 1906, reached his formative years in the Nineteen-Twenties. This was the decade of the great euphoria that ended in an economic collapse the like of which had never before been experienced by civilized men.

The decade started with almost universal hope that the world was finally entering the golden age of peace and prosperity forevermore. It boomed along to higher and higher heights of easy living. The auto, electricity, and the telephone, once luxuries for the few, became necessities for the many. Then, the decade ended with a depression that liquidated savings and left millions penniless and unemployed through no fault of their own.

With the advent of the Thirties, families, totally innocent of any wrongdoing, suffered unspeakable economic hardships with appearances of plenty all around them. On the farms, mortgages were foreclosed and families dispossessed from the homes of their ancestors. In the cities, jobless millions and their families became beggars for the means of survival.

The author's father came to this country in 1889, at the

age of 14. He had left Barbados, British West Indies, shortly after the death of his father, a plantation overseer. With only four years of schooling, the young immigrant took what jobs he could get. In 1904, he married a girl whose American ancestry went back to colonial days. Together, they worked hard for a quarter of a century to support their growing family.

In early 1929, it looked as though they were going to make it. The mortgage on the modest family home had been reduced. After forty years of employment, the father's job with a large steamship company seemed secure. The three oldest children were on their own. Only two more, one born in 1919 and another in 1920, needed to get through high school and become self-supporting. Then life would be easier.

However, the depression hit them in the spring of 1930. The father lost his job and could find no other employment. There were just no openings for unemployed men in their late fifties. The family's situation was pitiful. Unfortunately, their plight was typical of thousands of other New York City families.

The author of these lectures was the oldest son. He had been brought up on the gospel that free enterprise, free elections, and free perspiration paved the way to success. He had worked his way through college. Graduating *magna cum laude* in the spring of 1929, at the head of his class in business administration, he had the pick of jobs with many of the nation's most prosperous corporations. He accepted one where the prospects seemed bright. He was promptly enrolled in an ambitious junior executive training plan that promised him a raise every six months if he made the grade. Having majored in foreign trade, he had high hopes of spreading the glories of the American way of life to those benighted lands that still hampered business activity with trade restrictions, high taxes, and class distinctions that kept their people from moving up the ladder of success.

However, the depression brought a merger and soon the company had a surplus of experienced executives. The executive training program went out the window. The author survived another six months. He was given two months' pay and let go in the summer of 1932 — just weeks before the birth of his first son. Like his father, he could find no employment. With millions of older men walking from door to door in search for jobs, there were few openings for bright young men with little or no experience to offer. They were even rejected for low-paying jobs. Employers did not want to waste time breaking in those who would leave for more promising positions once the momentarily expected upturn arrived. But the upturn failed to appear.

Why, for long troublesome years, were so many, young and old, unable to find work at livable wages?

This gnawing question set the author off on a lifelong quest for an acceptable answer. First, he enrolled as a Doctor of Philosophy candidate in economics at Columbia University. Short of the desired degree, he was led by family economic pressures to accept a rare opportunity to work in Washington for the newly formed *United States News*. For two years (1934-36), he covered and reported the financial and economic upheavals by which the New Deal overthrew the traditions of our Founding Fathers. From Washington, he went to Europe as an executive for an American food company. There, he witnessed and experienced firsthand the ravages of Britain's mass unemployment, of France's *Front Populaire* with its sit-down strikes, and, last but not least, of the operation of Hitler's national socialist dictatorship in Germany.

All the time, he was searching for a logical answer to the problem of unemployment and misery among masses of innocent people eager for a chance to earn a decent livelihood.

Domiciled in Paris, he was paid in French francs. Within a short period his franc salary was raised 50 percent, but with the increasing French inflation and German monetary restrictions, he suffered a painful economic squeeze. Shortly before Munich, he resigned and returned to the United States to accept a public relations position with the nation's then largest life insurance company – a company which collected, invested, and made available, when needed most, the savings of millions of our fellow citizens.

The Federal Government was looking for new fields to conquer. Life insurance company assets were the largest private funds in the nation free from Federal regulation and control. The Temporary National Economic Committee (TNEC) proposed a new Federal regulatory body to supervise the assets that policyholders had entrusted to life insurance companies. The author was loaned to a life insurance industry committee to help prepare a rebuttal to this proposal. His research indicated that the high "cash surrenders" of poor families' insurance policies were not due to the alleged company pressure to sell them more insurance than their low incomes could safely support. In truth, such policy cash surrenders were due to the fact that the cash values of their policies were the only savings many poor families had to draw upon in times of financial emergency. If they had not had them to cash in, their lives would have been even more bleak.

His studies and experiences at home and abroad had confirmed his opposition to further government encroachments on the freedom of individuals in their personal and occupational pursuits of happiness. During World War II, he served as Research Director of the Republican National Committee, where he opposed the Administration's efforts to use the war as a cloak for the advancement of socialist measures. Early in 1945, when the Committee ceased its former opposition to the basic New Deal interventions and informed its employees that they could no longer work against public housing, Federal aid to education, or programs for socializing medicine, he resigned.

From the fall of 1945 to the summer of 1946, the author served as Chief of the Minority Staff for the Joint Congressional Committee on the Investigation of the Pearl Harbor Attack, and helped draft the Minority Report. Here, he learned how successful politicians are able to mislead the voters and keep their mistakes from public view. The following spring he served as Committee expert for the House Committee on Education and Labor. In this capacity, he attended all Committee hearings and helped prepare the first draft of what later became the National Labor Relations Act of 1947, more popularly known as the Taft-Hartley Law. For more than eight years (1950-58), the author served as Economic Advisor to the Christian Freedom Foundation and columnist for its publication, *Christian Economics*, at that time a fortnightly circulated to 200,000 Protestant clergy.

The author first became aware of Ludwig von Mises, the dean of free market (Austrian) economic theory, in 1944, when he read his *Bureaucracy* and *Omnipotent Government.* In 1950, he read Mises' great treatise, *Human Action*, for the first time. He has read it many times since. Shortly after coming to New York in 1950, the author registered for the fall term of the Mises graduate seminar at New York University. He continued as a regular and active participant until its last session, nineteen years later.

In the last twenty-two years, the author has developed a very close association with Mises. In the course of his studies, readings, and many conversations with Mises, he finally found answers that fully satisfied him as to the real causes of inflation, mass unemployment, and modern economic depressions. The Mises answers are very logical and most enlightening. If the public or its leaders could grasp their significance, the major miseries of our contemporary world would soon be greatly diminished.

During the last twenty-five years, the author has lectured widely to both private and academic groups. For several years in the 1950s, he presented a series of lectures at the Freedom School outside of Colorado Springs. From 1962 through 1967, he participated in the seminars of the Foundation for Economic Education, Inc. From 1965 to 1971, Mises and he formed the Economics Department of the newly created University of Plano. Mises usually gave the opening lectures, and then the author, as the Armstrong Professor of Economics, presented two courses of Misesian economics each semester. The author thus developed a certain facility for presenting the ideas of Mises in a language the layman can understand.

Early in 1969, Alberto Benegas Lynch, the president of Argentina's *Centro de Estudios sobre la Libertad*, invited the author to present a series of lectures in Buenos Aires later that year. The seven lectures that appear in this volume are the result. More and more people in many lands are now seriously worried about the monetary and inflationary problems of our time. Unfortunately, the pace of modern life leaves them little time for prolonged study. Many would like to get a satisfactory explanation in five or ten minutes, or at most in a single lecture. Unfortunately, the situation has become too complicated for that.

The study of money is at the apex of that mountain of human knowledge known as economics. To get to the top, one must first have a familiarity with what lies below it. The author thus contends that one must first understand the basic principles of human action and market processes before one can begin to comprehend the fundamental economic problem of our century. Unfortunately, these basic principles are seldom presented in the government-dominated school systems of our times. Our means of mass communication reflect the interventionist ideas of their unionized employees, who are legally privileged to block the employment of those committed to free market ideas. As a result, few people are familiar with such ideas. Accordingly, the first four lectures present basic elementary principles that must be fully grasped before one has a sufficient background to comprehend an analysis of our monetary problems.

The fifth lecture is an attempt to present in simple terms the free market theory of money. The sixth lecture is the longest. It analyzes the development of the 1929 depression from the viewpoint of Mises' Monetary Theory of the Trade Cycle. The last lecture brings that interpretation of monetary developments up through the events of 1968 and the end of the Johnson Administration.

Although the public prints and airwaves have devoted much attention to the inflation problem, there is seldom any mention of the basic underlying cause — the increase, by political manipulation, in the number of dollars, which are declared legal tender and must be accepted in payment of all debts and contracts. Most of the academic, political, and popular discussions dwell on the irrelevant pros and cons of proposed governmental fiscal and monetary policies, while ignoring the true cause of our troubles. Most steps proposed for ending inflation are just as fanciful as "the emperor's new clothes," in the famous tale of that name by Hans Christian Andersen.

For years, it has been generally assumed that governments

must manipulate the quantity of legal tender within the nation in order to maintain full employment and economic progress. It has been further assumed that they can do this and still have a free society. However, it is now being increasingly admitted that such debates over political policies of monetary management are actually debates over "how the government should manage the economy." It is thus slowly dawning on more and more people that all such policies are not the methods of a free society. They are, rather, the little understood tools of a government-managed economy. They were the tools that inevitably turned Hitler's National Socialism toward totalitarianism, war, and defeat. They can be just as disastrous for us.

On the late afternoon of November 14, 1968, New York University sponsored a "great debate" on *Monetary vs. Fiscal Policy,* between Professors Milton Friedman of the University of Chicago and Walter Heller of the University of Minnesota. There was an overflow audience and it was front page news in many papers. Printed copies were later sent to all economics professors with the suggestion that it was relevant for their courses as "a readable exchange between two of the nation's best-known economists who take contrasting views of *government's role in managing the national economy*." (Emphasis added.) Later that same evening, Mises' seminar met in a small room across the hall from the large main auditorium. It was early in the final teaching year of this great authority on monetary problems. Fewer than a dozen graduate students came to hear him. Such is the public blindness to economic truth — a blindness which is destroying our country's economic freedom.

At another seminar session, Mises was asked by a graduate student what he would have the government do during a depression. Mises replied in his quiet manner by presenting his free market position in a few well chosen words. The student, aghast, exclaimed: "You mean the government should do nothing?" Mises leaned back, as he frequently did, and said: "Yes, but I mean the government should start doing nothing much sooner!"

As Mises has written (1967): "Inflationism is not a variety of economic policies. It is an instrument of destruction; if not stopped very soon, it destroys the market entirely . . . . Inflationism cannot last; if not radically stopped in time, it must inexorably lead to a complete breakdown. It is an expedient of people who do not care a whit for the future of their nation and its civilization. It is Madame de Pompadour's policy: *Après nous le déluge.*"[1]

The policies of political money management have not brought the desired results. In short, they have failed, and the government has now moved, as Hitler did, into the direct control of prices and wages. The hour is already late. Those who are interested in preserving civilization and a free society would do well to take the time to read the lectures that follow. They present the problem and the solution from the long neglected free market viewpoint − a viewpoint which maintains that a free people should be free to choose their own money in the marketplace, even if they would choose GOLD. Before we succumb to a complete economic and political dictatorship, with its inevitable decline and fall of civilization, some attempt should be made to understand the processes of economic freedom, which have provided more people with the highest living standards ever known.

*   *   *

These lectures, originally presented in Buenos Aires, Argentina, were well attended. There were overflow crowds on all but two occasions. They were given *ad lib* in English and translated simultaneously for an audience provided with earphones. Both the English and Spanish versions were taped. Several of the lectures have already been published in Spanish and it is hoped they will eventually be available in a Spanish language book.

In closing, I want to thank each and every one who contributed to making these lectures a success, and particularly the members of the *Centro de Estudios sobre la Libertad* who sponsored them. I must also thank Mr. Prager, who, I am told, did an excellent job of translating them as they were given. Without him and the devoted activities of Sr. Alberto Benegas Lynch and his elder son, Alberto, *hijo*

---

1. *American Opinion*, March 1967.

(Jr.), who translated the questions, these lectures would have been impossible.

Needless to say, I owe undying thinks to my great teacher, Mises, who for years has put up with my everlasting questions in search of the answers I soon found only he could supply. It was he who gave me what understanding I have of these most important issues on which the future of civilization now hinges. I have tried to present his ideas as best I could. He is not, of course, responsible for the inevitable human errors that must have crept into my presentation.

Mises gave his last public lectures in 1970. It was my honor and privilege to travel and appear with him in three different parts of the country that year. On May 1st, a Seattle audience of 490 people gave him a standing ovation after hearing one of his best lectures ever on the twin dangers of inflation and a socialist dictatorship. Fortunately, this talk has been preserved on tape. Later, in the fall, when he was already in his ninetieth year, we presented two seminars on the monetary problem in the San Francisco area. In December, we went to Texas, where he answered questions from my students at the University of Plano for the last time.

By then, he had read the lectures which appear on the following pages. He had kind words for them, but in a private conversation in his Dallas hotel he chided those who first used the term "money supply." He pointed out that the word "supply" carries a subtle connotation of "the more, the better." Thus, the use of the term "money supply" carries with it the half-concealed suggestion that when a government increases the "money supply," it is providing society with more of the good things of life. Actually, an increase in the quantity of money does not supply more of the goods and services that people really want. It merely helps some at the expense of others, while upsetting the peaceful processes of a more bountiful free market society in a manner that makes a recession or depression inevitable. I took the hint and shall do my best not to use this misleading term in the future.

Last but not least, I must thank my beloved wife and fellow-student of Mises, Bettina Bien Greaves. Her understanding of and familiarity with the works of Mises, in German as well as English, has made her suggestions, contributions, and encouragement along the way most helpful. She has had the patience of Job and the indefatigable industry of a bee. In addition to her many functions as a Senior Staff member of the Foundation for Economic Education, Inc., an efficient housekeeper, a devoted daughter to a frail mother, and a dutiful wife, she transcribed these lectures from the original tapes and helped prepare and type the final copy for the publisher. She is solely responsible for the index. Without her help, cooperation, and persistence, this book would never have been possible.

Percy L. Greaves, Jr.

May 1972

Part I

What Is Economics?

It is indeed a great honor to be brought so many miles to speak to you here this week and next. I owe my thanks to Sr. Alberto Benegas Lynch and to the *Centro de Estudios sobre la Libertad.*

As he has said, I am a student of Ludwig von Mises. I consider him the greatest man of our century. If our civilization, the whole of Western Civilization, is to be saved, it will only be because his ideas come to be more generally accepted than they are today.

In this first lecture I have been asked to talk about the science of economics.

Economics: A Science of Means

Economics is sometimes thought of as a very dry and dismal subject dealing with dusty tomes of statistics about material goods and services. Economics is *not* a dry subject. It is *not* a dismal subject. It is *not* about statistics. It is about human life. It is about the ideas that motivate human beings. It is about how men act from birth until death. It is about the

1

most important and interesting drama of all — human action.

Since we must all be economists in one way or another, we all face the problem of how to become better economists in our daily work, in our family life, and as good citizens of our nation and of the world. The top educational problem of today is how to provide people with a better understanding of economics. All of our fundamental political problems, about which we have so many disagreements, are basically economic problems. Our prime problem is how to solve these economic problems. The best answers can be found only by resorting to the study of sound economic principles.

Many people think that economics is a matter of opinions. Economics is *not* a study of opinions. Economics is a science, and as a science it deals with eternal laws — laws that men are not able to change — laws that remain constant. If we want to improve our own satisfactions in life, we must improve our ability to know and use these laws of economics so as to attain more of the things we want. So, if the civilized world is to survive, people must learn more about this science of human action.

My great teacher, Ludwig Mises, called his great book *Human Action.* He reduces economic science to two words: Men act. From these two words he builds the whole science of economics. He points out that purposes direct all conscious human actions. We are not dealing here with the functions of the body that are performed without conscious guidance. We are dealing with the attempts of men to achieve the things they seek in life. This is what we are assembled here to learn a little bit more about.

In every act throughout our whole lifetime, we are always exchanging something we have for something we prefer. We may be exchanging our time, our energy, our money, or some other scarce good for what we want, but every one of our actions is an exchange — an exchange of something we have for something we prefer. We must learn to improve our actions if we are to get more of the things that we want in life.

The things we really want in life, both material and immaterial, our ultimate goals, are not chosen with the help of economics. Our ultimate aims and goals in life we choose ourselves. They are our decisions. We get our ideas of what we want in life from our parents, from our teachers, from our priests, from our philosophers, from our own thoughts and those of others who are in a position to help us make our own decisions on what we want. But we, each of us, know what is really important to us. No other man is capable of telling us what it is that we want or prefer. No dictator, no bureaucrat is able to tell us what we want. This is something we all decide for ourselves and which we alone know.

If we disagree among ourselves about what we want, we may come to blows. If the disagreement is important enough to us, we may attempt to settle the issue by combat. But most people agree on what is wanted. Our great differences are disagreements about how to go about getting what we all want. These are differences about means rather than ends. For such disagreements, economics provides the intelligent solutions.

Most of the people in the world want peace and prosperity. We want them, of course, for ourselves, our family, our country, and our world. Most of us realize that if we are to have peace for ourselves, our family, and our country, there must be peace for other people, for other families, for other countries. But when it comes to prosperity, there are great disagreements. Many people want it at the expense of others. There is, unfortunately, very little realization that if we are to have prosperity for ourselves, there must also be prosperity for others. Prosperity, like peace, is something that must be general — something that must be shared by all peoples.

So, we now get to the reason for studying economics.

Good Intentions Are Not Enough

The main objective of economics is to substitute consistently correct ideas and actions for the contradictory ideas and actions inherent in popular fallacies. Most people accept many of the popular fallacies that have come down over the years. In my next lecture I shall be dealing with one of the most important fallacies, if not the key fallacy — one that goes back to the days of Aristotle, and to which we owe many of our great difficulties. I shall then elaborate on the idea that many people have had, that the only fair exchange is an equal exchange.

Now the common man, the average man, any man, will change his ideas and actions whenever he is convinced that the change will better serve his interests. No man aims at failure. He always wants to use his available means in a manner that will bring him success in attaining whatever he wants most in life. This is true of all of us. There is no way we can avoid it.

Our job, and my job in particular, is to show that the science of economics, that is, the free market, rather than political intervention or socialism, will help all of us achieve more of the things that we want in life. So the better we understand the laws of the free market, and the better our fellow men understand them, the more successful we shall all be in attaining more of those things that each of us wants most in life.

However good our intentions may be, they can never make unsuitable means any more suitable for attaining desired ends. The world is full of people with good intentions. It is not only the people with bad intentions that we have to worry about. There are a few of them, to be sure, seeking power, seeking things which do not belong to them. Our great problem is the many people who have the best of intentions but who have been taken in by some popular fallacies.

Sometimes I tell a story to illustrate this point. It is about two American sailors in uniform who were spending a weekend in Stockholm. They had been brought up like most good American boys to go to church on Sunday. So they found a large Swedish church and went in. They found, of course, that the service was in Swedish, which neither of them understood. They took seats up front, behind a certain gentleman. They agreed between themselves that when this gentleman rose they would rise and when he knelt they would kneel. They would then worship God in their own way. This was all with the best of intentions.

Midway through the service, the gentleman in front of them stood up. So the two sailor boys in their American uniforms also stood up. The congregation then slowly broke into laughter. The boys were embarrassed and sat down. After the service was over, they spoke with the minister at the door. They found that he knew English. One of the sailors then asked him why the people had laughed when they stood up. The minister smiled, scratched his head a bit, and said, "I was announcing a baptism and I asked the father to stand." The boys had stood up with the best of intentions.

Many of us, like the sailors, do things when we do not know what we are doing. We do not know the results our actions will produce. We do not know how ridiculous they may make us look to somebody else.

So, good intentions are not enough, whether we are going to church, helping a neighbor, engaging in business, or even helping at home. The little child, trying to help her mother in the kitchen, puts her hand on a hot stove, and is burned. She is hurt just as badly no matter how good her intentions were. And so it is in life. It is not good intentions that count. It is reality. It is the fact that only correctly selected actions produce the results that you seek. What matters is not whether a doctrine is new, but whether it is sound.

The Future Can Be Changed

Men will neither seek nor support a free society until they are convinced that the voluntary cooperation of a free market can provide them with more of whatever they want than any other possible system of the division of labor.

This is the situation we face today. Many people throughout the world do not understand the operation of the free market society. They therefore ask for governmental intervention; they resort to force, rather than to the free and voluntary cooperation of the market place. They think they can get more from governmental intervention than from the free market.

Economics, as I have said, is about human action, and all life is human action. So what we are discussing is all life. Let me speak further here about these two words, human action.

To live implies action. Action implies choosing, that is, selection and rejection. Every time you select one action, you are rejecting all the other possible actions that you could take. When you decided to come to this lecture, you rejected the possibility of being in other places at this time. All of our actions imply a choice. We always take that action which we think is going to give us the greatest satisfaction. All action also implies change. It implies that the future can be changed. What we are constantly trying to do is to exchange something we have for something we prefer. We seek to change the future to the way we would prefer it to be. All human life is an attempt to change the future.

Some people sometimes say that they would like to know the future. For example, they would like to know what the prices are going to be in the stock market next week. Actually, we do not want to know the future. If you, or I, or anyone could know the future, this would mean it was set and we could no longer act to change it. All human activity is an attempt to change the future. We have a wide choice of actions that permit us to change the future. If we select the right actions for our purpose, we will produce the future conditions we desire.

All human action also implies imperfection. If we had perfection, there would be no reason to act – no reason to change the future. This means that if we had everything we wanted, there would be no reason to live. When the day comes that you have everything you want, let me know. I shall make arrangements to come to your funeral, because you will then be dead. So do not ever think that we can have perfection, or that we can have everything we want. Life is a series of choices of actions trying to improve the future, and the future always needs improvement from our point of view. Life is never perfect, but it is subject to change, and it is our hope that our actions will produce changes for the better rather than for the worse.

Human Actions Are Usually Unique

Every human action also implies a self-selected purpose. Every time you act, you have a goal, an end, in mind. This is implied whenever you act. You have chosen a goal and you are acting in an attempt to attain that goal. Every human action is an attempt to exchange something we have for something we prefer. I have said this before and I shall say it a number of times during the course of these lectures to try to drive home the point that that is what we are doing every time we act.

Now to go on with my definition of economics. Having stated that all life is human action, I state further that economics is a science of purposeful human actions. It is a science of means for attaining desired ends. It reveals the human actions that moral and intelligent men may take to attain their self-selected goals with the least use of their available time, energy, and scarce goods. My great teacher would say that, when I say "with the least use of their available time, energy, and scarce goods," I am being redundant, repeating myself, in that this is already implied in what has already been said.

As there is in this world no discernible regularity in the emergence and concatenation of ideas and judgments of value, and therefore also none in the succession and concatenation of human actions, the role that experience plays in the study of human action is radically different from the role it plays in the natural sciences. Experience in human action is history and only history. It is not like the natural sciences. It is never a situation that we can repeat with any assurance that we can always produce the same results. With new information, new facts, new associates, new knowledge, we react differently to the same situation; and, of course, it is impossible for us to duplicate exactly the same social situation.

Reason and experience show us that there are two separate realms: the external world of physical, chemical, and physiological phenomena, and the internal world, in our minds, of our thoughts, feelings, valuations, and purposes in life. There is no bridge connecting these two spheres. They are not connected automatically. We always have the right to choose our actions. Identical external events often produce different human reactions, and different external events sometimes produce identical human actions. We do not know why.

So, the science of human action is different from the physical sciences. We cannot experiment with human beings except in a physiological, medical, or biological sense. In the realm of ideas, we cannot experiment as we can in the physical sciences. We cannot duplicate situations in which all things are maintained the same as before. We cannot change one condition and always get the same consequences. We cannot experiment with human actions, because the world, its population, its knowledge, its resources are all constantly changing and cannot be held still.

In economics we must use our minds to deduce our conclusions. We have to say: Other things being equal, other things being the same, this change will produce such and such an effect. We have to trace in our minds the inevitable results of contemplated changes. We are dealing with changeable human beings. We cannot perform actual experiments, because the human conditions cannot be duplicated, controlled, or completely manipulated in real life like chemical experiments in a laboratory. Therefore, there are great differences between economics and the physical sciences. We cannot experiment and we cannot measure. There are no constants with which to measure the actions and the forces which determine the actions and the choices of men. In order to measure you must have a constant standard, and there is no constant standard for measuring the minds, the values, or the ideas of men.

Since we have great differences from the physical sciences, we have to use a different methodology. Economics cannot be empirical, because there are no constants and no measurements. For many years, people used to think that money or a monetary unit was a unit of measurement. I do not think that today, here in Argentina, you have to be told that the value of a monetary unit is not constant. So we do not have to deal with that problem. But there are people who do think it is constant. There are also people who think they can change the situation so that they can construct a constant, or some index number, which they think will measure the changes in the value of a monetary unit.

Science: A Search For Truth

Having spoken of some of the differences between

economics and the other sciences, I now want to speak about the characteristics that the science of economics, the science of human actions, purposeful human actions, has in common with all other sciences. Science always is and must be rational. It is the endeavor to attain a mental grasp of the phenomena of the universe by a systematic arrangement of the whole body of available knowledge. Science does not value. Economic science does not value. Science is always neutral with regard to values. Economic science is neutral with regard to values, but it provides acting man with all the information he may need with regard to forming his valuations.

Science is intent only upon discovering truth. It seeks to know reality. It is not dealing with opinions or value judgments. All science aims at tracing back every phenomenon to its cause. There will always be some irreducible and unanalyzable phenomena, some ultimate given, some a priori postulate beyond which you cannot go back any further. In all science, if it is "D" that you want and "C" produces "D," then you strive for "C." If you learn that "B" produces "C," you seek "B," and if "A" produces "B," you seek "A." You go back to "A." So that "A" gives you "B," which gives you "C," which gives you "D," which is what you want.

In science we go back *regressus in infinitum.* We go back to a point beyond which we cannot go back any further. This is true in economics as it is in every other science. In economics, human action is an ultimate given, and is one of the agencies capable of bringing about change. There are only two ways to bring about change. One is the automatic way of the physical sciences. We get in a car. We turn the key and it starts certain things moving automatically that can bring changes that we hope will make the car go. And if the car is in good working order, it will go. In human actions you have another agency for change, the purpose in the mind of the acting person. This purpose brings actions that produce changes, which the actor hopes will improve the future situation from his point of view.

Economics is the science which studies human behavior as a relationship between ends and scarce means that have alternative uses. Economics is a striving for efficiency in the use of means to attain selected ends and is essentially the theory of free enterprise.

A Priori Postulates

As I said, we go back as far as we can. Mises goes back to the two words, "men act." Everything in economics is contained in those two words. Because it is difficult for us to understand this, I have expanded these two words to what I call the three a priori postulates of economics, the science of human actions for attaining desired ends.

The first postulate is that *all men seek to improve their situation from their viewpoint.* This is what all of us are trying to do at all times. We constantly strive to attain something that improves our situation from our viewpoint. This postulate has been attacked by some who think it too materialistic. It includes, of course, the actions of men with materialistic purposes, but it does not apply solely to them. It also includes the actions of pure egoists, pure altruists, pure ascetics, pure sensualists, or – what is more likely – the actions of men whose purposes are a mixture of all of these motives. We all have some goals that may be ultra-selfish or ultra-altruist. What I am speaking of here is not actions seeking a maximization of monetary gains only, but actions seeking a maximization of those satisfactions we have selected from all the alternatives that were open to us.

Many of the things we want in life are not utterly selfish. Only a few months ago a brave young boy in Czechoslovakia laid down his life for a cause in which he believed. He thought he was giving it for freedom. His action was certainly not selfish or materialistic.

Many of us do many things for other than purely selfish purposes, but we always seek to improve the future situation from our viewpoint. Who gets the most satisfaction on Christmas morning, the children or the parents? These things you cannot measure. Is a man selfish when he buys life insurance to take care of his loved ones after he is gone? No! We do many things by which we seek to improve the future situation in many ways that are not purely or overly selfish.

Let us remember that the human satisfaction that we seek

is the most immaterial thing there is in the world. Nonetheless, we always have ultimate goals in all our acting. We are always seeking something that we want.

Even the criminal, when he commits a crime, is choosing an action which he thinks is best for him from his point of view. Let us remember that so-called materialism includes the wages of priests and musicians, the prices of art, concerts, and books on philosophy. The human satisfaction that all men seek is the most intangible thing in the world. It is not necessarily materialistic, although, of course, the material is included in the scope of this first postulate. I am not saying how I want it to be, nor how I think it should be. I am discussing a science, a search for the truth, reality. This is the way men are. This is what men do. This is why men act – to improve the future situation from their point of view.

Now the second of these postulates, which I hold are a priori and therefore evident to all men, is that *the factors available for improving men's situations are scarce.* This is a fact in the world. Long before Adam Smith wrote his great book, *The Wealth of Nations,* in 1776, it was known by all that nature, unassisted by man, is niggardly. There are not enough desirable things in this world to provide all of us with all we want. This poses the economic problem. Men have unsatisfied wants, and there are not enough of the things they want available for satisfying all their wants. So some of us have to go without many of the things we want, and all of us have to go without some of the things we want.

When I say things are scarce, I mean they are scarce in relation to men's wants. There is no quality in things that makes them economic goods except their relationship to the satisfaction of some human want. We say good eggs are scarce. There are not enough to satisfy the human demand for eggs. Eggs are economic goods and we have to pay for them. Some must go without all the eggs they want. There may be even fewer bad eggs, but we do not say that bad eggs are scarce. One bad egg is usually more than we want. Economic scarcity is always in relation to human wants. This is the important thing.

Before I go on with the third and last a priori postulate, let me give you this economic fact: TANSTAAFL. This is a series of letters that was popular in the United States during the New Deal days when everything was represented by alphabet letters. In English these letters stand for the words, "There ain't no such thing as a free lunch." This is a fact of life. If someone gets a free lunch, somebody else pays for it.

Going on to the third postulate: *Men make mistakes.* What we are all trying to do is to reduce our mistakes. Our aim here in studying economics is to replace the fallacies that we hold, many of which are popular, with economic truths — that is, we seek to reduce our very human errors.

All economics gets down to these three postulates. We seek to improve our situation with our limited means for doing so, and in our actions we make mistakes. I shall be dwelling on applications of these three postulates all through these lectures.

Men Seek Satisfaction

The burden of our time is that we do not know or realize what we are doing. Just like those two sailor boys in the Swedish church, we do things which produce consequences that we do not intend to produce. This is true of all of us. Our problem is how best to improve our situation. Perhaps the most general inconsistency of our time is the conflict in our market actions. *As consumers*, "we" buy the things we want at the lowest price we can find. By so acting we reward those who are most efficient in producing the things that we want. *As producers, as sellers*, and particularly *as members of labor unions*, "we" choose security and high prices and strive to protect inefficiency. These contradictory policies frustrate each other. They lead to split situations and split personalities. Economics brings the answers, the knowledge of means which are consistent with the desired ends. Actually, today, if we continue pursuing the policies we are now pursuing throughout the Western world, we shall bring an end to peace, and, if we do not change our present policies for better ones, we shall bring an end to the lives of millions of people now on earth.

Now, the vital question is: Are these assumed postulates right, or are they wrong? I hold that they are right. I hold that every man has to agree that in choosing his purposeful actions he seeks to improve the future situation in a way he expects will provide him a better future than if he chose any other actions open to him at that time. He has scarce goods. He has scarce time. He has scarce energy. He uses these scarce factors to produce more of those things high on his scale of values, and he makes mistakes.

Now, for this study of economics you do not need an expensive apparatus. All you need is to use that small space which is subject to the greatest unemployment in the world today: the short space between your two ears. Economics, like logic and mathematics, is a display of abstract reasoning. What we need is to use our minds intelligently and to think clearly in facing our problems. We need to look at them without bias. We need to know whether the actions and policies we choose are fit to accomplish what we seek. *The first thing necessary to correct an error is to discover it, the next is to admit it, and the last is to avoid it.*

Economics is concerned with the simple law of human nature that man strives to attain the maximum of satisfaction with the minimum of sacrifice. Human action is purposive. It always intends to increase human satisfaction. A free and unhampered market economy tends to produce or provide us with the highest possible human satisfactions. This is what I hope to show during the lectures which follow.

The purposefulness of human action is a category to which nothing in the physical sciences corresponds. The actions of nature have no purpose, except when men direct them. If there is a purpose in the actions of a tree growing, it is a purpose of the Deity. It is God who determines the purpose, if any, of the actions of nature. We learn the innate actions of nature by studying the physical sciences. Then, we can use them intelligently for our own purposes.

The Deduced Postulates

Going on from the three a priori postulates, we come to the deduced postulates. These flow from or are deduced from the a priori postulates. The first one, as stated here, is that *all*

men are rational beings. That is, we use our God-given minds
to attain our objectives. We always aim at success.

It is very popular to call someone else "irrational."
Scientifically, the only people who are irrational are people
who are out of their minds, people who are crazy. People
make mistakes. Yes, but they always choose the means which
they think are most likely to attain the ends they seek. They
never aim at failure. Their reasoning may be wrong, but it is
their best reasoning. If we want to call somebody else's
reasoning irrational because it is mistaken, we had better be
careful, because that means that anyone who makes a
mistake is irrational. We all make mistakes, and therefore, by
this line of reasoning, we are all irrational.

Our first great President of the United States, George
Washington, when he was on his death bed, was surrounded
by some of the best medical doctors obtainable. These
doctors decided that to prolong his life the best thing they
could do was to let out some of his blood. They did so, and
he died promptly. Today, if a doctor did that, we would call
him a murderer. But would you have called those doctors
irrational then? No. They were using their best reasoning.
The best reasoning of the most intelligent men is often
faulty. We are all always acting to attain success in whatever
we are trying to do. In this sense, all men are rational. We are
all attempting to improve our situation from our point of
view, and we are using our minds to our best ability with
what we know at the time.

The second deduced postulate here is that *all human
actions take time.* This seems perfectly obvious, that everything we do takes a certain amount of time, and our time is
capable of alternative uses. I shall not dwell on this at great
length now. I'll speak more about it in the next lecture. I do,
however, want to mention that the socialists forget to take
this fact into consideration. They do not take time into their
consideration of costs. The payment for time is interest, and
they ignore interest. In fact, many tax officials in the United
States consider interest to be "unearned income." There
are people, including the socialists, who want to abolish
what they call "unearned incomes." They do not realize
that they are suggesting an end to the payment for time,

which is a necessary factor in every human effort.

Next, *all human actions have consequences*. We, of course, would not act unless we thought we were going to produce a consequence that we preferred over the consequences that we could produce by any other action or non-action that we could choose. This involves means and ends. It involves cause and effect. Men's minds hold this idea of cause and effect. If we did not expect our actions to have consequences, there would be no reason to act.

There is a prime cause that we cannot ever know, because no man can conceive of something being created out of nothing. We know that everything we create has to come from some preceding good or action. We are always acting with this in mind. As mentioned earlier, there are only two ways to produce change: the purposeful actions of men and the mechanical actions of the physical sciences — physics, biology, chemistry, and other sciences that we call the natural or physical sciences. All human actions have consequences. It is not good intentions that decide the consequences. It is whether the doctrine is sound, whether it works. It is not whether I like it, nor whether I say it should be so, nor whether Mises says it should be so. It is solely a question of whether or not the chosen action will produce the desired consequences.

Choices Have Prices

Economics attempts to deal with reality and provide the means to help us attain the consequences that we desire. If we are going to attain them, we have to learn the actions that will produce the desired results. This always involves the sacrifice of something. There is a cost for everything we do. This means that every hur .an action has its economic aspect. When we choose one thing, we have to do without certain other things that we cannot have simultaneously. This is the economic aspect of choice: using our scarce means in the best way we know to produce the results we want most. This is the economic problem.

A technical problem exists when you have only one end and you want to know the best means to attain it. An economic problem exists when you have more than one end and must choose one or another from those that are open to you, recognizing that if you choose one you must go without certain others. It is not intelligent to want something without realizing and being willing to pay the cost. One of the great problems in the world today is that so many people want something for nothing, or something at the expense of others. We do not really want anything until we are willing to pay the full cost, or accept the consequences.

Going on to the next deduced postulate: *Men choose those actions they believe will best improve their situation.* Like the other postulates, this is, of course, a truism. It is not how I want it to be, nor how I say it should be. It is how men act. They choose actions which they believe will best improve their situation from their viewpoint. Now, their actions may try to improve somebody else's situation. They may get a satisfaction out of helping others or advancing a cause, as our friend Señor Benegas Lynch gets satisfaction from bringing speakers to you who strive to advance the cause of *la libertad* (liberty).

Importance Of Theory

We all want things that are not necessarily essential, but *we always choose those actions which we think will best improve the situation from our viewpoint. This means that the ideas that men hold determine their choice of actions. This means that the most important thing in the world is ideas.* John Locke, the philosopher, once said, "I have always thought that the actions of men were the best interpreters of their thoughts." Böhm Bawerk, the teacher of Mises, said, "I cannot profitably discuss the 'practical' side of the subject until there is a complete clarity with respect to the theoretical side."

We hear a lot of disparaging remarks about theory or about something being theoretical. This is unfortunately so, because so many of the economic theories that have guided people in recent years have been bad theories — theories that do not work. Consequently, we seem to look down on theory and seek what is "practical." Actually, it is not a question of theory versus practice. It is good theory versus bad theory. The disparagement of theory is unfortunate, because it is theory that motivates us all. It is ideas that guide all our actions. Let us remember that you cannot shoot ideas. The only way you can stop bad ideas is by satisfying their holders that other ideas are better – that is, more effective for attaining their objectives. What we need in the field of economics more than anything else is better ideas, ideas that stand up, ideas that work, ideas that cannot be successfully challenged.

The conclusion to be drawn from these additional postulates is that the ideas men hold determine their actions. The great problem, then, is to hold the right ideas. Sound theory is most important. We never act without a theory. We never act without an idea that the selected action will improve our situation from our point of view. This is what economics is all about, the freedom to choose our actions. The essence of freedom is that people be free, not only to select their actions, but also to deviate from traditional ways of thinking and acting, so that they may plan for themselves rather than have an established authority plan for them and prevent them from planning in their own way.

We all gain from the planning and the freedom of others. Many of us are using things that we ourselves could not invent or produce. I flew down here in a jet airplane. I have no way of knowing how to make a jet, and yet I benefit from the freedom of the people who made it. We all benefit from the freedom of the people who made the earphones that most of you have on today.[1] We all benefit from the freedom others have enjoyed. Many inventors in days past had their difficulties. We benefit from Mr. Gutenberg's freedom, which produced the invaluable printing press, so misused by national treasuries today.

So freedom is important to us not only for our own use, but also for our use of the products of the freedom of others who can improve our situation. Those of us who live in today's age have the highest standard of living that men have ever had in life on this earth. I was last down here in

1. These lectures were simultaneously translated into Spanish for those who did not understand English.

Argentina in 1925 as a young man. I have seen a great many changes in the forty-four years that have passed. Many of these changes have been brought about by people in your country and many by people outside your country. We have all advanced our standard of living because those people had the freedom to invent and to produce in new ways and did not have to stay with the ways of yesteryear.

The problem in economics is one of feeding into the human mind the right ideas, the applicable assumptions, and then thinking straight, thinking soundly with the data we have. The job of the economist is to recognize the decisive causal chains within the tangles of given data. As there are changes in the data, changes in the means available, changes in the things we want, we have to have new ideas, new thoughts, new solutions.

Applied economics consists of propositions such as, "If you want this, then you must do that – if such and such is the ultimate good, then this is clearly incompatible with it and you must drop it out."

Keynes On Ideas

Now I shall quote from a gentleman with whom I do not always agree. In fact, I disagree with him rather basically in many ways. However, I am in agreement with this statement that the late Lord Keynes wrote on the last page of his *General Theory*[2] : "The ideas of the economists and political philosophers, both when they are right and when they are wrong, are more powerful than is commonly understood. Indeed the world is ruled by little else. Practical men, who believe themselves to be quite exempt from any intellectual influences, are usually the slaves of some defunct economist."

Going out of the quote, early this year, the London *Economist* reported that Lord Keynes is now a "defunct economist."

Continuing the quotation: "Madmen in authority, who hear voices in the air, are distilling their frenzy from some

---

2. John Maynard Keynes, *The General Theory of Employment, Interest and Money* (Macmillan & Co., Ltd., London, 1936).

academic scribbler of a few years back. I am sure that the power of vested interests is vastly exaggerated compared with the gradual encroachment of ideas. Not, indeed, immediately, but after a certain interval; for in the field of economic and political philosophy there are not many who are influenced by new theories after they are twenty-five or thirty years of age, so that the ideas which civil servants and politicians and even agitators apply to current events are not likely to be the newest. But soon or late, it is ideas, not vested interests, which are dangerous for good or evil."

Many of the ideas that people practice today are the ideas of Karl Marx, although very few of the people who practice them realize it. They do not understand that the problem is one of getting the right ideas, ideas that work, and that good intentions are not enough.

Logical thinking and real life are not two separate orbits. Logic is for man the only means he has to master the problems of reality. What is contradictory in theory is also contradictory in reality. Man must fight error by exposing spurious doctrines, by expounding the truth. The problems involved are purely intellectual. We have to repeat the truth again and again and again, because those who expound fallacies are repeating them again and again and again.

Human Action

We always aim at success. The logic with which we think is the logic with which we act. Reason and action are two aspects of the same thing. Action is an offshoot of reason. We start with an end in mind and eliminate all possible actions not consistent with it. What remains, if anything, is the action we take, and we hope that this will produce the situation that we prefer.

In closing, I repeat what I said earlier, that however good our intentions may be, they can never make unsuitable means more suitable for obtaining our desired ends. What matters is not whether a doctrine is new, but whether it is sound. Bad ideas can be killed only by showing men that new and better ideas will advance them further toward whatever it is they want. Those who are interested in having a free society and a free world have to realize that men will not seek and support a free society until they are convinced that the voluntary cooperation of a free market can provide them with more of whatever they want than any other possible system of the division of labor.

The main reason for studying economics is to substitute consistent, correct ideas for the inconsistent, fallacious ideas so popular among the uninformed. As Henry Hazlitt says in his great little book, *Economics In One Lesson*, before acting we should consider all of the inevitable results of the proposed action. What we need more than anything else in this world is sound economic thinking. If we start with a correct assumption, and proceed with sound logic, we will attain the results at which we aim with a minimum sacrifice of our limited and therefore valuable time, energy, money, and other scarce goods.

QUESTIONS AND ANSWERS

We have some time for questions. We ask that you stay within the subject of the lecture. The question and answer period following the last lecture will be open to any question that I may be able to answer.

What I have tried to say in this lecture, of course, is that we all aim at success. Our problem is learning how to attain that success. In the next lecture I will be speaking on "value," the great errors that exist in that field, as well as the best ideas known to man.

Henry Hazlitt, who has spoken here, has written a great book, *Economics in One Lesson*, which I believe is available in Spanish. That one great lesson is that we should look at all of the inevitable effects that must flow from any proposed action. Too many of our people look only at the short-run effects, or the effects on one group, and not at the effects on other groups or the effects on the long run. I hope I have made myself clear and that you understand me. I have tried to state the situation, as far as I have gone, in a way with which I do not think honest men can disagree.

Why A Free Market?

Q. Why must we be convinced that a free market is the best way to obtain more of what we want ?

A. If we believe in freedom and we want to persuade others to believe in freedom, we have to show them that freedom will get them more of the things they want. How long could any of us live on what we ourselves produce? We have a high standard of living because of the division of labor, because we cooperate in helping each other. We are not like animals in a forest, fighting each other. We cooperate. It is because other men want the same things we do that we can have mass production at low cost, and mass production means mass consumption.

What would it cost us if each of us had to produce his own automobile? It is social cooperation that increases the production of the things that consumers want. Most people do not understand that it is only under freedom that they can have more of these things. It is the job of those of us who understand this, those of us who want freedom, those of us who want more things, to convince others that this is the best way. The benefits of freedom cannot be enjoyed without general agreement. Now in the physical sciences, one person can make something by himself that is better than what was previously available and gradually convince a few people that it is better. But in the field of human action, we have to have majority agreement before we can change our system or improve our laws. We must have agreement. So, if we are going to get agreement, if we are going to move toward freedom, if we are going to move toward peace, if we are going to move toward prosperity, we must convince the majority of people of the best way to attain these things they want. They do not disagree on the ends. They disagree on the means. They think that they can get more of the things they want by taking them from someone else. We shall discuss this further in the next lecture.

Is Keynesianism Defunct?

Q. What is the present status of Keynesianism and why did you say it was defunct?

A. First, let me make a correction. I did not say it was
defunct. It is not defunct. I said that the London *Economist*
said Keynes is now a "defunct economist," that is, he is dead.
But his ideas are still alive. The quotation was, "Practical men
who believe themselves to be quite exempt from any
intellectual influences are usually the slaves of some defunct
economist." My aside remark was more to the effect that
many of us today, and many unfortunately in positions of
political power, are the slaves of Mr. Keynes. Some of us are
also slaves of the thinking of Marx, who is certainly defunct
physically. What this says is that their ideas live on when the
men have passed away. The ideas of Marx live today and the
ideas of Keynes live today. We will be dealing with Keynes in
future lectures, particularly when we get into the monetary
phase.

Is Freedom The Same?

Q. Is the freedom of the inventor who invents the plane the
same as the freedom of the man who produces the plane, and
the same as the freedom of the person who uses the plane?

A. First, let me say that freedom is indivisible. You cannot
lose a part of your freedom, the freedom of speech, the
freedom to buy, the freedom to print, without eventually
losing all of your freedom. Of course, all freedom is based on
economic freedom. Freedom is indivisible. No one man
invented the airplane. It took many, many men to invent
today's jet. It took a lot of history, a lot of just minor
improvements.

My great teacher, Mises, asks, "What is the automobile of
1969?" He answers his own question: "It is just the
automobile of 1909 with thousands upon thousands of minor
improvements." Everyone who suggested an improvement
did it with the hope that he would make a profit. Many made
suggestions that fell by the wayside. But it was the freedom
of those men to work on improving the automobile that
has given us the automobile that we have today. No one man
invented it, neither did one man produce it.

It takes a roomful of plans or specifications to make a jet

airplane. It takes men of many different talents. As one of the speakers brought here before you many years ago, Leonard Read, has said, no one man can make even such a simple thing as a pencil. There is not a man alive who can take it all the way from the original raw materials to the finished pencil with its eraser. There isn't a man alive who could make a jet plane. It takes the cooperation of hundreds, possibly thousands. We who want to use the jet need freedom for them, so that we may use our freedom to use the production of their minds, while they are striving to help themselves by helping us. Some of this we will get into in our next lecture.

On Defining Economics

Q. Isn't it better to define economics as a means of voluntary peaceful cooperation? Isn't that better than defining it as maximizing benefits and minimizing costs?

A. I do not see any conflict. What I have tried to do is to explain the same thing in different words. The free market is a peaceful voluntary cooperation. We shall be discussing that in the next two lectures. The free market economy is the actual application of the Golden Rule; we help others as we help ourselves. As we help others more, we help ourselves more. As we help ourselves more, we help others more. This will come out rather clearly, I think, in the third lecture.

How Is Freedom Spread?

Q. What is the best way to extend the ideas of freedom?

A. You have had Leonard Read here. One of his great contributions is on this matter of methodology. As I have tried to stress tonight, the most important thing is ideas. As I have said, you cannot shoot ideas and you cannot jam them into another person's mind. Men have to be ready for ideas. They have to want them. They have to know where they can get them. We have a great responsibility for ourselves, our loved ones and our own families. Our problem is to learn more about freedom ourselves, to the extent that others will come and ask us. In that way we can spread the word.

We cannot go around using force to impose our ideas on others. It has to be done by education. Education is possible only when the people to be educated are willing, when their minds are open. Then, they have to see, hear, or read the right things. We have to make these materials available for the people who want them. This, I believe, is one of the great services that our friends here at the *Centro de Estudios sobre la Libertad* are providing to you by sponsoring these lectures. I am sure they have publications that will help you to obtain a better understanding, and help other people when they want to know more about *la libertad.*

Do Ideas Always Precede Action?

Q. Do ideas always precede action?

A. I said that ideas precede action. We do not always have time to study a problem before action is required. Of course, ideas are formed in advance. We must get our education beforehand. We shouldn't wait until there is a fire in our house to know how to get out of it in a hurry. We have to be prepared in advance. Our problem is getting the ideas before we need to act on them. You cannot spend two days studying when you've got to act tomorrow. You have to know these things a certain time in advance. You have to have certain basic ideas. Of course, you cannot afford to spend too much time in making minor decisions, such as whether to cross the street at one point or another. You have to judge each problem as to how important the decision is and how much time you can take before making the decision. Frequently you don't have any time. Something comes at you quickly. You have to make a quick decision and you have to make it on the basis of the intelligence you have at that moment.

Is Too Much Freedom Harmful?

Q. Cannot excessive freedom in certain aspects of economic

activity — such as advertising — lead to a waste of resources, human effort, money lavishly spent, etc.?

A. It's hard for me to see what excessive freedom is. I speak of freedom that is equal for all men, but not freedom for one man to harm another. I would admit that freedom means that men are going to make mistakes; but men will make mistakes with or without freedom. However, in a free society you have competition. If one person makes a mistake, perhaps in a suggestion he thinks will improve the automobile, and the suggestion is not accepted by others, he will not make a profit. It is only that one man who loses. Others are still free to advance society. Without freedom, only the dictator can try out his ideas. As I have said, men make mistakes, and they make mistakes in advertising as they do in other occupations, but once you permit the censoring of advertising for reasons other than fraud or misrepresentation, you are going to censor the freedom of speech. Who is to decide what is truth? As John Stuart Mill said, freedom for one man's ideas is often important. Who is to decide whose ideas are to be printed and whose are not? There is no one who can decide this, except the consumer. When men advertise, they advertise with the hope that they are going to sell a product. If there is fraud, if their advertising misrepresents, they may make a few sales, but they will soon go out of business. In my great country, and I suppose it is true down here too, many of the large companies making products which are sold over and over again, give away free samples just to get people to try their products. What makes a business successful is having a good product and getting repeat orders for it from satisfied consumers. Consequently, a company that misrepresents its product is not going to stay in business long. We don't have to worry about it much. Of course, I do not approve of fraud, nor do free market principles sanction misrepresentation.

The Role Of
Value In
Human Action

In this lecture we address ourselves to the role of value in economics.

Some people, thinking economics merely a matter of opinions, question the "value" of economists. When people are sick or have trouble with their bodies, they consult a doctor. They ask him what to do and what not to do. They take whatever bitter medicine the doctor prescribes, pay him, and thank him. When the same people have economic problems they rarely consult an economist. When they do, and he tells them that a popular expense will have undesirable consequences, they scorn his advice and call him "an enemy of the people." As one prominent economist once implied, it is almost impossible for a man to be both a true patriot and a popular economist at the same time. If an economist is popular with the economically ignorant, it may well be that his advice is not sound.

We are addressing ourselves tonight to a phase of economics that is responsible for many of our problems. Most people do not understand the full importance and significance of value in human action. This ignorance goes back many centuries. We must first deal with some popular fallacies, before presenting the positive theory that must become more popular if our civilization is to be saved. But let's go back to where we left off in the last lecture.

All life is change. For men, life is a series of choices by which we seek to exchange something we have for something we prefer. We know what we prefer. No other man or bureaucrat is capable of telling us what we prefer. Our preferences are our values. They provide us with a compass by which we steer all our purposeful actions. Because few people fully understand this, we have some serious economic problems.

Aristotle Misunderstood Exchange

Part of our trouble goes back all the way to Aristotle (384-322 B.C.), who in some asides in his books suggested a fallacious idea which many people now accept as gospel truth — the idea that the only fair exchange is an equal exchange, or, stated the other way around, that an equal exchange is the only fair exchange. This sounds reasonable but it contains the seeds of many fallacies concerning value, trade, and exchange.

Nonetheless, this idea has been held by many people over the years. It is still held by millions today. It is responsible for a great deal of the feeling against profits and against successful businessmen. It is generally felt that profits and business success are obtained only at the expense of workers or customers. In the popular mind it seems to follow, as night follows the day, that if someone gains, someone else must have lost.

This is, of course, a very basic error. It goes back at least to Montaigne. My great teacher, Mises, calls it "the Montaigne dogma." Montaigne, who lived in the sixteenth century, once wrote in his famous essays, "*Le profit de l'on est le dommage de l'autre.*" Translated, this says, "The gain of one is the loss of another." This thought was and is very popular.

It was even promoted by Voltaire. In 1764, Voltaire wrote, "To be a good patriot means to wish that one's community shall acquire riches through trade and power through its arms . . . . It is obvious that a country cannot profit but by the disadvantage of another country, and cannot be victorious but by making other people miserable."

That is a terrible thought to have to live by or with: the idea that all gains in life must come from the suffering of other people. But this is what many people think about the success of others. In the times of the Scholastics, even good Christians held the idea of a "just price" and a "just wage" that never changed. Saint Thomas Aquinas held such ideas. He thought that if it took one hour to produce "A" and two hours to produce "B," then two units of "A" should always be equal to and always exchange for one unit of "B." According to this idea, any other exchange rate was "unfair."

Classical Economists Misunderstood Value

The early classical economists did little to clear up this fallacy. Even Adam Smith, the founder of the Classical School of English economics, has this to say in his great work of 1776[1]: "Labour is the real measure of the exchangeable value of all commodities." By this he was trying to say, as were those who earlier favored the "just price," that there is a basis for calculating equal exchange rates, and this basis is the labor time it takes to produce what is being exchanged. Any other exchange rate favors one party at the expense of the other.

This, of course, agreed with the Montaigne dogma: If someone is rich, he must have become so at the expense of others. This is still the attitude of many toward businessmen who become rich in the service of the many. Unfortunately this was also the thinking of many of the early economists.

Adam Smith was followed by David Ricardo, who lived from 1772 to 1823. In his *Principles of Political Economy and Taxation* (1817), he wrote: "The natural price" — I stress here the

1. Adam Smith, *The Wealth of Nations,* edited, with an introduction, notes, marginal summary and an enlarged index, by Edwin Cannan (Modern Library, 1937), p. 30. See also p. 33: "Labour alone, therefore, never varying in its own value, is alone the ultimate and real standard by which the value of all commodities can at all times and places be estimated and compared." Also, p. 36: "Labour . . . is the only universal, as well as the only accurate measure of value, or the only standard by which we can compare the values of different commodities at all times and places."

word "natural," because this was a time in history when everyone believed there were both natural laws and natural prices that men could not alter — "The natural price of labour is that price which is necessary to enable the labourers to subsist and to perpetuate their race, without either increase or diminution . . . . The natural price of labour, therefore, depends on the price of food, necessaries and conveniences required for the support of the labourer and his family."[2]

This was merely a specific application of the general rule that the cost of anything was the amount of labor that went into its production. Ricardo thought this meant that the cost of labor itself must be the cost of the amount of labor needed for the production of the goods needed to produce and support a constant labor supply. This is what Ricardo called the *natural* price of labor — the price toward which he thought wage rates would always tend to be set.

Then, he went on in the next few pages to define the market price. He wrote: "The market price of labour is the price which is really paid for it, from the natural operation of the proportion of the supply to the demand; labour is dear when it is scarce and cheap when it is plentiful. However much the market price of labour may deviate from its natural price, it has, like commodities, a tendency to conform to it . . . . When, however, by the encouragement which high wages give to the increase of the population, the number of labourers is increased, wages again fall to their natural price, and indeed from a reaction sometimes fall below it."[3]

This was in accordance with the thought that whenever there was too much production of something, competition would send its price below the cost of production. Then, businessmen would reduce production and the price would tend to rise to its "natural price." Ricardo thought these same principles applied to labor. When employers paid higher wages than workers needed to live and reproduce another generation of workers, workers would only raise more children to the working age. Then when these additional

2. David Ricardo, *The Principles of Political Economy and Taxation* (Everyman's Library Edition, E.P. Dutton, 1911), p. 52.
3. *Ibid.*, p. 53.

children became workers, their competition against each other would drive their wages down toward the "natural wage," and sometimes even below the "natural wage." As a result, some workers would somehow have to be eliminated, probably by war, famine, or epidemics.

This was the philosophy of the Classical School. This was the essence of their ideas about labor, wages, and value. In those days, millions of infants and children never lived to become adults. In fact, one of England's nobles is reported to have named six or seven of his sons after himself, all with the same name, hoping that one of them might live to become an adult and carry on his name.

It was capitalism that reduced the infant mortality rate.

But getting back to this early nineteenth century period, this concept of the classical economists presented a very, very gloomy outlook. It meant, according to the doctrines of Malthus too, that any increase in population would only produce great distress. It meant that under the market system of capitalism, it was hopeless to try to raise the real wages, or living standards, of labor. If you raised their wages, they would only have to be lowered eventually, resulting in great suffering and many deaths. This was the thinking of the best economists all through the first half of the nineteenth century.

They had other problems they couldn't solve. There was, of course, the great paradox of value. Iron and its products were much more useful to men than gold, yet gold was more valuable in the market place. This fact was a paradox the economists of those days could not understand or solve. They couldn't see why gold sold at a higher price than iron, when iron was the more useful metal. Their writings did not solve this problem of value. Instead, they struggled with the labor theory of value, the idea that the value of anything was the value of the hours of labor that went into its production.

Marx's Value Theory

This was the status of economic thought when Karl Marx appeared on the scene. His *Das Kapital* was based entirely on this labor theory of value. In the first volume of *Das Kapital*, he wrote: "The value of labour power, like that of every other commodity, is determined by the working-time necessary for its production, consequently also for its reproduction. Labour power exists solely as an attribute of a live individual, and hence it presupposes the latter's existence. A live individual needs a certain amount of necessaries in order to sustain himself. The working-time necessary for the production of labour power resolves itself, therefore, into the working-time required for the production of such necessaries of life, in other words, *the value of labour power is the value of the necessaries required to sustain its proprietor."*[4]

This was completely consistent with the economic theory taught by the better known economists of that time. Perhaps we tend to blame Marx too much for this. He later had his troubles trying to defend this labor theory of values. However, when he published the first volume, he was merely adopting the value theory which leading economists then held. Under this labor theory of value, there was no hope that workers could improve their conditions in a market society. Marx thought that under capitalism the rich would become richer and fewer while the poor would become poorer and more numerous. With such fallacious ideas, it was only natural for Marx and his followers to oppose the market society. He sought its overthrow as the only way to improve the conditions of the masses. These ideas, including the labor theory of value, are part of the problem we face today in the United States, and they are also popular in other countries, including Argentina.

If labor is the sole source of value, then when there is an increase in wealth, all the increase must rightfully belong to labor. When any wealth or value is created, it is created by

---

4. Karl Marx, *Capital, The Communist Manifesto, and Other Writings,* edited by Max Eastman (Carlton House, 1932), p. 36. See also his *Capital,* edited by Frederick Engels and later by Ernest Untermann (Kerr, 1906-1909), Vol. I. pp. 190-191:

"The owner of labour-power is mortal. If then his appearance in the market is to be continuous . . . the seller of labour-power must perpetuate himself . . . . The labour-power withdrawn from the market by wear and tear and death, must be continually replaced by, at the very least, an equal amount of fresh labour-power. Hence the sum of the means of subsistence necessary for the production of labour-power must include the means necessary for the labourer's substitutes, *i.e.,* his children, in order that this race of peculiar commodity-owners may perpetuate its appearance in the market."

labor. Any businessman or investor who takes or receives an increased income is appropriating an unearned income. According to the Marxian theory, he is getting what really belongs to the workers.

When economists speak of indirect exchange, they mean exchange with the use of money. Direct exchange is barter, an exchange of goods for goods, or goods for services, directly, without the use of a medium of exchange. When you exchange goods for money and then exchange the money for other goods or services, it is an indirect exchange.

Marx said that a fair exchange existed when people took a commodity to the market, exchanged it for an equal value of money, and then exchanged this money for an equal value of another commodity they wanted. This, he considered, was a fair indirect exchange. This is what Marx and his followers thought the situation had been and should continue to be.

But those terrible capitalists came along and changed the system. What did they do? They changed the system by starting out with a definite quantity of money. They first bought commodities at market prices and hired workers at market wages. Then what did they do? They sold the finished products for more money than they had paid for the labor and commodities that went into their production. This was an unequal exchange. This was an "unfair" exchange. The capitalists got more back than they paid out.

Marx Opposed Profit

Marx wrote in Volume I of *Das Kapital*: "But how can profit derive 'spontaneously' from capital? For the production of any commodity the capitalist needs a certain sum, say $25. In this sum are included all the costs of the production . . . . He subsequently sells the finished commodity for $27.50 . . . . The idea of something being thus created out of nothing is unacceptable to human reason. . . . When this process is finished the capitalist has only in his possession an object of the same value as previously." [5]

---

5. Marx (Eastman ed.), pp. 24-25. See also Marx (Kerr ed.), Vol. 1, Chs. V & VII; Vol. III, Ch. I.

Later, he wrote in Volume III: "It is inexplicable that more value should come out of production than went into it, for something cannot come out of nothing."[6] In other words, it's nonsense to say that goods are sold for a higher price than they are worth. So if they are sold for $27.50 they must have been worth $27.50 in the beginning, and that $27.50, except for the cost of raw materials and depreciation, should all be paid to labor.

So, according to Marx, the capitalists cheated the workers. This was supposedly done in this manner: Under the market system, the workers earned enough to buy the food and other essentials needed to sustain themselves, their wives, and their children, in so many hours. Let us assume this was nine hours. Then the businessmen worked them ten or eleven hours and kept the full value of what was produced in the overtime. This was all in harmony with the idea that all value was created by labor only. According to this view, there is no other way to create values. This, of course, brought forth the idea that so many people hold today, the idea that anyone who gets rich from trade or business is doing so at the expense of the workers. This feeling is very, very common in the world today. It is the underlying official doctrine of most labor unions and political parties.

We do not have time to discuss all of the faults of this labor theory of value. However, let me say that Marx wrote his three volumes of *Das Kapital* in the 1860's. Volume I appeared in 1867, based on this labor theory of value. Volumes II and III were also based on it. But Marx was wise enough not to publish Volumes II and III during his lifetime. It was not until after his death that Engels found and edited Marx's original manuscripts. Volume II appeared in 1885, two years after Marx's death. The third volume appeared in 1894, eleven years after Marx's death. Economists then studied these last two volumes to see if Marx had been able to defend the labor theory of value, because in the early 1870's economists had come out with a new theory of value, which superseded the labor theory. We shall be speaking of this new theory in a moment.

---

6. Marx (Kerr ed.), Vol. III, p. 51.

Böhm Bawerk, one of the greatest economists of all times, and the teacher of my great teacher, Mises, pointed out in 1896 the principal error in the Classical School's labor theory of value, which is the basis of all Marxian thinking, and which is still popular today. Table I gives an example illustrating the main error involved in the labor theory of value. This example, of course, is oversimplified, but it should help you to understand the fallacy in the Marxian thinking so prevalent today in the ideas of labor union leaders, the masses of unskilled workers, and even university professors, as well as the political leaders of all nations.

We are going to divide the production of some consumer goods into five processes. (See Table I.) The first process is obtaining raw materials from mining or agriculture. We shall assume that we hire twenty men who work this first year obtaining the needed raw materials. The wages of each man come to $5,000 a year, for a total labor cost of $100,000.

We assume that the second year we move on to the second process, the making of simple tools. For this we also employ twenty men. We pay them $5,000 each per year, for another expense of $100,000.

The third year, we make machinery with twenty men at a cost of another $100,000. The fourth year we manufacture the consumer goods with twenty men at $5,000 a year each,

PRODUCTION PROCESS (Assuming five processes)

Year	Process	Men at $5,000 per year	Labor Bill
I	Obtaining raw materials (Agriculture & Mining)	20	$100,000
II	Making simple tools	20	100,000
III	Making machinery	20	100,000
IV	Manufacturing consumer goods	20	100,000
V	Selling period	20	100,000
	Total	100	$500,000

Table I

ASSUME:
100,000 Consumer Units are produced at $5.00 each = $500,000.

for a total labor cost of $100,000 more. The fifth year is a selling period, during which twenty men sell the goods at a cost of another $100,000.

So we have a total of 100 man-years, and a total labor cost of $500,000. Assuming that they produce 100,000 consumer units, each unit would then have cost $5 to produce. If they are sold for that price, it would return the total labor cost of $500,000.

This is all in conformity with the theory that only labor creates value. The total values produced then belong to the laborers. They are the only ones who contributed to increasing the values of the raw materials. Capitalists should get back only the costs they actually paid.

But is this the way men act? This would mean that those gentlemen who worked a full year in the first process would have to wait until the goods were sold, four years later, to receive their wages. Where is the money going to come from for them to live on until their raw materials are transformed into consumer goods and sold? What about the men employed for the second, third, and fourth processes?

Of course, today, the answer is very simple. Let the government pay them. Everybody understands this today, but where was the government going to get the money in the days before governments learned how to print money and produce "paper gold"? In real life, do workers wait years for their wages? No. This is not the way men act. If we are going to have an advanced civilization, one engaged in multiple production processes, beyond the simple stages of catching fish and picking wild berries, some people must be induced to consume less than they produce, and then make their savings available to pay those who engage in the early processes of a complicated, time-consuming production system.

Costs Include Interest

Somebody has to pay the men engaged in the first process four years before the goods will be paid for by consumers. Somebody has to pay the men in the second process three years before the goods are available, and the men engaged in the third process two years ahead of sales receipts, and the men in the fourth process one full year in advance of the final sale of the finished products.

This requires savings. This requires not only that somebody must save money, but also that he must be willing to make it available to others. Man is so constituted that he will not regularly make his savings, his money, his wealth, available to strangers for nothing. He must have some inducement. In this case (see Table II), and in Böhm Bawerk's examples, this inducement takes the form of interest. Interest is payment for time. You pay interest to get something now rather than wait until later for it.

As I mentioned last night, time is a part of every human action. It is a cost that must be taken into account in every business transaction. It comes before any allowance for profit or loss, which is something else entirely – profits or losses depend upon whether or not consumers will buy the goods or services produced at a price that covers the costs.

Here we are discussing an element in the cost of all goods, the payment for time, or interest. Let us assume an interest rate of 5 percent. I am merely doing here what Böhm Bawerk did many years ago. Five percent is today an historical interest rate. Using a 5 percent per year interest rate, and leaving it at simple interest, without going into the complexities of compound interest as we would have to do in real life, the interest charge would come to $5,000 for every year for which $100,000 was advanced to pay wages. We would have $20,000 interest expenses for the first twenty men, who have to be paid four years in advance; $15,000 for those engaged in the second process; $10,000 for those in the third process; and $5,000 for those in the fourth process. We thus get a total interest expense of $50,000.

So the total cost, without any profit or loss, is not $500,000, the labor cost. It is $550,000, which includes an additional 50 cents per consumer unit. The real cost of production is thus $5.50 per unit.

Now interest expense is something that communists and socialists neglect, because they still hold the labor theory of value. Today you hear this theory frequently. When increased capital investment helps workers increase production, it is argued that the increased values should all go to labor. This

		PRODUCTION PROCESS, INTEREST INCLUDED (Assuming five processes)		
Year	Process	Men at $5,000 per year	Labor Bill	Simple Interest at 5%
I	Obtaining raw materials (Agriculture & Mining)	20	$100,000	$20,000
II	Making simple tools	20	100,000	15,000
III	Making machinery	20	100,000	10,000
IV	Manufacturing consumer goods	20	100,000	5,000
V	Selling period	20	100,000	———
	Totals	100	$500,000	$50,000

ASSUME: 100,000 consumer units at labor cost of $500,000, plus interest cost of $50,000 = $550,000, or $5.50 per consumer unit.

Table II

policy has even been sponsored by former occupants of the White House. If production goes up, it is held that increased values all belong to the workers and it is not "fair" if they do not get them.

This is not, of course, in accord with the way men really act. We shall shortly be discussing a better, more modern, but less well-known analysis of this problem. However, this more modern economic theory was known among economists while Marx himself was still living. Perhaps it was one of the reasons why he did not permit Volumes II and III of *Das Kapital* to be released while he lived.

Modern Value Theory

The sound solution of this problem requires an understanding of the modern theory of value, the subjective or marginal theory of value. This theory holds that value is in the minds of men. Value is not objective. It is subjective. We value things according to our understanding of their ability to satisfy some human need or want. Economists have developed this theory over the centuries. It was not discovered all at once. In fact, it has only been in this century that Professor Mises has applied this theory thoroughly and precisely to the theory of money. This, unfortunately, is little understood. It will be the subject of my fifth lecture.

One of the first men to come up with this subjective theory was a German by the name of Hermann Gossen (1810-1858). He wrote a book whose title, translated into English, is *The Development of the Laws of Exchange Among Men and of the Resulting Rules of Human Actions.* This book appeared in 1854, thirteen years before the first volume of Karl Marx's *Das Kapital* appeared in 1867. But neither Marx nor economists in general were aware of this book. The author, considering his work a failure, had the publisher return to him the unsold copies, which he destroyed before his death in 1858. However, his book was mentioned in an 1858 German history of political economy that was read by an English economist, who advertised for a copy for several years before getting one in 1878. Although Gossen was not the first economist to bring these principles to public notice, he was the first to publish a book devoted solely to presenting this modern theory.

In his book he presented three laws, now known as the three laws of Gossen. The first holds that the amount of satisfaction derived from the consumption of a good decreases with each additional unit or atom of the same good until satiety is reached. The second maintains that, in order to attain the maximum of satisfaction, a man, who is in a position to choose several goods whose consumption gives him satisfaction, must choose part of each of the several goods before he satisfies completely his total desire for the good he first desires most. In short, he must choose portions or quantities of each desired good in such proportions that at the moment his consumption ceases the satisfaction from each good chosen is the same. The third states that subjective use value attaches to a good only when the supply of the good is smaller than the quantity demanded. As more units — Gossen's word was "atoms" — are supplied, the subjective value of the additional unit approaches zero.

These were Gossen's ideas or contributions. But as previously indicated, his book was not discovered until years after others had presented somewhat similar ideas in their own words. The first to do so, in 1871, was Carl Menger, an Austrian and the founder of the Austrian School of economics whose theories I am trying to present in these lectures under the sponsorship of the *Centro de Estudios sobre la Libertad*. This modern marginal theory of value was also brought forth separately by an Englishman, William Stanley Jevons, who published his book in late 1871. In 1874, Léon Walras, a Frenchman living in Switzerland, published a similar book on the same subject. Unfortunately, Walras and, to a lesser extent, Jevons resorted to the use of mathematics in their defense of the idea that the value of any one unit is to be found in the value of the marginal unit. As shown in the first lecture, mathematics cannot and does not apply to economic theory, because there are no constants or standards by which ideas or values can be measured.

These three men, working and writing independently of each other, came to the same general conclusions. They held that value is the significance a good has for the well-being of a human being or beings, and that the value of any specific good or service is determined by the importance attached to the utility of the marginal, or last available, unit in satisfying some human longing.

An economic good is a good in short supply, a good for which the quantity available is less than the demand for it. When there is a sufficient quantity to supply every human want, it is a free good, like the air in this room. When it is an economic good, the value of each unit comes from the use to which the last unit is put, because that is the lowest value that the available supply can satisfy. That is the value lost if one unit is lost or destroyed.

Value of Marginal Unit

Now, what is the definition of this last unit that determines marginal value? There has been some refinement in the definition over the years. Here are the definitions of the top economists of their time. First, Gossen wrote in 1854 that the marginal value was "the value of the last atom."[7] In 1871, Menger's book stated that marginal value was "the importance of the satisfactions of least importance among those assured by the whole quantity and achieved with any equal portion."[8]

Jevons, whose book was published a few months later in 1871, not then knowing what Menger had stated, wrote that the marginal value is "the final degree of utility, the degree of utility of the last addition, or the next possible addition of a very small, or infinitely small quantity to the existing stock."[9]

Walras, writing in 1874, without knowledge of what either Menger or Jevons had written, used the French term *rareté*, which he got from his father, another economist. This he defined as "the source of the effective utility on account of the quantity owned . . . the intensity of the last need satisfied by any given quantity consumed of a commodity." [10]

We move on to Böhm Bawerk (1851-1914), who followed Menger in the Austrian School and was the teacher of Mises. He defined the value of the marginal unit as "that concrete want or partial want which has the lowest degree of urgency among the wants that can be covered by the available supply of goods of the same kind." [11]

Now we come to my teacher, Mises (1881-   ). In 1949, Mises wrote in *Human Action* that the marginal value is the "value attached to one unit of a homogeneous supply on the basis of the value of the least important use of the units of the whole supply." [12]

This is how we value all economic goods, according to the value of the last unit. I shall go into this in a little more detail in my presentation of the modern positive theory. But first let me paraphrase Böhm Bawerk:

7. In the terminology of Hermann Heinrich Gossen, "*Werth der letzten Atome.*"
8. Carl Menger, *Principles of Economics* (Free Press, 1950), p. 132.
9. W. Stanley Jevons, *The Theory of Political Economy* (Macmillan, 1924), p. 51.
10. Léon Walras, *Elements of Pure Economics* (Allen & Unwin, 1954), pp. 119 & 146.
11. Eugen von Böhm Bawerk, *Capital and Interest* (Libertarian Press, 1959), Vol. II, pp. 142-143.
12. Ludwig von Mises, *Human Action*, 3rd Ed. (Regnery, 1966), p.123.

> Goods acquire value when the total available supply of that
> kind is so limited as to be insufficient to cover all the demands
> which call for satisfaction by those goods, or so nearly insuffi-
> cient that the withdrawal of the units being valued would render
> the supply insufficient. Goods are valueless when they are
> superabundant.

Actually, of course, when you increase the supply of any
particular good, the use value of each available unit of that
good goes down. There can come a time when you have more
units than you want. That particular good then becomes a
free good of no economic value. The additional units may
even become a liability — a minus value. This is something
that those who believe in the labor theory of value fail to
take into account. Nor are these facts taken into account by
the so-called Mathematical School of economics, those who
try to calculate the gross national product, or what we call
the "GNP." Actually, the larger the quantity you have of
anything, the lower the value of each unit must be. If you
increase production of a good by 10 per cent in quantity,
other things being equal, you do not increase the value of the
production by 10 per cent. This is difficult for many people
to understand. Some need must depend on each unit. Since
each additional unit satisfies a less important need, its value
must be less.

Value and Exchange Postulates

Now, having given you this introduction to the subjective,
marginal theory of value, permit me to return to the
presentation of some more deduced postulates of human
action. These are what I call the postulates of value and
exchange. They are deduced from the a priori postulates that
men act to improve their situation, that the factors available
for doing this are limited, and that men make mistakes.

The first of these is that *men have value scales.* As stated
earlier, you know what you want. You know the order of the
importance of different things to you. Nobody else can tell
you what that order is. This isn't true only of goods. You
also know the relative importance to you of non-market
factors. You place your own order of importance on your

honor, your glory, your virtue, your health, as well as things that touch only your heart. You know the order of their importance to you. They are either ends in your life or goods of the first order whose relative values are immediately known to you.

Our problems come in calculating the value of raw materials, wage rates, and interest rates — the factors that are needed for the processes which, in an advanced market society, ultimately produce consumer goods and services. For these, we need economic calculation. But in our daily lives, in buying the things we need as consumers, we know which things are most important to us. We know the order of their importance to us. Allowing for the fact that we make mistakes, this order is always known to us.

Values are formed in our minds. They change with changing conditions. Let me give you an example of what I am trying to say.

The assumed marginal utility scales of Mr. Smith, who owns four horses and four cows, are presented graphically in Table III. He ranks them in this order: first, a cow; second, a

---

MARGINAL UTILITY SCALES

ASSUME: Mr. Smith owns { 4 Horses (H) / 4 Cows (C)

RANKS

1 – C
2 – H   Simple if choice is to lose a Horse or a Cow,
3 – C   or to lose 2 Horses or 2 Cows.

4 – H   But if his choice is to lose all of his Horses or
5 – H   all of his Cows,
6 – H

7 – C   then Mr. Smith must rerank (*revalue*) into
8 – C   (*new*) units according to the actual situation.

Value is comparison — not measurement.

Table
III

horse; third, a cow; fourth, fifth and sixth, horses; and at the bottom, seventh and eighth, cows. Assume that he is faced with the choice of losing one animal, a horse or a cow, or of losing two animals, two horses or two cows. His decision is very obvious. He would get along with one or two less cows.

Now, suppose he is faced with this situation: He has his horses and his cows in a barn. It is constructed so that the horses come out at one end, and the cows come out at the other end. Assume the building catches on fire and Mr. Smith has the choice of rescuing either the horses or the cows. Which does he rescue?

The value scale in Table III does not help us at all. He is faced with a new situation. He is no longer considering units of one horse or one cow. He has to revalue the situation. He must re-rank his units. The units are now only two, one of four cows and the other of four horses. He instantly forms a new scale of values. Under this new condition he immediately makes his decision as to which is the more valuable unit, which he will rescue.

What I want to stress here is that values are compared. They are not measured. You cannot say how much you value one thing more than another. You have no constant standard for measuring such differences. Valuing is expressing a preference. It is like love. Can you say how much you love one person more than another? There is no unit for measuring love. There is no unit for measuring value. It is always a comparison under the conditions that exist at the time. It is not permanent. It is subject to change constantly. We shall soon be discussing that at greater length.

Each Additional Unit Worth Less

Going back to the postulates of value and exchange, the second asserts that *each additional unit of any economic good is of diminishing importance, or use value.*

We live in an automobile age. Here in Argentina, as well as in my country, you try to cross the street and you realize it. So perhaps you can understand this better if I use the example of automobiles. If you are a one-car family, you have to be careful about the use of that car. It can only be used for the most important uses of the family. In my country, the most important use of a family car is for the dates of our teenage children. This comes first. All other uses of the family car have to wait.

If you are prosperous enough to have two cars, then Mama also has a car. She can be the family chauffeur and take the other family members around. If you are plutocrats and have three cars in the family, then, as we say in the States, the old man gets a car. He can go about his business or even play golf on the weekends without consulting his children. There is a story of one father who got so furious that he actually said to his son: "The next time I want the car I'm just going to take it!"

This is the problem we have in fully understanding that each additional unit of the identical thing has a lower use value. Let me give you an example from Böhm Bawerk to help make this clear. (See Table IV.) This is basically his, though I must admit there is one change, which I shall mention later. Assuming an isolated farmer, this is his value scale for six bags of grain, according to the importance of the uses he expects to make of them: He plans to use the first bag as food to sustain his life, and the second bag as food for good health, so that he will be more robust. The third bag he expects to put aside for seed. The fourth he will use to produce meat, that is, he will feed it to cattle or chickens to improve his diet. The fifth bag he will use as food for pets, and the sixth he will use to make whiskey.

The one change that I have made is that Böhm Bawerk ranks whiskey as No. 5, above the pets, which he ranks as No. 6. The first time I presented this example, a lady in the audience objected that she preferred pets to whiskey. So,

VALUE SCALE FOR USE OF SIX BAGS OF GRAIN	
No. 1	Food to sustain life.
No. 2	Food for good health.
No. 3	Seed.
No. 4	Meat — feed for cattle or chickens.
No. 5	Food for pets.
No. 6	To make whiskey.

Table IV

in deference to her, I changed it. This gives me an opportunity to show that we all have different value scales.

Now suppose the farmer has labeled those bags 1, 2, 3, 4, 5, and 6 and a rat got into, let us say, bag No. 3. Would the farmer have lost his seed? Or would he have lost the bag on which he placed the lowest value, in this case whiskey? All of the bags were identical. When you lose one of any number of identical units, no matter which one it is physically, the value you lose is the value at the bottom or margin of your value scale.

This should make it clear that the use value of every additional unit of anything is less, because it is put to what you consider a less important use. In life we are usually considering whether to add one more unit or to get along with one less unit.

Values Not Computable

Now this tells us something else. It shows that values of the same things differ according to the number of units being valued. This means that there is no way of calculating the total value of a supply, if only the value of a part of the supply is known. Likewise, there is no means of establishing the value of a part of a supply, if only the value of the total supply is known. Many people, including many so-called economists, make the mistake of trying to find total values by adding or multiplying the known values of certain units. This is a basic error in all national income and gross national product (GNP) figures. They are completely unrealistic.

You probably can see it more easily with stock exchange quotations. Assume that you can buy a hundred shares of a particular stock for, let us say, 200,000 pesos. Does that mean that you could buy *all* the shares of that corporation at the same price per hundred shares? Suppose you wanted to buy 51 per cent control of a firm. As you bought more and more shares, you would have to pay higher and higher prices. Likewise if you are selling shares, the more shares you sell the lower prices you will get.

This whole idea of dividing total values and multiplying part values does not apply in real life. This is an error many people make, including so-called economists, particularly those known as "mathematical economists." Judgments of value refer only to the supply with which a concrete act of choice is concerned. Men decide on the basis of the value of the least important use they expect to make of the supply under consideration. For them, that is the marginal unit.

This is the reasoning that supplies the answer to the paradox of iron and gold. Nobody wants all the iron or all the gold. People want a specific quantity of iron, or a specific quantity of gold. They value only the quantity that is important to them. Therefore, although all iron may be more useful than all gold to men, men acting in the market do not compare the values of all iron with all gold. They compare the values of specific quantities that interest them and not the values of the total supply. Given the available supplies of gold and iron and the many uses to which these supplies can be put, one pound of gold is usually worth much more than one pound of iron to most men.

We are constantly thinking in terms of the value to us of one more unit or one less unit. The use values to us of one more unit or one less unit are two entirely different values, even though the units are identical. In considering these varying values we have no standard, no constants, for measuring the differences in their value. It is always a matter of comparing. If you have N units, you must consider N plus one or N minus one unit. You are always considering the importance to you of that one more or one less unit, that is, the least urgent or marginal use to which you put that unit. No other result is thinkable.

This is the subjective use value, the value that is in the minds of men who are eager to satisfy their most urgent wants according to their own value scales. So, the magnitude, the size, of value is relative and depends upon the importance of the concrete want that will be satisfied by the unit under consideration. This unit that is being valued is always the marginal unit. An identical unit has one value in selling and another value in buying. The value of goods may be ranked, but only with the ranking of specific concrete wants. Wants are fractionable, divisible, and of different importance, and we know the importance of each one to us.

Values Differ

Now, getting back again to the postulates of value and exchange, we come to the third one: *Different men have different value scales and the same men have different value scales at different times.*

You know yourselves that you have different value scales from those you had ten years ago. In fact you now have different value scales from those you had this morning. Perhaps, when you got up this morning, the first thing on your value scale was a cup of coffee. Once you had that coffee, it went down lower on your value scale. Your value scale is constantly changing. As you satisfy one want, as conditions change, or as you get new information, your value scale changes.

Likewise, different men have different value scales. Perhaps you can see this if you consider a factory where 100 men are employed to do the same type of work and all are paid the same wages. I would feel safe in making a bet that no two of the 100 families involved would spend those wages in the same way. They would all have different wants. Some would have babies. Some would have special hobbies. Some would have in-laws to support. Some would have sick members and doctors to pay. Also, some would like one kind of meat, while others would prefer another kind, or fish, or something else. No two of them would spend their earnings exactly the same way.

It is also true that values change as conditions change. For example, would you place a higher value on a gallon of water or a pound of gold? In a modern society, you would, of course, put the higher value on the pound of gold, if you were legally allowed to own it. But if you were in a desert far from civilization, a gallon of water would be worth much more to you than a pound of gold. As conditions change, our values change. Since conditions are constantly changing, so are our values and value scales.

Perhaps one of the most dramatic changes in values in all history occurred at eleven o'clock on the morning of November 11, 1918, when the World War I Armistice was signed. At that time, the values of the whole Western civilization changed. To celebrate the occasion, I was let out of school, but that wasn't important. The important thing was that up to that moment Western civilization had for several years valued highly anything and everything that would help win World War I. After the Armistice was signed, those things immediately lost value. They could only be sold at a loss. The government was soon selling off food and other Army supplies for less than 30 percent of what it had paid for them. Army uniforms were very cheap. There was no market at all for battleships.

Values are changing constantly. Values change with new inventions, new knowledge, new desires. All of these things are constantly changing. Sometimes a commodity has value. Sometimes it does not have value. Take uranium. Twenty or thirty years ago there was no known use for uranium. Now people are looking for it all over the world. Values of many things are constantly changing. Except as people meet in the market place, it is difficult to compare their ever-changing values. This, of course, is one of the fallacies behind the Marxian progressive income tax. The burden of an increased tax is different for each individual, and there is no way to compare these burdens.

Market Exchanges Mutually Profitable

Let us pass now to perhaps the most important postulate of value and exchange: *Only men with different value scales can and do exchange for mutual advantage.*

When people fully understand the significance of this postulate, they really understand the importance of the free market economy. Only people with different value scales can and do exchange for mutual advantage.

Let me explain. Suppose you want a suit. You go into a tailor shop and see a suit you like. The price on it, let us say, is $100. You decide to buy this suit. Why do you buy that suit? Because the suit is worth more to you than $100. In fact, it is worth more to you than anything else in the world that you could then buy for $100. Otherwise you would not buy the suit. Instead you would buy whatever you considered more valuable. Now, take the man who sells you that suit. For him, $100 is worth more than the suit. Otherwise, he would not sell it for that price.

Both parties give up the asset on which they place the lower value and receive in return the asset on which they place the higher value. In other words, free and voluntary exchanges occur only when two people place different relative values on two different specific assets. In the market, one of these assets is usually a quantity of money.

You go into a department store. You see goods and their prices all around you. When you see a price on a good which is lower than the value of that good to you, you buy, and you buy additional units of that good until you reach the point at which another unit is not worth that price to you. It is the same in a grocery store. It is the same in any store.

Likewise, when you see a market price you think is high, so high that you think you can buy or make the good for much less, you go into the business of making or reselling that particular product. You offer it for a little more than your costs and a little less than your competition. No one buys or sells unless he believes he is improving his situation.

It is these differences in the value scales of different individuals that make the market function. It is these differences in value scales that keep the free and unhampered market economy in harmony with the Golden Rule. In every market transaction you improve your situation, and the other party is also improving his or her situation, barring force, fraud, or human error. In a free market, there is no use of force. Some people may resort to force or fraud, but it is the function of government to keep the use of force or fraud to a minimum. As previously mentioned, all men make mistakes, but they try to keep their mistakes to a minimum.

You may take the suit out in the daylight and find it is not quite the color you thought it was. Or you may take it home and try it on in front of your spouse. He or she may not like it. He or she may say, "I won't be seen in public with you in that suit." Then you know you have made a mistake. But barring force, fraud, or human error, you never enter into a free market transaction unless you expect to improve your situation. This is also true of all other parties to the transaction.

This is true not only of buying and selling, but also of hiring an employee or taking a job. In a free market you take a job because in your judgment that job gives you the best return of all the jobs open to you. The advantages may not be monetary only. They may be the hours you prefer, the kind of work you like, or the location you desire. You take all conditions that you value into consideration, and you make a choice — you choose the one that gives you, from your viewpoint, according to your value scale, the greatest returns. Similarly, if you employ someone, you hire that available person who you expect is going to give you the greatest return for the money you pay out.

The same is true in borrowing or making a loan. You borrow $100 at 10 per cent interest, because you prefer having $100, or what you can buy for $100, now, to having $110 a year from now. The man who lends you the money has a different value scale. He may want the money for some future trip or to send his child to college next year. He prefers to part with his $100 for a year in return for $110 a year from now.

Exchanges Increase Wealth

All free market transactions are exchanges of two sets of assets, in which each set of assets moves from those who place a lower value on it to those who place a higher value on it. These are all comparisons. They are not measurements. There is no way to say how much more you value that suit than $100. Possibly you would have paid $105. Possibly you would have paid $110. But in real life you do not waste time thinking about what does not matter.

You always try to use your available means so as to get the greatest possible satisfaction that you think you can get for them. You never try to waste your assets. You never exchange them for assets on which you place a lower value. We are always trying to improve our situation. We are always trying to eliminate some uneasiness. We are always trying to exchange something we have, our time, our energy, our scarce goods, or our money, for other things we prefer.

We have been talking about the use values of consumers' goods. Our use values are our value scales and the result of our own ever-changing judgments. In a market society, there is also a market price, or market value, for every economic asset. *In a market economy, identical assets always have the same price, or market value, at the same time and place.* The exchange value of an asset is its capacity to obtain in exchange a certain quantity of other assets.

In life we are constantly comparing our use values with market values. The clothes you have on have a higher use value for you than their market value. When their use value to you falls below their market value as second-hand clothes, you will sell them. Everything you have that you don't want to sell has a higher use value to you than it has to anyone else. Otherwise you would sell or exchange it. When you find something whose use value is higher to you than its market value, you buy. On the other hand, when someone offers you more for your automobile, or anything else you own, than its use value to you, you will sell it.

One of the important things to remember about a free and unhampered market is that goods and services are always moving through market exchanges from those who place a lower value on them to those who place a higher value on them. *In a market economy, all the factors of production are allocated, by voluntary exchanges of mutual advantage, to those alternative uses that are expected to yield the greatest human satisfaction. By free market transactions every economic good is moving to persons and places where it is more valuable.*

Political Intervention Reduces Human Satisfaction

What does all this mean in terms of political or governmental intervention, or higher costs of any kind? Suppose the politicians in power have a welfare program that they want to finance to help them win the next election. Suppose they levy a sales tax of 10 per cent on that suit we discussed. Then instead of paying $100 for it you would have to pay $110. There will be a lot of people who would prefer that suit to $100, but who may not prefer it to $110 – particularly those who have only $100. They must then buy something that is less valuable to them. They will have to accept what they consider a lesser satisfaction. Likewise, the man who would have sold the suit has to get along with a lesser satisfaction. This also applies to the men or women who make suits. In fact, the farmer who raises the sheep from which the wool is taken to make the fabric would also suffer as a result of this governmental tax.

Let me say here, taxes needed for the protection of life, property, and the market place are not a burden on the market. The market needs protection. It can only operate under peaceful conditions. Such taxes are just as necessary as the costs of any of the factors of production.

However, every unnecessary rise in costs or prices, every unnecessary increase in taxes, and every governmental intervention must reduce the first-choice transactions of consumers. They must also reduce the sales of those who are otherwise best able to satisfy consumers. Such interferences with the free market must therefore reduce human satisfactions below their highest possible potential.

This has to be so. This is not a question of my opinion, of how I think it should be. Every use of force for other purposes than the equal protection of all must prevent people from getting the highest potential satisfaction that they would enjoy in a free market.

Values are an order of preference, a value scale that registers your preferences. You cannot measure values. You can only compare them. If you cannot get the assets you value most, you must accept assets that are less valuable to you. When governmental interventions hinder or prevent market transactions that benefit all parties, they must necessarily reduce human satisfaction.

Such political interventions are not only taxes or higher costs. They may be laws that stop you from buying something that someone wanted to sell you. Your work may prevent you from going to a barber or hairdresser except on evenings or Saturdays. So, a law that requires the barbers and hairdressers to be closed on evenings or Saturdays hurts both you and those who might like to serve you. Every governmental intervention, that is not necessary for the protection of life, property, and the market place, or for a peaceful adjudication of disputes between citizens, must reduce the satisfactions of all those affected by the intervention.

Summary

To review, briefly: Value is the significance a good has for the well-being of a human being or beings. The value of a good is determined by the importance attached to the utility of the marginal unit in satisfying some human want.

All life is change. For men, life is a series of choices by which we seek to exchange something we have for something we prefer. We know what we prefer. No other man or bureaucrat is capable of telling us what we prefer. Our preferences are our values. They provide us with the compass by which we steer all our purposeful actions. And last but not least, a fair exchange is not an equal exchange. A fair exchange is an unequal exchange from which all parties expect to gain.

Barring force, fraud, or human error, every free market transaction provides all parties with a psychic profit or higher value, according to their own scale of values. Anything that raises cost or hinders the free and voluntary transactions of the market place must keep human satisfactions from reaching their highest potential. Today the greatest obstructions to the attainment of higher human satisfactions are the well-meaning but futile political interferences with the mutually beneficial transactions of a free market economy.

QUESTIONS AND ANSWERS

We shall be glad to entertain some questions and answer them to the best of our ability. I've tried to be clear, but it isn't always easy to present this subject simply, particularly when working with a foreign language and in a country where ideas and conditions may differ. But we are all human beings and we are discussing the immutable laws of human action. Being a human being, I must make mistakes. If you can call them to my attention, I shall certainly appreciate it, as I want to improve my understanding of these matters.

Progressive Income Tax

Q. Please expand on what you said about the progressive income tax and its relation to the marginal theory of value.

A. Well, you can compare the value scales of different people only when they meet in the market place. Then, when they have different relative values for two different things under consideration, they will trade. The progressive income tax is based on the fallacy that all men have similar value scales, and thus any tax on a higher-income group will mean only a sacrifice of unessential things which lower-income groups cannot afford. Thus the tax will not affect or burden tax-payer satisfactions as much as taxes levied on those in all income groups. This, of course has several fallacies in it.

Perhaps the most important popular fallacy that supports the progressive income tax is ignorance of the fact that, in a market society, where prices, wages, and interest rates are free to shift so as to reflect shifts in supply and demand, the progressive income tax does not necessarily burden most those in the higher tax brackets. The truth is that it is a tax on every participant in the market, and the market determines how the burden is distributed. It breeds friction. It breeds bad feeling. It leads low-income people to think the rich should pay still more, and it leads high-income people to think they are paying more than their share. Both groups are wrong.

In a market economy, the market determines who bears the burden of the tax. If a corporation has to pay a business executive, say the president of a shoe company, $200,000 a year so he can take home $50,000, the executive is merely a tax collector for the $150,000 tax. Much of the tax will work its way into the price of shoes. A higher price for shoes means that fewer people can afford shoes. Then fewer people will be employed in that shoe factory. The burden of that tax will fall on the consumers, the workers, the investors, and the high-income executives too. But *how* it falls on all these people will depend upon market conditions and not on who sends the check to the Treasury.

Getting back to the question of the relation of the progressive income tax to marginal value: For a man with a low income, who spends everything he gets, a higher tax may mean that he drinks a little less beer or smokes a few less cigarettes. But a man with a high income, let us say $50,000 a year, may have committed a large part of his income to specific payments. He may have bought a house with regular mortgage payments. He has life insurance, with regular premiums to pay. He has entered into other investment and payment agreements based on an expected income of $50,000, less whatever current taxes are then in force, say $10,000. Suppose his taxes are doubled, to $20,000. That extra $10,000 may be marginal to the point that it means he has to lose his house and/or his life insurance. It may mean something very drastic to him, possibly bankruptcy. His situation is not the same as that of the low-income man. Men's situations and value scales are different in every case, and there is no way that you can make them the same.

Actually, of course, the best income tax is one with the same rate on everyone. Such a tax would not cause the frictions, the class warfare, that the progressive tax causes. Then, if anyone proposed increasing government expenses by 10 per cent, everyone would know that his taxes would go up 10 per cent. He could compare the expected benefits with his costs, and thus be able to vote more intelligently on the issue. Today, in my country and in many other countries, many spending measures become popular because most people think that only the rich and the corporations will pay for them. But actually everyone pays for them, and the people who feel it the most are the low-income people who have to pay more for their bread and shoes.

Is Intervention Necessary?

Q. Is government intervention necessary to modify the demand to promote welfare?

A. Well, I should have to say that government intervention, as I define government intervention, is never necessary. It is never generally helpful. Of course, if there is a crime, a murder, a theft, or a fraud, governmental action is needed. But such governmental actions are not interferences or interventions into the peaceful operation of the market. However, all so-called "welfare" interventions do interfere with the market. Their purpose is always to help some people at the expense of others. Such interventions are not necessary. What we call "welfare" today is a burden on all individuals, and not a mutually helpful governmental function, as is the suppression of violence. We now have the socialistic idea that the rich and the corporations should take care of the poor. Actually such measures are making more people poor every day. Ever-increasing numbers of poor people now believe they have a legal right to welfare and that therefore they do not have to work any more. In my country, in New York City, we have one million people on one program – public relief. This is about one person in eight. In many cases they consider that living on relief is better than working. Of course, some women have more illegitimate children because then they get higher welfare checks.

If this were taken care of by private charity and the churches, the poor would feel thankful for it and try to get off welfare. Now, they spend their time trying to find ways to get more welfare. In my country the welfare recipients are organizing into unions and demanding more things. They have to have a telephone, because somebody might get sick and need to call a doctor. They have to have raincoats, because they could catch colds and then they would be a further expense to the government.

Last year there were two rather extreme examples of this. The women on relief invaded department stores, disrupting business and demanding charge accounts. They also wanted enough money for the "American standard of living," including Christmas toys for their children. When there are large numbers of unemployed and other difficulties, "we" have fallen into the rut of thinking that the answer is always more government. In later lectures I shall be dealing with this problem. In my fourth lecture I shall also be discussing why we have so much distress, why we have so much unemployment, and why we have ever-increasing demands for welfare. This is always the result of prior government intervention, and I hope to make this clear.

Influence of Henry Ford

Q. What has been the influence of the ideas of Henry Ford

on the money cost of wages in the economy of the United States?

A. Of course, I must first ask which Henry Ford you mean. The old gentleman and his grandson are two entirely different individuals of two different philosophies. If you mean the elder Henry Ford, he was not a perfect economist, but he was a very intelligent human being. He did not advocate paying unneeded men to stay on a farm. He offered former farm workers the high wage of $5 a day, which was then much more than they could earn on the farm, to make automobiles. He then sold those automobiles at prices which were considered bargains by those who bought the cars. He helped both the workers and the buyers of automobiles while incidentally making himself rich.

If you want to become rich, find something with which you can save people the equivalent of ten pesos. Then make a million of them, split the profit of ten pesos on each with your customers, and you will have five million pesos, while every person who buys one of your products is five pesos better off. Henry Ford, the original Henry, contributed to the American success in ending the depression after World War I without any serious governmental intervention. His grandson, the present head of the Ford Motor Company, does not have these ideas. His grandson believes in, and advocates, many of the governmental interventionist policies. These, of course, are leading to a different end in the United States.

Equality Before the Law

Q. Why don't you speak a little more about equality before the law rather than equality of fortunes?

A. Of course, what I've been trying to say is that I believe in equality before the law. Equality before the law means that we are going to be unequal. Actually, there is no way to make men equal. This is very fortunate, because some people have certain talents and can contribute certain things which others cannot contribute. We are all different and we profit from these differences. We are very unequal and there is no means to make us equal. These socialistic attempts to level fortunes, to level money income and wealth, are the basic problem of the day. They derive from the fact that we no longer believe in equality before the law. It used to be that we depicted Justice as a woman with a blindfold over her eyes so that she could not see who was in front of her. But now, as one of my friends[13] says, Justice lifts up the blindfold and peeks to see who stands before her for judgment. If it is a member of a labor union, she renders one decision. If it is a member of the business community, she renders another decision. We no longer have equality before the law. This is one of our great difficulties in all countries. I know it is so in mine.

Youths Seek Truth

Q. What do the young people in the developed countries think about the principles that you have talked about?

A. Well, unfortunately, I do not have a very large audience, but those whom I have had in my classes, those I've had for a sufficient time, have grasped these basic principles with enthusiasm. But the means of mass education and the means of mass communication are largely in the hands of those with different ideas. The young want the truth, but they seldom find it today. This is one of the reasons for the unrest in the universities.

Increased Production Benefits All

Q. What is the difference between something you desire and something that is a necessity?

A. The questioner seems to feel that there is a difference between something you desire and something you consider a necessity. There is no difference between these in either theory or action. Actually, as we shall be revealing as we go

13. Professor Benjamin A. Rogge, Wabash College.

along, there will be more production of what people really want under a free market society. The more production there is, the less burden taxes are on production and the more everyone will have, including those down at the bottom of the ladder. They are the ones who suffer most from this welfare state approach. Everybody suffers, but the well-to-do can stop producing and go play golf, retire early, or take a long vacation, when they think income taxes are too high for the extra effort involved.

If a high-income doctor is approached to take an appendix out, he can say: "I should get $500 for that. It is November, and I am now in the 50 percent bracket, so I will have to charge $1,000." Who pays that $500 tax, the patient or the doctor? The doctor can quit and go play golf. Then the patient has to go to a less competent doctor who charges less and whom he can afford under those conditions. Both the doctor and the patient are hurt by the tax, but the poor patient feels it more.

In a free society everyone is benefited by increased production, and the greatest answer to poverty is the increased production of a free market. The standard of living in the Western world, and in my country particularly, has risen because of the free market. Starvation exists in the socialist and communist countries, the countries that do not have the free market, such as China, India, and places of that type. Where you have a market economy, no one need starve.

I wish I had the time to tell you the story of the early communist attempts in America. Communism was tried in our very first colonies, at both Jamestown and Plymouth. For three years they put everything into the common warehouse and doled it out according to what the ruling powers decided were the needs of the different individuals and families. In every one of those first three years, in both Plymouth and Jamestown, more than 50 percent of the people starved to death. The rest of them were saved only because new shipments of food and necessities came from Europe. When they adopted the private enterprise principle that each family could keep what it produced, there was no longer any starvation. The women, the children, and all of them put forth their utmost effort, where previously they had stolen food from the fields before it was even ripe.

Mathematics and Economics

Q. Is mathematics absolutely divorced from economics?

A. Mathematics in the field of economics is always statistics, and statistics are always history. Mathematics cannot and does not enter into measuring the ideas or values that determine human action. There are no constants in these. There is no equality in market transactions. Therefore, mathematics does not apply. The use of mathematics requires constants. Mathematics cannot be used in economic theory. Mathematics can be used in economic calculation, but this depends upon a monetary unit whose purchasing power does not fluctuate violently. Mathematics may be helpful in presenting economic history, but not economic theory, on which all human action is based.

Effect of Progressive Income Taxes

Q. What about the progressive income tax in relation to the decrease in the marginal value of incomes?

A. What I've tried to say is that everyone has different value scales. These different value scales cannot be compared except when those who hold them go into the market and compare their use values with market values. When they find two different relative values, they trade. Then you know the buyer places a higher value on the product than he does on the price, while the seller places opposite relative values on these two items.

The problem of the progressive income tax arises, of course, with changes in tax rates. A change in the tax rates affects different people differently, according to their particular conditions at the time of the change. When a tax is set and not changed, market prices already reflect the tax burden. We make our plans and our choices in accordance with the existing taxes. We make our long-term contracts, buying things over a period of time, investing, renting, or leasing, with the present tax burden in mind. Now a new and higher tax becomes law. It affects most the persons who have these long-term commitments. They are less able to adjust than a person who does not have such commitments. So frequent changes in taxes upwards — and that's the only way they go these days — are the source of our troubles. This means that people who have learned to expect higher taxes will hesitate to make long-term commitments. Such commitments are necessary for a high standard of living. It takes years to produce some of the things that we now want. That means that savers and investors should feel confident, in making long-term contracts, that their calculations are not going to be upset by new taxes after they have made their commitments. Of course, if we did everything just on a day-to-day basis, this effect of tax changes would not be there. But then, we would have to live in a day-to-day economy, and would not be able to make long-term plans or enjoy products that require long-term planning and production processes.

"Welfare" Measures Reduce Wealth

Q. What do you think about welfare economics?

A. I hold that free market economics is the only system of the division of labor that advances the general welfare of all the people. It is in accordance with the Golden Rule. We advance ourselves as we help others. The more we help others, the more we receive in return. This is an incentive to increase production. Everyone does the best he can. People have choices of action, and they usually choose to make those market contributions which they expect will bring them the greatest returns.

The welfare state relies upon taking from some and giving to others. It reduces the production of those who get something for nothing, and it reduces the production of those who know their increased production will be heavily taxed. Reducing production does not increase the general welfare. The general welfare is served by policies which increase production. Most important, as I said in the last lecture, is the fact that all increased savings invested in production for the market must increase wages, increase production, and reduce prices. Thus increased savings help everyone. If we want to help the poor people, we should adopt policies that increase savings. This would increase the bidding for labor, increase the production of wealth, and lower prices. As a result everyone who participates in the market would get more for his or her contribution.

How Prices
Are Determined

There was once a Russian school child whose cat had a family of kittens. When asked to write a paper for her class, the child wrote about the mother cat and the kittens. The next day she read her paper to the class. In it she told about how these kittens were born. There were five of them and they were all good little Communists. The teacher liked the paper, and when, a week later, one of the Moscow inspectors visited the school, the teacher, proud of her pupil, asked the child to read it again. The child read the paper. When she came to the part about the kittens she said there were five kittens and two of them were Communists. The teacher was quite surprised. The child had previously said all five were Communists; so the teacher asked the child why she had changed it. "Well," the little girl said, "three of them have opened their eyes."

One of the things we are trying to do in these lectures presented by the *Centro de Estudios sobre la Libertad* is to open the eyes of people who have heard so much about the promises of socialists and government interventionists to use political power to improve the economic situation of the poor, the sick, the young, the aged, and all others with whom they seek popularity. Actually, the only way for governments to improve the economic condition of their citizens is to provide equal protection of life, property, and the market place for everyone, while peacefully adjudicating disputes which might otherwise lead to frictions and infractions of the peace. Using the force of government to take from some to provide special privileges for favored groups will never improve the general welfare. Governments that play favorites sow the seeds of their own destruction and reduce the production of both the poor and the rich.

For each of us, life is a problem of how to use our limited means to produce more of the things that provide us and our loved ones with the greatest possible satisfaction. We daily strive to satisfy our most important wants before we try to satisfy those we consider less important. In short, we constantly seek to improve our situation by exchanging something we have for something we prefer. The prime function of government is to provide an atmosphere in which more and more mutually beneficial exchanges can take place.

Division of Labor

As individuals we cannot produce all the things we want. So we tend to specialize, and produce things that other people want. We then exchange the products of our efforts in the market place for the things that we want. This involves what economists call the division of labor.

In his great book, *The Wealth of Nations*, Adam Smith, the founder of English classical economics, tells how we can all have more if we specialize and trade. As mentioned in our previous lectures, it is our value scales that direct us in making our choices of how to use our limited means to attain more of the things we want most.

If man finds it easier to get what he wants by specializing his contributions and trading his specialties with those who produce what he wants, he will do so. He will take the easiest way he knows to improve his situation. Consequently, civilized men have resorted to specialization in production and the subsequent trading of the specialties they have produced. Such trading necessitates the use of a medium of exchange, or money. In our fifth lecture, we shall be dealing with that very serious part of the market problem. But it is money *prices* that we are talking about now. Most people are confused about prices. They seem to think that prices are set by producers and sellers, that they add up their costs and then add something more for their profit. This is how most people think prices are set.

Actually, the successful businessman looks for something that the people want, something he thinks he can produce for less than people will pay for it. So in the final analysis it is the values businessmen believe people have in their minds that determine what goods they will make, and how much they will make of each particular scarce good.

This question of what to make is one of the important problems that the socialists neglect. Marx thought there was no such problem. So did Lenin. They thought the only businessmen you needed were bookkeepers to keep the accounts. Nobody had to decide what needed to be produced. This was supposedly evident to everyone. The masses needed more food, more clothing, and more housing. For Marx and other socialists, the choice of what to make was no problem at all.

But this, of course, is not so. We cannot make everything people want. The most important decisions in this world are those that determine what should be made and what should not be made. These decisions seek to determine what things give the greatest human satisfactions, so that our scarce means of production are not wasted making things that people do not want as much as other things that could have been made with the available supplies of labor and raw materials.

In a market society, individual subjective values allocate the available supply of every scarce good so as to satisfy human wants in the descending order of their importance, whereby the particular want last satisfied is the one with the marginal utility. From beginning to end, price, and thus economic calculation, is the product of subjective valuations. Price is the result of the reciprocal impact of the subjective values placed on the good and on money by all interested parties. The resulting market prices must benefit all who exchange.

As we have said before, but should never forget, all life is a series of choices whereby we try to exchange something we have for something else that we prefer. The fewer the obstacles placed in our way in the form of higher costs, taxes, or other governmental interventions, the more exchanges we can make for the mutual advantage of all the participants.

The Economic Problem

We are constantly faced with the economic problem. The economic problem is, of course, the problem of human beings, the problem of life. This problem is how to employ our available means in such a way that no important want is left unsatisfied because the means for attaining it were used to satisfy a less important want. Such a misuse of scarce means would provide less human satisfaction. It would be wasting valuable wealth. Acting man wants to know how to use what he has to provide the greatest attainable human satisfactions. This is the problem that concerns all of us. This is the problem that the market solves.

In trying to get what we want, we are directed by our ideologies. Ideologies are our ideas about how we think society operates. Sometimes we are influenced directly by an ideology. If we believe certain actions will produce the results we want, we take those actions. Ideas, as we stressed in the first lecture, are very important. But sometimes in our social activities, an ideology influences us indirectly. We follow certain procedures which by themselves we do not consider very helpful, because we do not want to offend those around us. We go along with certain widely held myths, certain popular prejudices, or certain accepted folkways, rather than take the actions we consider most efficient. We do this because we have to live with our fellow men and cannot always do things that we ourselves might consider best.

For a good to have value it must assure the satisfaction of a need or want of some human being. Thus, if that good did not exist, there would be some human want that would have to go unsatisfied. Every loss of an economic good means that there is one less human satisfaction attained. Goods can have a direct value, that is a use value, to us. Or they can have an indirect value, that is an exchange value, which means they have a use value to someone else. In that case, we can exchange them for something which has a use value to us.

In the market place it is the use value or the exchange value, whichever is greater, that determines our choice of actions. When we see something that is more valuable to us than its market price, we buy. When we have something that is more valuable in the market than it is to us, we sell. We do not trade for the fun of it. Otherwise we might trade back and forth all day long. We consider every exchange, every transaction, beforehand, and we continue exchanging up to the point or limit beyond which we do not expect to gain any further.

Trade Increases Wealth

Since all men are eager to satisfy their more important wants, those which are higher on their value scales, before they satisfy their less important wants, those which are lower on their value scales, they trade whenever they can find anyone who has opposite or contrary views on the relative values of two goods or services. By an exchange transaction, each good or service moves to that person who places the higher value on it. The wealth of each party is thus increased. They have both gotten a psychic profit, that is, a gain that they themselves consider a profit. This psychic profit cannot be measured, but it is a very real increase in satisfaction in the minds of the parties participating in the exchange. Market exchanges are not equal exchanges. They are unequal exchanges, from which both parties expect to gain.

So trade is productive of value. In a market economy goods are constantly moving from those who place a lower value on them to those who place a higher value on them. This is a fact of economic life that is not taken into consideration by mathematical economists. They seem to think that economic goods have a certain fixed value, usually based on the cost of production. They calculate this value as an unchanging fact, not realizing that when a good shifts from one person or place to another its value has been increased. The physical goods have greater value when they are owned by people for whom they can provide greater satisfaction.

It is the unequalness of the use and exchange values of different people that leads to exchange. These differences cannot be measured, only compared. They are in the mind. They are psychic. It is always a matter of greater or less. If the value of what you expect to receive is not greater for you than the value of what you will have to give up, then there is no trade. The differing use and exchange values of different individuals result in the emergence of prices – market prices. There are no other kinds of prices, only market prices.

Most scarce goods have many uses, or a use value for many people. The economic problem is to allocate them so as to give more human satisfaction to all concerned. Voluntary exchange is the only possible way in which all can benefit. It is the only system that allocates each scarce item to that use or person where it has the highest relative value. It is the only system that tends to minimize waste and maximize human satisfaction.

How Men Act in the Market

In life we are faced with two questions as we go to the market place. These questions are whether or not to exchange, and if so, on what terms. The answers can be simple. There are three rules or postulates for answering these questions:

1. *Man will exchange only if he can exchange for an advantage.*

2. *Man will exchange for a greater advantage, in preference to an exchange for a lesser advantage.* If you can buy something for 250 pesos, you are not going to pay 275 pesos. You will always take that price which gives you the greatest advantage. Of course, sometimes it is not merely a matter of money. It may be primarily a matter of convenience. You may pay a slightly higher price for something in your neighborhood rather than take the time to go downtown, where you might get it for a few pesos less. Or you might pay

a little more to a person or group you wanted to help, considering the difference a charitable contribution.

3. *Man will exchange for a small advantage in preference to not exchanging at all.*

These three rules or postulates provide all the answers we need to solve the problems we face in the market place. Can you get an advantage? You can. Okay, you exchange. If you can get a greater advantage, you take it in preference to a lesser one, but you will take a small advantage in preference to no advantage at all. You are trying to improve your situation as best you can from your point of view.

Now here are a number of rather simple problems to show how prices evolve and how our value scales contribute to their emergence. Here we are going to assume that you have a use value for several objects you do not own, and that this value scale is:

```
1st . . . . . . . . . . . . . . . .A
2nd . . . . . . . . . . . . . . . .B
3rd . . . . . . . . . . . . . . . .C
4th . . . . . . . . . . . . . . . .D
```

Then you learn that you can exchange a "D" for an "A." This is new information, information you did not have when you had this original value scale. This new information changes your value scale and it becomes now:

```
1st . . . . . . . . . . . . . . . .A
2nd . . . . . . . . . . . . . . .D
3rd . . . . . . . . . . . . . . .B
4th . . . . . . . . . . . . . . .C
5th . . . . . . . . . a second D
```

A "D" has gone up to second place, not because of its use value but because of its exchange value. You can exchange it for an "A." The fact that you have to take the trouble to exchange it to get the "A" places it below the "A." The second "D" would be valued for the use value of a "D."

So your value scales change as you get new information. You find out that you can buy something cheaper at another place, or you find that something unexpected has happened, or you learn that something new has been invented. You then have a new situation and it calls for a new value scale.

Simple Barter

Table V presents a slightly more complicated, but still very simple, situation. These problems illustrate the principles that determine how prices are formed and how they are constantly being changed. We start here with an assumption that Smith has four horses. They appear in the first column. In the second column we have his value scales for horses and cows. If he had only four animals he would prefer first a horse, second a cow, third a second horse, and fourth a second cow.

Señor Black, in the third column, has four cows, and his value scale for horses and cows, in the last column, is in this order: first he would like a cow, second a horse, third a second cow, and fourth a second horse.

These two men meet. What happens? One owns four horses. The other owns four cows. When they come together, they soon find out that Smith will gladly trade his fourth horse for a cow. And Black will gladly trade his fourth cow for a horse. They make the exchange. They have both improved their holdings of these two kinds of animals.

In fact, they will go further, in a second step — Step B. Smith will gladly trade his third horse for a second cow, while Black will gladly trade his third cow for a second horse.

	SIMPLE BARTER		
Mr. SMITH		Mr. BLACK	
has 4 horses:	his value scale for horses & cows:	has 4 cows:	his value scale for horses & cows:
1st H	1st H	1st C	1st C
2nd H	2nd C	2nd C	2nd H
3rd H	3rd H	3rd C	3rd C
4th H	4th C	4th C	4th H

Table V

STEP A: Smith will gladly trade 4th horse for a cow.
Black will gladly trade 4th cow for a horse.

STEP B: Smith will gladly trade 3rd horse for a 2nd cow.
Black will gladly trade 3rd cow for a 2nd horse.

STEP C: No further trades of mutual advantage possible.

Then, they both have improved their situations and satisfied their value scales so far as this problem goes. Under these assumptions, no further trades are possible, because there is no advantage to be gained from any other transaction. They have each satisfied their value scales. If their value scales changed, you would have another problem, another situation. So much for that.

Satisfying a Value Scale

Now we go into another more complicated problem, shown in Table VI. We assume here that Smith has six horses and Black six cows. In the column on the left we assume that they both have the same value scales. First they would like a horse, second a second horse, third a first cow, fourth a second cow, fifth a third horse, sixth a fourth horse, and down on to the bottom of the column, as you can see.

These two gentlemen come together. What happens? Now

MORE COMPLEX BARTER			
Value Scale of both		Mr. Smith (S) has 6 horses (H) Mr. Black (B) has 6 cows (C)	
1st	1st H	S has his 1st, 2nd, 5th, 6th, 7th and 8th preferences;	
2nd	2nd H	B has his 3rd, 4th, 9th, 10th, 11th and 12th.	
3rd	1st C	Smith trades 6th H for Black's 6th C.	
4th	2nd C		
5th	3rd H	Then Smith has 5 horses and 1 cow:	
6th	4th H	his 1st, 2nd, *3rd,* 5th, 6th and 7th preferences. Black has 5 cows and 1 horse:	Table
7th	5th H	his *1st,* 3rd, 4th, 9th, 10th and 11th preferences.	VI
8th	6th H	Smith trades 5th H for Black's 5th C.	
9th	3rd C		
10th	4th C	Then Smith has 4 horses and 2 cows:	
11th	5th C	his 1st, 2nd, 3rd, *4th,* 5th and 6th preferences. Black has 4 cows and 2 horses:	
12th	6th C	his 1st, *2nd,* 3rd, 4th, 9th and 10th preferences.	
Smith would not gain, so no further trades with this value scale.			
If the 5th preference on the value scale were a cow, one more trade would give each his first 6 preferences.			

looking at these value scales we find that, in the existing situation, Smith has his 1st, 2nd, 5th, 6th, 7th, and 8th preferences, while Black has his 3rd, 4th, 9th, 10th, 11th, and 12th preferences. Under those circumstances, these two gentlemen meet. What happens?

They certainly will be happy to make an exchange. So Smith trades his sixth horse for Black's sixth cow. Then we have a situation in which Smith has five horses and one cow. Now he has advanced his situation to the point that he has his 1st, 2nd, and *3rd* (thanks to the trade), as well as his 5th, 6th, and 7th preferences. He has given up his eighth preference to obtain his third preference. He has improved his situation by getting the third item on his value scale in exchange for one that was lower down, in eighth place.

On the other hand, Black now has five cows and one horse. He has gotten his *first* preference and continues to have his 3rd, 4th, 9th, 10th, and 11th preferences. He has exchanged his 12th preference for his first preference. He, too, has certainly improved his situation from his own point of view.

Under these given conditions, it is also profitable for both of them to make another trade. Smith gladly trades his fifth horse for Black's fifth cow. Then Smith has four horses and two cows. He now has his 1st, 2nd, 3rd, *4th*, 5th, and 6th preferences. He has exchanged his 7th preference for his 4th preference. He now has all of his first six preferences. He cannot improve his satisfaction with only six animals.

On the other hand, Black has four cows and two horses. He has his 1st, *2nd*, 3rd, 4th, 9th, and 10th preferences. He has exchanged his 11th preference for his 2nd preference. He has his first four preferences, but he does not have his 5th, 6th, 7th, or 8th preferences. He would like to improve his situation further, but in the market you cannot improve your situation, you cannot have a transaction, unless both parties expect to gain. Since Smith could not gain from another trade, there will be no further trades with this value scale. Under these assumptions we have reached the end of the trading.

However, if the 5th or 6th preference on this value scale shifts to a cow, one more trade would give each of them their first six preferences. So this shows that as value scales change, the possible trades change. Value scales affect everything that can occur in the market place. Each person tends to trade up to the point beyond which he cannot gain any more. But he has to find somebody else who will also gain, or there will be no transaction.

We have been talking about barter, the exchange of goods for goods. In a market economy we usually exchange goods for money or vice versa. Now we want to consider exchanges with the use of money, getting into what we call prices. A price can be defined as a quantity of money.

A Böhm Bawerk Contribution

Much of the material for this lecture has been adapted from the works of Böhm Bawerk. He was not only one of the greatest economists ever, but he was also a teacher of my great teacher, Mises. Böhm Bawerk found it useful to compare the formation of prices to the breaking of waves and surf on the sea coast. Both are complex phenomena that seem to be completely "without rule or regularity," yet they are both subject to the strict operation of immutable laws.

When waves break on a rockbound coast, the path every drop of water follows may seem haphazard, but, given the essential data, the laws of physics can explain where every particle goes. Given the force of each wave, given the exact shape and resilience of the coast, and given the velocity and the direction of each gust of wind, there could only be one possible result. The laws of physics could then tell us where every drop of water must fall.

Likewise in economics, if we could know the ever-shifting value scales of every individual, and the available supplies of goods and services in the market place, then economic laws, the laws of human action, could tell us where every price would have to fall. Of course, in real life we cannot know the ever-changing value scales of all people. We can find them out in part, but only by reference to market exchanges.

When you go into a store, you do not usually tell the shopkeeper how much you might be willing to pay for a desired good. You try to find out the lowest price for which you can buy it. So when we participate in market trans-actions we seldom reveal how high we might go for the goods on our value scale. Therefore these values are seldom evident. But value scales determine all actions in the market place.

In developing man's understanding of economics, the British classical economists reduced everything to supply and demand. They took supply and demand as given. When they talked about supply and demand, they advocated that the businessman should strive to buy low and sell high. That is good business. But they did not go back to what creates supply and demand. This is a contribution of the Austrian School of economics.

Consumers Determine Prices

As I mentioned in my first lecture, science traces cause and effect by going back and back and back until one cannot go back any further. The Austrian economists demonstrated that you can go back behind supply and demand, and find out what it is that leads to both of them. Demand is determined by the value scales of consumers, while supply is determined by businessmen seeking to foresee, as accurately as they can, the future value scales of consumers. In the end, it is the value scales of consumers that determine both demand and supply and thus the prices of all goods and services sold in the market place.

Supply and demand are vague shibboleths that do not provide enough information. The central factor that explains price is found entirely in the subjective values of men. Market competition forces the pricing process into a zone between the subjective values of the border or marginal pairs, where the quantity offered for sale exactly equals the quantity there is a desire to buy at the market price. At that price, supply and demand are bound to be equal. You cannot buy more than are sold, but the price has to be one that benefits all who buy or sell.

Isolated Exchange

Now I'm going to present a few problems using money. You will pardon me if I use dollars here. It makes little difference which monetary unit is used. The first is a case of isolated exchange. (See Table VII.) There are just two men involved. Farmer Brown needs a horse. A horse is worth more to him than $300 — that is, he will pay for a horse up to, but not more than, $300. If he has to pay more, it will not be worth while for him to buy it. Neighbor Smith has a horse with a use value to him of only $100.

These two men meet. What happens? Naturally it is to the advantage of both of them to make an exchange. We posed the essential questions earlier: whether or not they should exchange, and if so, at what terms. We have determined that these men should exchange. The question then becomes, at what price will the horse be sold.

Given this situation, will they trade? If so, at what terms? Every price from $100 to $300 is possible. The actual price within that range will depend upon the bargaining abilities of the two men. But a price below $100 is impossible. Smith would not sell for less, because the horse is worth that much to him. At a lower price he would use the horse rather than sell it. A price over $300 would not lead to a transaction because the horse is not worth sufficiently more than $300 for Farmer Brown to pay the higher price. So the price must fall between $100 and $300.

There is a rule that applies. It is not my opinion. It is not what I think it should be. It is a fact. It is an economic law. It

---

ISOLATED EXCHANGE

Farmer Brown needs a horse. A horse is worth more than $300 to him, but not enough more for him to pay more than $300.

Neighbor Smith has a horse with a use value to him of $100.

Will they trade?   If so, at what terms?

Every price between $100 and $300 is possible. The actual price, within that range, will depend on the bargaining abilities of the two men.

RULE: The price must be between the buyer's *Subjective Value* and the seller's *Subjective Value.*

Table VII

is how men operate. The rule is that the price must fall between the buyer's subjective value and the seller's subjective value. Any other price is impossible. This seems simple and I hope it is understood. The price must benefit both parties.

One-Sided Competition Among Buyers

We move on to a little bit more complicated problem. We take now an example of one-sided competition among buyers. And the question is: Who will buy and within what price range? (See Table VIII.) Smith has a horse, as before, with a use value to him of $100. As before, a horse is worth more than $300 to Brown. But this time we also have a Mr. Carey for whom a horse is worth just a bit over $200. Who buys Smith's horse? And what will be the price range?

Given this situation, Brown will buy at a price between $200 and $300. Any other price is unthinkable. If the price were below $200, Brown would have competition from

Table VIII

ONE–SIDED COMPETITION AMONG BUYERS

QUESTION: Who will buy and within what price range?

ASSUME: Smith has a horse with a use value to him of $100.

A horse is worth just over $300 to Brown.
A horse is worth just over $200 to Carey.

Brown will buy at a price between $200 and $300.

ASSUME FURTHER: A horse is worth more than $260 to Dell.

Brown will buy between $260 and $300.

ASSUME FURTHER: A horse is worth more than $320 to Ely.

Ely will buy at a price between $300 and $320.

RULE: The potential buyer who places the highest value on the good gets it at a price below his own valuation and above the highest value of all his competitors.

Carey. If the price were over $300 the horse would not be worth it to him. So the only sale that can take place, given these assumptions, is between the prices of $200 and $300.

Now assume another man, Señor Dell, comes along. He wants to buy a horse, and a horse is worth more than $260 to him. What does this do to the situation? Who will buy the horse, and what price will he pay?

Mr. Brown will buy the horse, but he will have to pay more than $200 under these circumstances. He will have to outbid Mr. Dell. He will have to pay a higher price than $260, but of course he will still not pay more than $300.

Now assume further that another gentleman, Mr. Ely, comes along. For him a horse is worth more than $320. Now what happens? What is the answer to the question of who will buy and within what price range? It should be obvious by now that Mr. Ely will buy the horse. What price will he pay? He has to outbid our friend Mr. Brown. So he will have to pay more than $300, but he will not pay more than $320.

Now, these are not my opinions. This is not how I say it should be. But this is how men act. They try to get what they want at the best price they can, and they do not pay more than the good is worth to them. The rule for this type of exchange is that the potential buyer who places the highest value on the good gets it at a price below his own valuation and above the highest value placed on the good by any of his competitors.

What we are saying is simply that the market allocates scarce goods to those who place the highest values on them, to those prepared to make the greatest sacrifice to attain them. Here we have had competition on one side, competition among multiple buyers for one horse.

One-Sided Competition Among Sellers

Now, we move to the very opposite situation, one-sided competition among sellers. (See Table IX.) There is one buyer and there are many potential sellers. The question here is, who will sell and within what price range? Potential buyer Brown places a subjective use value of $300 on a horse. Potential seller Fort places a subjective value of $140 on his horse, while Green places a subjective use value of $200 on his, and another potential seller, Mr. Hall, has a subjective use value of $250 for his horse. Who will sell the horse to Mr. Brown, and within what price range?

It should now become obvious that it is not a question of my opinion. Every one of us should come to the same conclusion, because this is a matter of how all men act. It is an application of economic law.

Mr. Brown will buy the horse as cheaply as he can. He will not pay $200 if he can get a horse for less than $200. So, based on these assumptions, he will pay less than Mr. Green is asking. Mr. Fort will sell his horse to Mr. Brown at a price between $140 and $200. Any other price is unthinkable.

Moving on, we assume further that another gentleman, a Mr. Jate, wants to sell a horse. He places a subjective value of

---

ONE-SIDED COMPETITION AMONG SELLERS

QUESTION: Who will sell and within what price range?

ASSUME: Potential Buyer Brown places a subjective value (S/V) of $300 on a horse.

Potential Seller Fort with a Subjective Value of $140.
Potential Seller Green with a Subjective Value of $200.
Potential Seller Hall with a Subjective Value of $250.

Table
IX

Fort will sell at a price between $140 and $200.

ASSUME FURTHER: Potential Seller Jate with a S/V of $180.

Fort will sell at a price between $140 and $180.

ASSUME FURTHER: Potential Seller Korn with a S/V of $120.

Korn will sell at a price between $120 and $140.

RULE: The potential seller who places the lowest subjective value on the good sells it at a price above his own valuation and below the lowest subjective value of all his competitors.

$180 on his horse. What does this do to the situation? It reduces the price that Mr. Fort will be able to ask. He will still sell his horse to Mr. Brown. But now it will NOT be between $140 and $200, but, according to his bargaining ability, between $140 and $180.

We assume another gentleman comes along, a seller, Mr. Korn, who places a subjective use value of $120 on his horse. Applying the same reasoning, Mr. Brown wants a horse, which is worth more than $300 to him, but he still doesn't want to pay any more than he has to. He puts these men into competition bidding against each other. The bidding goes down below the previous high price of $180. Mr. Brown can now buy a horse at a price between $120 and $140.

The rule here is that the potential seller who places the lowest subjective value on the good sells it at a price above his own subjective valuation and below the lowest subjective value placed on the good by any of his competitors. And so a horse moves from the potential seller who places the lowest value on a horse to the man who places the highest value on one. That is how the market works.

These problems have been relatively simple. The value of money is a factor in all of these. This too is not constant. The value of money is always shifting. As the values of horses and money shift, the value scales of people shift. They get different ideas about what is to their advantage. But they only trade when they expect to gain. In these examples we have assumed that their value judgments remain constant until the transactions are completed. The prices that resulted were formed under the impact of the entire quantity of horses on the value scales of all present at the market. All the competing suppliers and buyers had a chance to act to improve their situation according to their value scales as the market conditions permitted. Competition forced every successful buyer and seller to set his price with full regard to the relative subjective values of all concerned.

Bilateral Competition

Now we come to an example of bilateral competition, as I call it. (See Table X.) This is a more complex situation, in which there is competition between both multiple buyers and multiple sellers for a limited quantity of goods, in this case, thirteen taxicabs.

<table>
<tr><td colspan="6" align="center">**BILATERAL COMPETITION**
(Problem posed)
Assumed subjective valuation of similar taxis</td></tr>
<tr><td colspan="3" align="center">**Owners of 13 taxis**</td><td colspan="3" align="center">**Potential Buyers**</td></tr>
<tr><td>Ace's</td><td>1st</td><td>$4,000</td><td>Law's</td><td>3rd</td><td>$2,750</td></tr>
<tr><td>Bag's</td><td>1st</td><td>3,800</td><td>Moon's</td><td>2nd</td><td>2,920</td></tr>
<tr><td>Cod's</td><td>1st</td><td>3,750</td><td>Nid's</td><td>2nd</td><td>3,080</td></tr>
<tr><td></td><td></td><td></td><td></td><td></td><td></td></tr>
<tr><td>Ace's</td><td>2nd</td><td>3,600</td><td>Law's</td><td>2nd</td><td>3,130</td></tr>
<tr><td>Dove's</td><td>1st</td><td>3,500</td><td>Ott's</td><td>1st</td><td>3,400</td></tr>
<tr><td>Eby's</td><td>1st</td><td>3,450</td><td>Pry's</td><td>2nd</td><td>3,550</td></tr>
<tr><td></td><td></td><td></td><td></td><td></td><td></td></tr>
<tr><td>Bag's</td><td>2nd</td><td>3,380</td><td>Moon's</td><td>1st</td><td>3,680</td></tr>
<tr><td>Ace's</td><td>3rd</td><td>3,360</td><td>Law's</td><td>1st</td><td>3,780</td></tr>
<tr><td>Fork's</td><td>1st</td><td>3,330</td><td>Pry's</td><td>1st</td><td>4,100</td></tr>
<tr><td></td><td></td><td></td><td></td><td></td><td></td></tr>
<tr><td>Gay's</td><td>1st</td><td>3,250</td><td>Nid's</td><td>1st</td><td>4,250</td></tr>
<tr><td>Ace's</td><td>4th</td><td>3,050</td><td></td><td></td><td></td></tr>
<tr><td>Bag's</td><td>3rd</td><td>2,800</td><td></td><td></td><td></td></tr>
<tr><td>Dove's</td><td>2nd</td><td>2,600</td><td></td><td></td><td></td></tr>
</table>

Part 1 – How many sold? Within what price range?

Part 2 – Assume (a) sales tax of $50; (b) 10% tax.

Table X

In the column on the left-hand side are the owners of thirteen taxicabs or taxis. Seven men own these thirteen taxis; four of them are owned by Mr. Ace. In the next column we have the assumed subjective values these owners place on their taxis, that is, the figures below which they would not sell the taxis. If they can get a higher price for any one of the taxis than the figure shown in this column, they will sell that cab. On the right-hand side, we have some potential buyers and the highest prices they would pay, the subjective valuations they place on owning a taxicab. If they can get taxicabs for these figures, they will buy. If they cannot, they will not buy.

There are thirteen cabs. We shall assume they are identical cabs with no material differences that need to be taken into account. The potential buyers and potential sellers all come together at one time and place. There are potential bidders here, ten, I believe. The questions are: How many of the cabs will be sold? How many will not be sold? And within what price range will the sales be made?

The answer is rather simple. There are many ways you can go about getting it. You can be quite complex and start the bidding low. Of course, no one will offer to sell a taxi for $2,600. If Mr. Dove tries to get, say, $2,700 for his second one, he will have every one of these ten potential buyers bidding for it. They are not going to let it be sold for $2,700. They are going to bid it up. As they bid it up, Mr. Bag comes in when it gets to a price above $2,800. Before then, Mr. Law's demand has dropped out. As the bidding goes higher, other cabs become available, and other potential cab buyers drop out. This goes on until you get into a price range where the number of cabs offered for sale and the number of potential buyers who will buy become equal.

Or you can start with the top. Mr. Ace would be glad to sell his top cab for $4,150 to Mr. Nid. But he is not going to get $4,150 because Mr. Nid is not going to pay $4,150, when all these other cab owners are competing to sell one for less. Competitive bidding will bring the price down, making fewer cars available for sale as it drops below the points in the left-hand column. At the same time, competition will increase the number of the potential buyers as it drops below points in the right-hand column. This will go on until the price reaches the price range where again the number offered for sale equals the number potential buyers will buy.

In this market place, we assume all these cabs are similar. There are no known differences, no dents in the fenders as in real life. There will be one price at which the owners will exchange all the cabs that are exchanged. The question is: How many will be exchanged and at what price? The answer is simple.

The best and easiest way to find the answer is to apply

what I have already said about the market. This is the fact that the market allocates all scarce goods to those who place the highest values on them. You have thirteen taxicabs. You have twenty-three desires for the taxicabs. Who ends up with the taxicabs? Those who place the thirteen highest values on them.

So all you have to do is to find out quickly which are the thirteen highest values. The answer to this problem is that six taxicabs will be sold, and the price will be between $3,360 and $3,380. All three methods reach the same result. No other answer or price is thinkable. (See Table XI.)

At a lower price, Mr. Ace would not sell his third cab. At a higher price, Mr. Bag would try to sell his second cab. There would be seven potential sellers, but there would not be seven potential buyers. There would thus not be equality

Table
XI

BILATERAL COMPETITION
(*First part of problem answered*)

Assumed subjective valuation of similar taxis

Owners of 13 taxis			Potential Buyers		
Aces's	1st	$4,000	Law's	3rd	$2,750
Bag's	1st	3,800	Moon's	2nd	2,920
Cod's	1st	3,750	Nid's	2nd	3,080
Ace's	2nd	3,600	ⓧ Law's	2nd	3,130
Dove's	1st	3,500	☒ Ott's	1st	3,400
Eby's	1st	3,450	Pry's	2nd	3,550
Bag's	2nd	3,380 ☒	Moon's	1st	3,680
Ace's	3rd	3,360 ⓧ	Law's	1st	3,780
Fork's	1st	3,330	Pry's	1st	4,100
Gay's	1st	3,250	Nid's	1st	4,250
Ace's	4th	3,050			
Bag's	3rd	2,800			
Dove's	2nd	2,600			

How many sold?	Within what price range?
6	**$3,360 to $3,380**

between the number offered for sale and the number that would be bought. The bidding would go on until that number was equal, because would-be sellers can never sell more than potential buyers will buy.

So the subjective values of the market participants limit the price range, and the market allocates the scarce taxis to those who place the highest values on them. The thirteen who place the highest values on them are those above the line on the left side and those below the line on the right side. When the transactions are completed, these parties are the ones who are going to own cabs. Given this assumed state of the market, the people on the left below the line do not value cabs enough to keep them, while the people on the right above the line do not value cabs enough to buy them.

If there were a fourteenth cab, one more desire for a cab could be satisfied. If there were fifteen cabs, two more desires could be satisfied. But the reality of life on this earth is that there is a scarcity of the things men want, and the economic problem is to decide who gets these scarce goods and who must go without.

Law of Price

In the market economy, this decision as to who gets the limited number of taxicabs, who goes without, and what the price will be, is determined by the Law of Price. The Law of Price is not opinion. It is not what I think it should be. Nor is it a law I would like the government to pass. It describes how men act, in a market situation, each man trying to improve his situation as best he can from his point of view. It is, however, just as immutable as any law of physics.

Under bilateral competition, market prices must fall within a range between upper and lower limits that are determined by the available supply and the subjective values of the interested parties. The upper limit is set by the subjective valuations of the lowest successful bidder and the lowest excluded potential seller, whichever is lower. The lower limit is set by the subjective valuations of the highest successful offerer and the highest excluded potential buyer, whichever is higher.

Prices are determined by the subjective valuations of the two marginal pairs, and must fall within the range between the middle two of these four valuations. Valuations above and below these middle two marginal pair valuations have no effect on the market price.

Now let us look at Table XI again and run through this Law of Price with the figures before us. According to the Law of Price, under bilateral competition, market prices must fall within a range between an upper limit and a lower limit. The upper limit is set by the lower of the pair with the X in the squares. Of those two, the lower one is the $3,380 figure. That is the upper limit.

The lower limit is set by the higher of the pair with the X in the circles. In this case, the higher is the $3,360. So the price has to fall between these middle two, $3,360 and $3,380.

At any other price, there would not be equal numbers willing to buy and willing to sell. This is not my opinion. It is how all men act. They will not buy unless they expect to improve their situation by getting something they value higher than they value the sum of money they pay for it. They will not sell unless they value the money received higher than they value the good they offer for sale. Every participant expects to gain from every transaction, and there must be a buyer for each unit sold. Likewise, men will not pay more than market conditions demand; nor will they sell for less than competitive market conditions compel potential buyers to pay.

Effect of Taxes

Now we shall try to show what happens when the government places a tax on the transaction. First we shall assume a sales tax of $50 on every sale of a taxicab. That means you have to add $50 to the subjective value each potential seller places on his taxicab. He will have to get at least that much before he improves his situation by selling. What happens with this problem?

Under the assumed conditions, only five cabs would be sold, and the price would be in the range from $3,350 to

$3,360. With the tax included, this price range would be from $3,400 to $3,410. (See Table XII.)

BILATERAL COMPETITION
(Second part of problem answered)
Effect Of Taxes
Assume sales tax added to sales price of each taxi in Table XI.

Table XII

If a flat rate of $50 per taxi:	If a 10% sales tax rate:
5 taxis will be sold at a price of $3,350 – 3,360 ; with tax included, $3,400 – 3,410.	4 taxis will be sold at $3,250 – 3,330; with tax included, $3,575 – 3,663.

If the tax were 10 percent of the sales price, only four cabs would be sold, and the price range, with the tax included, would be between $3,575 and $3,663.

Now we have seen what would happen to the price. It goes up. We have also seen what would happen to the number of transactions. Fewer cabs are sold. This means that under the first assumption, the $50 tax, one taxicab has to remain with a man who places a lower value on it than another man, a potential buyer, does. Because of the tax, the taxicab cannot be transferred to the potential buyer who places a higher value on it, but for whom it is not worth the extra $50 he must now pay.

When the tax goes up as high as 10 percent of the sales price, two taxicabs have to remain with men who place a lower value on them than would be the case in a market where the taxes did not exist. So sales taxes stand in the way of transactions that would increase the satisfactions of both potential buyers and potential sellers.

Of course, those taxes might be necessary for the market to operate. In that case they are a necessary cost of doing business. But when they are just an interference with the market, or a tax to provide a subsidy for some privileged group, rather than an expense for the equal protection of all, they must diminish the satisfactions of the people operating in the market place. Every transaction prevented reduces the satisfaction of a potential buyer and a potential seller. In addition, it results in a rearrangement of market conditions in a manner that must reduce the highest potential satisfaction of human beings.

This is how prices come about. They emerge from the concatenation of the subjective values of all the people participating in the market place, each one trying to improve his situation as best he can from his own point of view. Except for the valuations of the middle marginal pair, changes in the valuations of the other parties have no influence, as long as they do not cross the price range of the middle marginal pair. If one of the potential buyers below the line was willing to pay up to $10,000 for a cab, it would have absolutely no influence on this particular situation, because he will not in fact pay more than he needs to pay, that is, the market price.

Remember that price must benefit all who trade. You do not trade unless you expect to benefit. Price must also allocate the available units to those who place the highest value on them. And every interference with free market prices is an interference that must diminish the human satisfaction of moral persons. It leaves things where they are worth less than they would have been worth if the market had been free to transfer them to those placing the highest value on them.

The same is true of laws that do not directly affect price, but do directly affect what you can trade, the hours during which you can trade, or where you can trade. All such laws reduce transactions and must therefore reduce human satisfactions.

Economic Calculation

We have been talking about consumers' goods, or things that people seek for their own use satisfactions. Let us go into the more complicated part of the market — producers' goods, or goods that are eventually used to make consumers' goods. When valuing producers' or capital goods, men transfer values of consumers' goods to their factors of production, that is, to the various things that are needed to make the consumer goods. It is thus the market value of consumers' goods that determines the value of labor, machines, and raw materials. For this, economic calculation is necessary.

Under socialism, economic calculation is not possible. Without a market, socialists cannot calculate what goods will give the most satisfaction, or the most efficient way to make whatever they decide to make. Since the government owns and controls all the factors of production, there can be no competitive market bidding for scarce materials to decide how they should be allocated. This is a function of prices in a market economy. But there is no market for raw materials or other factors of production in a socialist or communist society.

In a socialist or communist society, those who want to find out whether steel is more expensive than aluminum or some other metal have to buy a newspaper from a country that has a market. Even then, the prices in that paper will reflect the relative values of that country's market and not those within the borders of the socialist area, where supply and demand conditions may be very different. Socialists have no other way of knowing relative values. They must rely on the opinion of some bureaucrat, someone with authority. Without competitive prices, planning production is like trying to solve a puzzle without an answer. Because it monopolizes raw materials, the government receives no help from competitors in determining relative values.

In our market calculations we grade, prefer, and set aside. Values are ordinal and comparative. Now let's take an example of what happens in the market with one of the factors of production. Take iron, for example.

The price of iron originates in the businessmen's appraisal of the consumers' subjective valuations of iron products, products of which iron is a part. After all, businessmen cannot sell their products unless consumers consider them a bargain. So their ideas of consumers' valuations determine how high they will go in bidding for iron and the other factors needed to make their product.

The available supply of iron, like that of taxicabs, always

goes to the highest bidders, those who expect their use of the iron will bring the highest price from consumers. Of course, the larger the quantity offered for sale, the fewer the potential buyers who are disappointed. Money is the common denominator for calculating the most profitable uses of the limited supply, that is, the best-paid uses, the highest prices on the market.

The available iron is sold to the highest bidders, with the marginal buyer determining its price and thus the cost to all buyers, even those who might have been willing to pay more. The competition of sellers drives prices down on all iron products. If there are high profits, there will soon be more suppliers competing. General market bidding thus allocates all the available supplies of all factors of production so as to satisfy the highest not yet satisfied consumer wants. High market prices for a product induce businessmen to increase production of that product, while low market prices cause businessmen to use the factors of production to make other consumers' goods for which they expect prices to be higher.

Market Effect of Savings

Whenever additional savings are available, these new savings start a bidding for the factors of production needed to supply the highest not yet satisfied wants on consumers' value scales. This bidding raises costs, including wages, and ultimately results in more production, which tends to lower prices and squeeze or eliminate profits.

If the cost of some factor of production is too high for businessmen, it means there is another use for it for which consumers are expected to pay a higher price. Prices are expressions of relative scarcity in relation to demand. Values are not quantities but arrangements in order of importance in satisfying human wants. Adding values, like adding love, is crazy. We can only compare them.

As consumers' value scales change, the kinds of wealth produced must change. Market prices are the indicators that direct businessmen to change their production. Businessmen tend to produce units of every article up to the point at which they expect consumers to pay all costs of production, including interest. A profitable industry tends to expand to that point; an unprofitable one tends to shrink to that point. Thus consumers, by their buying or non-buying at or above the cost of production, determine how much should be produced in every branch of industry.

There prevails upon the unhampered market a tendency for consumers to encourage production in every industry up to that point at which the marginal producer or producers make neither a profit nor a loss. Flexible market prices are the means for revealing that point to producers. Any outside interference with freely flexible prices must misdirect production and lead to diminished satisfaction of consumers.

Subjective Values Determine Prices

As stated in the beginning, it is the subjective values of individuals which allocate the available supply of every good, so as to satisfy human wants in the descending order of their importance, whereby the particular want last satisfied is the one with the marginal utility. From beginning to end, prices, and thus economic calculations, are the products of subjective valuations. They are the results of the reciprocal impact of the subjective values placed on the goods and those placed on a quantity of money by all interested parties. Every price must benefit all who exchange.

There is nothing automatic or mysterious in the operation of the market. The only forces determining the continually fluctuating up-and-down state of the market are the value judgments of interested individuals, and their actions as directed by their value judgments. The ultimate factor in the market is the striving of each man to satisfy his needs and wants in the most economical way possible or known to him. The supremacy of the market is in fact a supremacy of the consumers. Interfering with the market interferes with the satisfactions of consumers.

QUESTIONS AND ANSWERS

Effect of Consumers' Values on Producers

Q. What you have explained is all right for products which already exist. But does it apply to those that don't exist – to new ones?

A. Certainly it does! As I have said, people's wants are never fully satisfied. There are always some things they want that they do not have. When there are new savings in a market society, the saver becomes an investor. He tries to invest his savings in a way that will produce more goods. What goods? Those goods next lower on consumers' value scales, for which their needs have not yet been satisfied. These are the goods that businessmen expect consumers will pay more for in the future than their current cost of production. When he produces these new goods, he has got to bid for labor. He has got to bid for raw materials. Thus he pushes those wages and prices up to take the labor and raw materials away from other uses. Then he produces goods that have to be sold in competition with all existing goods. With more goods and no change in the quantity of money, prices are lower than they would have been, and everyone gets more for his own limited amounts of money. To answer the question more specifically, every businessman must pay attention to consumers' values – to what consumers want and will pay. This may mean producing larger quantities of presently available goods or entirely new items not previously available. In either case, more human wants are satisfied. If a businessman does not pay attention to consumers' wants, he will soon be out of business.

Morality of Speculation

Q. The majority of people consider speculation immoral. What do you have to say about that?

A. Calling speculation "immoral" is saying that all men are immoral, because we are all speculators. It is even a speculation to cross the streets in Buenos Aires — or New York. No one knows the future. We have to speculate. All of our choices and actions are speculations.

It is true that many consider immoral those "terrible" people who make money speculating. Do you know that you cannot make money speculating unless you serve society? If you speculate on the future and do not serve society, you lose. The normal process for successful speculation is to buy something cheap at one period and sell it high at a later period. Speculators make a profit when they can do this. But when they buy, they have no assurance that it is going to be higher later. It could be lower and then they lose. Try it in the stock market sometime and you will find out.

If the speculators buy something when its price is low, they are buying it when it is in relatively large supply and, because the price is low, people are using it as a cheap good. If they sell it later at a higher price, it is because it is then scarcer in relation to the demand for it. It is, therefore, worth more and serves human uses that are more valuable. So what the speculator does to earn his money is to buy the good when it is cheap and store it for when he hopes it may be more expensive. If this is something that is needed for life, like the grain in the story of Joseph in the Bible, when the seven plenteous years were followed by seven years of famine, the service to society becomes evident. Those who save goods when there is a plentiful supply and make it available when there is a famine, or no other supply, are speculators who make money by serving society. If, on the other hand, there is, later on, a larger supply, the speculator has to sell his stored supply at a cheaper price, pay for the warehouse, pay interest on his investment, and thus he loses. A speculator can make money only when he serves society. A speculator is a person who tries to foresee the future situation and prepare for it. Only if he sees and acts relatively more effectively than other people in satisfying human wants, does he make a market profit from his speculation. Serving society is never immoral.

On Effects of Intrinsic Value and Quality

Q. What do you have to say about the influence of intrinsic value? And about the influence of quality?

A. Those are really two different questions. In economics, there is no such thing as intrinsic value. This is a very common error, particularly concerning the precious metals, including gold. Nothing has value in the market unless it satisfies some human want or need. The value of something is in a person's mind. It is not in the product. Of course, the physical qualities of a good contribute to its usefulness to men. However, it is only when men can see a use for a scarce good that it has value.

Now, of course, the quality of a good is an essence of its value. Rotten eggs have little value. There are people who will pay more for a higher quality. But the seller can charge a higher price for a higher quality only if people want the higher quality. Most of us, of course, prefer higher quality. We do not go around in rags. We buy suits that are made to fit us. We buy suits that look better on us than simple lengths of cloth that we could wind around us to keep us warm, and we pay more for them. It is the consumers who determine both the values and the qualities that are found in the market.

Competition and Monopoly

Q. What happens to the Golden Rule when there is no perfect competition, that is to say, under oligopoly and monopoly?

A. First, about this "perfect competition," we could spend a whole evening on the fallacies embraced by that idea. There is no such thing as perfect competition. But in a market society there is always competition. In one sense everything in the market is in competition with everything else for the consumers' dollars.

We could spend another couple of evenings on the

question of competition and monopoly. Actually, the only monopolies we have to fear are those that are monopolies because they have a special privilege from a government. If there is freedom to compete in the market place, you can maintain a monopoly only as long as you are superior to every prospective competitor. In a free market society, you do not have a monopoly unless you are doing something better than any other person or group of persons could do it.

In one sense, we are all monopolists. We each have a monopoly on our own services. The man who is the best prize fighter, the champion of the world, has a monopoly on that title. The opera singer who can sing the highest note has a monopoly and gets the highest price. The man who owns the only gasoline station in a community has a monopoly. In a free market society, if anyone can do better, he is free to compete.

The problems of monopoly get down to the question of monopoly prices. No one has to pay a monopoly price unless he is satisfied that doing so improves his situation. In a free market anyone should be able to compete, if he thinks he can compete.

Most of our monopoly problems come from special privileges granted by law. The answer there is always to take away the special privilege. With equality before the law, which was mentioned in one question following the first lecture, there is no significant monopoly problem. Everybody should have an equal right to compete. Then those who give consumers the greatest satisfaction will be the ones who succeed. If they get fat, lazy, and rich from their success, then somebody else will come along, compete, and knock them down. In a free market, newcomers are constantly trying to replace the giant firms on the top.

One of the worst effects of the New Deal in my country and of welfare state processes in other countries is that they keep at the top those who are already there. Interventionism tends to protect them from the competition of those at the bottom who would like to replace them.

For example, it is now impossible in my country to do what Henry Ford did forty years ago. What Henry Ford did was to employ men to make more automobiles for more people, who bought them all at prices that they considered bargains. He paid the workers higher wages than they could get anywhere else. He made these automobiles for the masses and became rich. What did he do with his wealth? He plowed it back into more or bigger factories, hiring still more men to make still more cars.

Today, with present tax rates, the government takes a good part of all profits, including more than half of the profits made by corporations. As a result a businessman in the United States can no longer expand as fast as Henry Ford could. He therefore cannot compete as easily against the giants already at the top. So these laws, supposedly directed against the top people, are more against the new, smaller, struggling competitors. They prevent newcomers from competing with those already on the top as efficiently as they could if they were permitted to keep and plow back into the business more of their early profits.

Calculation Under Communism

Q. Considering the actual value scales existing in Communist Russia, must not the Communists calculate economic values on the basis of the cost of production?

A. They have no cost of production, or rather, their cost of production is the sweat and blood of their people. It is an order: You do this, or you do that, or you do something else. They cannot calculate market costs because they have no market to tell them costs. Their calculations have to be based on the judgments of a czar, the czar of each particular industry.

Some ten years ago, I put together an article that was largely quotations from Russian papers, *Pravda* and others. It related several interesting incidents, which indicated that these papers were not entirely happy with the operation of their own Russian Soviet system. It seems there was one industry that had to move goods from the north to the south on the Volga River. So they built a fleet of boats to move these goods from the north to the south, and the boats returned north empty. There was also another industry that had to move goods from the south to the north. So this industry built another fleet of boats that returned south empty.

Now in a market economy, there would be common carriers, or advertising that would bring the two industries together. In either case, the market economy would not waste its scarce labor and its scarce materials by building two fleets of ships to do what one could do.

Another interesting article was about the Soviet railroad organization. It was paid to carry things on the railroads. The railroads had some tank cars. If they moved oil in one direction, they got paid for it. If they came back empty, they did not get paid for it. So on the return trips they would fill up the tank cars with water. That way they got paid for the return trip. How can you calculate costs under such a system? There are many examples of such uneconomic actions. I shall cite one in a later talk. It concerns a trade agreement arranged between East Germany and the Soviet Union that resulted in a suicide.

The communists have no means of calculation unless they look outside the country to market economies. Then they have the relationship of supply and demand that exists within the other country. The communist system, because it has no economic calculation, has to be inefficient. Communists can never be forerunners. They must always be followers. When people understand this, they will no longer be afraid of them as an economic power. If communism were a good and strong economic system, we should adopt it. But the communists are not strong. They are weak. They are now trying to copy capitalistic production methods, but they cannot do so while the government controls and allocates all the factors of production. Without markets, they are blind as to real costs.

Christianity and Capitalism

Q. Do you think that Protestantism has helped free market principles?

A. Well, I am a very staunch believer that free market principles are in full harmony with Christian principles and that the free market is the only economic system that is consistent with Christian or Judeo-Christian principles. I must say that in recent years the organized churches, both the Protestant and the Roman Catholic, have not been in harmony with free market teachings, nor have they been in harmony with what I must hold are the principles taught in the Bible. The organized churches have largely accepted the welfare state ideology so popular today. This ideology has changed the original meaning of the Ten Commandments. I could give you quite a speech on that. However, I want to make just this one point. There is the Commandment which in English is only four words: "Thou shalt not steal." Today, most of our people think that it has been expanded to eight words. They think it is: "Thou shalt not steal except by majority vote." They seem to think that any stealing done by majority vote is all right.

Except when necessary for defense, neither capitalism nor Christianity approves of the use of force or coercion. The fundamental principle of the free market, voluntary social cooperation for mutual advantage, is in full conformity with Judeo-Christian teachings.

Anti-trust Law Interventions

Q. What do you think about the anti-trust laws?

A. How many weeks can we have to answer that? Anti-trust laws are like all other interventions. They help certain interests and they hurt others. They always hurt the consumers. In my country the anti-trust laws originated because the government had given privileges to certain industries, and the companies, particularly the railroads, used these privileges to enrich themselves at the expense of the consumers. By law, the railroads were handed monopoly privileges that protected them from competition. Once they had this monopoly, they raised rates above those that would have attracted competition; but no competitor could come in to lower them. Then the people and the government said, "We have to control these greedy monopolies!" This led to the creation of the so-called anti-trust laws.

Most of the anti-trust laws are aimed at trying to undo the damage created by earlier government laws. I have written an article on this subject, particularly with relation to labor unions. It is entitled, "Is Further Intervention a Cure for Prior Intervention?"[1] My answer is "No." Marx wanted such interventions because, as he correctly stated in the Communist Manifesto, they will make matters worse, create a demand for more and more intervention, until they result in overturning the capitalistic system. This is what is happening in many countries today. When people think the remedy for anything they do not like is another law, you get more and more laws until there is no freedom left. Every one of these governmental interventions makes matters worse from the point of view of those who advocate them. Try and think of one that does not.

Are High Prices Helpful?

Q. Do you think that the producer who sells his product at high prices benefits the community?

A. Yes, if he can get them. If the high prices mean a high profit, he is soon going to have competitors who will gradually bring the price down pretty close to the actual costs of production. Let me cite an example that has been before the world just recently, the case of the few doctors who are able to transplant human hearts. Suppose you only allowed them to charge $100 per operation, and they could only perform one operation a week, and there was need for many more. Who would be selected, and how many young doctors would train to learn that operation, if $100 once a week were all they could make? On the other hand, if they were allowed to charge the highest price they could get, the market would select their customers. If that price were really high, many young doctors would want to learn to perform

---

1. First published in *On Freedom and Free Enterprise: Essays in Honor of Ludwig von Mises,* ed. by Mary Sennholz. (Princeton, New Jersey, D. Van Nostrand Co., Inc., 1956. Reprinted separately by the Foundation for Economic Education, Inc., Irvington-on-Hudson, N.Y.).

that very intricate operation. In a short period of time, more doctors would be able to perform the operation; the price would come down and more people could benefit from that type of operation, if it could help them.

The remedy for high prices is prices high enough to attract competition. When you lower prices by law, you not only fail to attract new producers, but you also make it unprofitable for marginal producers to continue in business. So production goes down, and consumers are provided with less satisfaction.

We have seen that in my country in connection with the question of rent control. During World War II, they said we had to take care of the poor people and keep rents low. So they froze rents then in effect across the nation. Wartime inflation raised the costs of construction. What happened? Nobody built any houses for rent, not even after the war, when construction materials were again available for peacetime uses. Did that help the boys who came back from the war, married, and started new families? No. It only created a still greater shortage of rental housing.

What was the political solution? Another law – public housing. First, there was public housing for politically selected low-income families. Now it is public housing for politically selected middle-income families. Like the public schools a century earlier, it may be public housing for all incomes before long. In Russia, you take the housing the government assigns you. In Sweden, married couples sign up for space on a waiting list. By the time they get something they are ready for divorce.

On Politics and Poverty

Q. How do you explain the fact that today, although we live in a free market economy, every day there are fewer rich and every day more and more poor?

A. I do not know where the questioner lives! In my country and other countries of the Western civilization, we have had more and more wealth under *relatively* free market economies. It is only where government intervention results in capital consumption that there is less wealth produced. Marx certainly never envisioned the automobiles you have running around the streets here. He thought that before the end of the nineteenth century people were going to be starving, and that then they would rise up, throw off their chains, and create a dictatorship of the proletariat.

Now the automobiles that you have in Buenos Aires are not for the rich only. Those who are really poor today are poor largely because government intervention keeps them from competing for jobs. I, of course, am no authority on your economy, but I do know that in my country the poor, and particularly the Negroes, are kept poor because the labor unions can legally keep them out of jobs. We shall be saying more on this subject in the next lecture. It is the interventionist laws that prevent the poor from getting on the bottom rung of the ladder so that they can start the climb up. The stress of poverty is greatest when production goes down, and this usually occurs as a result of government interferences with a market economy.

We may not have a free market economy but we do have a market economy. We have what my great teacher calls a hampered market economy. It *is* hampered. Its operations are hindered by governmental interferences. Under this situation we all have less. Both the rich and the poor have less, but the poor suffer more. The rich can get along comfortably with a little less, but many of the poor cannot take that less. Most government intervention is intended to help the poor at the expense of the rich, but, short of a dictatorship, it is always at the expense of everyone, including the poor.

Speculators and Scarcity

Q. Do you agree that a speculator can artificially create scarcity so as to sell at a high price?

A. No, I would not agree that he can artificially create scarcity except in a very, very temporary local situation. We had a case in New York. Some of you may remember that a couple of years ago our electricity went off late one

afternoon, and remained off for some fifteen hours. People
were caught in elevators. Everything was dark. Radios and
TVs were silent. No one knew why. The only news I could
hear was the radio in my automobile, and the local stations
were going off the air. All of our electricity had gone off.
There was a scarcity of electricity, to put it mildly. Those
people who had flashlights and candles to sell were in a
position to make a nice little profit. But if those flashlights
and candles had not been there, the people could not have
had them. People can make these profits only when they
foresee the future better than their competitors. In a free
society everybody has the right to be a speculator. If you
think the price of cotton is going to double by next year, buy
it now. Sell it next year. You have as much right to do it as
anybody else. But what if you do, and the price goes down?
This is the chance the speculator takes. If someone destroys
his own property to raise prices, he is going to invite
competition, so that any gain will be short-lived.

Price Controls

Q. What are the consequences of imposing maximum and
minimum prices?

A. Imposing a maximum price – that is, holding prices below those of the market – means that the marginal producer
will not cover his costs and will go out of business. Imposing
a minimum price – that is, holding prices above those of the
market – has the opposite effect. It means that more will be
produced than can be sold at the minimum price.

Mises tells the story of how they like to introduce these
maximum prices by putting them on something that is very
much needed, say milk for babies. The poor people need
cheap milk. So we lower the price of milk by law. And what
do the people who have the cows do? They use the milk to
make cheese and ice cream, which are not under price
control. So to keep the price of milk down you have to apply
the price controls to cheese and ice cream. The controls then
must be applied to the expenses of the dairy industry, and

eventually from one product to another, until you get to the point that Hitler reached in Nazi Germany.

Establishing minimum prices, by which the government guarantees a higher-than-free-market minimum price to producers, as we have done in our farm programs in my country, means that you soon have surpluses piling up in warehouses. The taxpayers then have to pay subsidies to the farmers, storage, and higher interest charges, as well as higher prices for their food and cotton goods. In fact, all over the world new areas are now growing cotton and taking our former markets away from us. The free market would direct those now producing the surpluses to make something else that consumers prefer rather than more of the goods for which prices are held artificially high.

The maximum prices reduce production and the availability of the goods. The minimum prices increase production beyond what people want at prices that cover the marginal cost of production. Then the product has to be warehoused or destroyed. In your neighboring country, Brazil, they simply burned their surpluses of coffee.

Existence of a Free Market Economy

Q. In the United States, do you have a free market economy, and if so, tell us since when?

A. The free market economy is like Christianity. It is a goal to move toward but human beings never quite attain it. We have never had a completely free economy in the United States. It was only relatively freer than any that had ever existed in the world before. It protected private property and brought us great capital accumulation, on which we are now living. The nearer you approach to the free market economy, the higher the standard of living will be.

Product Durability vs. Higher Sales

Q. Would you be so kind as to discuss briefly the soundness

of a policy of manufacturing goods that do not last too long, thus insuring a continuing demand, creating manufacturing volume, and thereby reducing both costs and selling prices?

A. Well, a manufacturer's purpose is, of course, to maximize his profits. He has to compete with businessmen who may have different ideas of production. It is always the consumers who will decide which manufacturer gets the profits. I am the son of a Britisher and this question led to debates I used to have with my father about automobiles. As a Britisher, he defended the Rolls Royce, which did not change its models every year, had higher quality, and lasted almost a lifetime. In the United States, we change our automobile models almost every year in some way. The consumers then decide which of the two they will buy, the one that will wear out quickly, or the one that lasts a longer time.

The same thing is true of styles. In my country, as in other countries, the women's wear industry has persuaded women to change their styles almost every year so the industry will have more sales. They are now trying to do it with the men. Clothing manufacturers would like us to throw our clothes away because they are out of style rather than because they are worn out. Any business can attempt this, but the final decision is always made by the consumers as they spend their money. So in the long run, the manufacturer has no choice; he must provide what the consumers will buy.

Right to Destroy Wealth

Q. Has the producer the right to destroy the products he produces?

A. The question is: Does he own them? If he has paid for them, he has the right to do that; and I suppose he has the right to commit suicide too. If you have something of value and want to destroy it without harming anyone else, that is your right. But if it has a market value, there is no inducement to destroy it.

The Effect
Of Wage Rate
Interventions

This lecture is primarily on the subject of labor, wages, and employment. A good deal of what was said about prices in the last lecture applies also to the subject of wage rates. Unfortunately, there is more emotion in this area, because it is a bit more personal. Here, too, of course, we also find evidence of the great sin of economic ignorance. In seeking solutions, economic science is largely neglected. As a result, many governments attempt to solve these problems by means that will not accomplish the desired ends.

Please do not think, as many do, that economics – which is a science – takes sides on this issue. This is not a question that can be settled by bias, that is, by taking one side or the other. It is always a question of what helps everybody, and what policies will help to produce the ends that people want most.

All of us in this world want peace and prosperity. No one wants poverty even for other people.

Free Market: An Application of the Golden Rule

A major question that we face is the problem of reducing or eliminating poverty. I suggest that free market policies have eliminated more poverty than any other policy or system that has ever been known to man. In a truly free society, everyone enjoys the fruits of his own labor, and no one is entitled to special privileges. Everyone is free to choose his own actions. Everyone is free to take that job open to him that he believes will provide him with the greatest compensations. In a free society we constantly tend to act according to the Golden Rule, that is, by serving others as we serve ourselves.

This is, of course, true in the area of employment as it is true in all other market areas. However, there is a good deal of misunderstanding about this. Many think that we can raise wages by merely passing laws. This is an impossible thing to do for everyone. In fact, every law that raises wages for some lowers them for others. It seems to be very difficult for people to realize that all wages and employment cannot be increased by the mere passing of laws.

As mentioned last night, most people seem to think that producers and sellers set prices. Likewise, they seem to think that employers set wage rates. They think employers get rich by setting low wages for their employees and high prices for their products. This is a very popular fallacy, which we shall be discussing as we move on.

I understand that Argentina has a minimum wage law similar to ours in the United States. They tell the story in my country about a man who is running a small business. The inspector from the Minimum Wage Office in Washington comes out and asks him about his three employees. The inspector wants to know how much he pays them, the hours they work, and what they do. He examines closely the books of the little firm, checking to find out if the wages paid are above the minimum specified by law. Then he asks: "Is there anyone around here who gets less than the minimum wage?" The businessman answers: "Yes! There is." The inspector, all alert, says: "Let me speak to him." The owner of the business replies: "You are talking to him now. I work for my keep and very little more."

This touches on the problem that we are discussing, for small business owners who cannot make as much as their employees will soon stop hiring workers and start competing as employees.

There is a popular thought today that employers can be compelled to raise workers' wages at the expense of the owners of a business. This has been done in an increasing number of cases for a short period of time, but such wage increases cannot be maintained in the long run. As we have said before, in analyzing every economic problem it is necessary to examine all of the effects, and not only the short-run effects, but also the long-run effects, and not only the effects on those whom you seek to benefit, but also the effects on those who have to pay the costs. You should always weigh all of these inevitable effects before reaching your decision.

Freedom Permits Responsible Choices

Man differs from other animals in that he has foresight. He can think of consequences that extend beyond the immediate day. If a man feels cold one night in his home, he does not burn up the furniture just to get warm. A wise man looks ahead. He will have firewood or a furnace on hand. Unfortunately not enough people look far enough ahead. In this area of labor, wages, and employment, very few people look ahead and think the problems through to their logical conclusions. This is where economics can help us. Economics is a science that starts with the assumed conditions and then reasons, step by step, to the desired conclusions. If your assumptions and your reasoning are correct, you will produce the results you seek. Unfortunately, in this area of labor, wages, and employment, the greatest area of unemployment is that little narrow space between men's ears. There is little evidence of the intelligent employment of men's minds in the popular solutions of these problems.

In a free market you are free to take any of many jobs open to you. Each man takes that one which, from his point of view, he considers best. When everybody is free to do this, and no one is permitted to trample on the equal freedom of others to do so, when no one or no group can prevent others from taking jobs regarding which they and the potential employers reach mutually satisfactory agreements, then the Golden Rule will prevail. More workers will be producing more goods for others and everyone will have more for himself. The result will be ever-increasing production and human satisfaction. Of course, in a free market society, men will still make mistakes. But free market practices tend to reduce such mistakes by penalizing those who make them.

We may also have a few unfortunate people who need assistance from their fellow men. For such few cases, the free market not only encourages religious and other private charities; it also provides the means by which these charitable organizations can take care of the unfortunate. So these unfortunate few do not have to become a burden on the government. We are free to act voluntarily as good Christians and take care of our neighbors who are in trouble. It is our private duty to help those in distress over their troubles.

Unpopular Governments Fall

In any society, in any group of men, there will also be some who will try to help themselves at the expense of others. There will be some who wish to steal, or misrepresent, or resort to force. To protect peaceful, productive citizens against those who resort to such antisocial actions, governments are necessary, and very necessary.

Government, by definition, is a monopoly of force. It represents the combined strength of the community in suppressing those things which the community opposes. In the long run, a government must always be popular. There is no such thing, in the long run, as an unpopular government.[1]

---

1. A question has been raised as to whether a police state dictatorship is an exception to this general statement. It is not. No dictator can long remain in power without popular acquiescence that he remains the best available alternative. Modern dictators and would-be dictators recognize this when they reach for control of the mass media and educational systems, while seeking to suppress their articulate opposition. Those who fail to attain and maintain popular acceptance are soon removed from office. Lenin, Stalin, and Hitler insisted on

In the long run, we get the governments we deserve. No matter what those in political power may think, they cannot long do things that are not popular. We should remember this when we criticize some of those who are in office, because their powers to act are always limited by what the public is ready to accept.

Unfortunately, free market economics is not generally taught today. Consequently, very few people learn the ideas of the free market economy and understand what they mean for mankind. Many people think of my country as great and strong, but they do not realize that its greatness and strength came from years of practicing free market principles, many of which it has deserted in recent years.

Consumers Determine Wage Rates

There is today a popular idea that employers exploit the workers. This fallacy has been growing ever more popular since the days of Marx. My second lecture touched upon it briefly when I discussed the labor theory of value and Marx's idea that employers overworked employees, paying them less than the values they produced, while keeping the difference for themselves. According to this theory, the rich employers get richer and richer while the poor workers get poorer and poorer. The time would come, Marx held, when the workers would break the chains that bound them to their employers and set up a socialist utopia. According to this idea, in a market society the poor worker is helpless. He has no choice. He must take the wage that is offered to him. There is no other employer who might bid for his services.

---

thorough indoctrination of the young, complete control of all media, and ruthless elimination of any presentation of an opposing ideology. By such means they successfully thwarted the efforts of their internal minority opposition to become a majority.

In this connection, it should be noted that price and wage controls, once anathema to freedom-loving Americans, were accepted on August 15, 1971, with hardly a whimper of dissent. They continue to be acceptable because the majority of Americans now acquiesce in this part of the statist ideology that has been promoted by those interventionist-minded persons who control our mass media and educational system. This passive acceptance of the controlled economy pulls the rug out from under those Americans who so indignantly criticized the Germans for their peaceful acceptance of Hitler.

Actually, of course, that is not so. Free market economics teaches that in the absence of any social interference, workers tend to get the full value that consumers will pay for their contribution. It is the interferences by governments and the interferences by labor unions, supported by public opinion, even without the strength of laws, that prevent all potential workers from getting those market values they could contribute to society.

If the idea that unions help all workers is popular, then we are powerless to stop them from hampering the market competition. However, in an unhampered free market economy, competition tends to allocate to every factor of production, including workers, all that they contribute. It is the values that the ultimate consumers place on each particular contribution to total production that determine what businessmen can pay for that particular contribution. We tried to show this in the last lecture in relation to prices. The same principles apply to the wages paid for labor that apply to the sums paid for raw materials or any other factor of production.

In a free market, each employer seeks to hire as many workers as he profitably can. He hires employees up to the point at which it is no longer profitable for him to hire an additional worker because he cannot sell the product of that additional worker for the wage he must pay. As he hires more workers, the wage rate tends to rise, and as more units are produced, the market price he can get per unit tends to fall. This is the market tendency we tried to illustrate in the last lecture. The more workers you hire, the higher the wage rate you will have to pay. And you must pay the higher wage to all who do similar work.

As you produce and offer more goods on the market, you can sell them only at lower prices. Eventually you reach the marginal point, where you make no profit on the last man you hire. Wage rates are ultimately set by the marginal productivity of labor, that is, the market value added to the product produced by the marginal employee, the last man hired. This is the way the free market would work, if it were allowed to work. Unfortunately, as mentioned last night, the free market is something that we have never had completely at any time and may never have. However, the nearer we get to it, the better off we shall all be.

Given the conditions the employer faces, he must pay workers pretty much the values that consumers place on their contributions. If the employer pays a higher wage, he suffers a loss. If he does not then reduce his wage rate, his number of employees, and his production to the point where he can sell all his products at a price that covers his costs, he will eventually be forced out of business. No businessman can long pay costs that he cannot get back from consumers.

In the long run it is the consumers who pay the wages. The businessman is merely a middleman. He tries to make a profit as a middleman, buying raw materials, hiring workers, and selling the products to consumers. He makes his profit, if any, by holding what he pays for the factors of production below what consumers will pay for the final product. However, once a profit appears, competitors continually bid up what must be paid for each factor of production, including labor. There is always a tendency in a free market for profits to be squeezed and disappear. This includes any profits obtained by paying workers wages lower than the market value of their contributions.

Free Competition Protects Workers

It cannot be denied that employers would always like to pay lower than market wages. In his great book, *The Wealth of Nations*, published in 1776, Adam Smith mentioned that whenever businessmen get together they try to set wages and hold them down. However, in the free market, they are unable to do so. It is just not possible for all employers to get together and hold wage rates down by agreement for any length of time. Once one employer finds he can profit by breaking such an agreement he will probably do so. If none breaks the agreement, and if it is a free market society wherein anybody can become an employer, new employers will soon appear to take advantage of the situation by offering workers higher wages.

If the employer pays a wage lower than the market wage, that is, less than the product of the worker can bring in the market, his profits will be such that he can expand his production and his number of employees. If he fails to do so, and fails to raise his wage rates in doing so, he will invite new competition. In either case, market competition will raise the wage rates to the value produced by the marginal employee. And there is always a marginal employee.

In most industries there are also marginal companies. These are the companies that are just breaking even. If their costs go up a little bit, they will suffer a loss. Then they will soon be out of business, because money losers cannot stay in business indefinitely.

No businessman in a free market society can long pay a worker 50 pesos an hour and sell his product for 100 pesos an hour. Why not? Because you and I and thousands of others like us would be very happy to go into that business, pay those men 60 pesos and sell their product for 100 pesos if we could. Others would soon offer to pay them 70, 80, or 90 pesos. In fact, large corporations would be very happy to make a profit of just one peso an hour for every worker they employ. They are just not able to pay them much less than the market value of their product. The last one employed would not yield them any profit, particularly in a free society where anyone who thinks he sees a chance to make a profit can come in and bid away any employee who is paid less than the market value of his contribution.

A frequent refutation is, "Yes, but most people do not have the capital to start a business." Let's remember that there are many savers eager to invest their money where they can earn more. If they can be shown a situation where they can earn more, they will be happy to make the needed capital available. All you need to do is to show them where a profit higher than current interest rates can be made.

Whenever there is a profit in a free market society, it attracts competition, and competition always reduces prices. This is constantly going on in the market. If you do not believe this, get into the stock market and learn what is happening there as the result of competition among the many investors eager for higher returns on their savings.

Savings Raise Wages

The real secret of higher wages is increased savings per capita. Increased savings are a result of producing more than is consumed. If more goods and services are produced than are consumed, then these unconsumed goods and services are available for making tools, factories, and other things needed to help increase production. In my great country, living standards have gone up in the past because generation after generation of North Americans provided their children with more than they themselves had had. The history of our country has largely been that the first generation of immigrants provided their children with an elementary school education, the next generation saved enough to give their children a high school education, and the third generation sent their children through college. Now many are going on to graduate work. In this way each generation provided the next generation with a higher standard of living. In each case the higher education was the result of increased savings. The earlier generations just could not afford to provide their children with as much as later generations could.

When there are savings in a capitalistic system, people do not put them under a mattress. They do not dig a hole and hide them as people do in India or China, where savers are afraid that if they put up a factory, the property would be seized. No, in a capitalistic society people invest their savings where they hope they will earn a return. In a capitalistic society, capital savings are not accumulated by the rich only. One of the great advantages of a capitalistic society is that low-income people can also invest their savings and earn a return on them. They can buy savings bonds. They can put their money in the savings banks. They can buy life insurance. Then, the banks and the life insurance companies make their savings available to large businesses seeking more capital in order to offer more or better goods or services.

As a matter of fact, it is the low-income people who are the great creditors of our day. They are the ones who are hurt the most by low interest rates. It is largely the higher-income people who are debtors and who benefit from low interest rates. They are stockholders, and their corporations borrow the money saved by low-income people. One of the great advantages of the free market system is that it provides a way for low-income people to participate in the earnings that savings provide.

When I graduated from college in 1929, my first employer gave me a schedule for savings. It provided that a young man save 10 percent of his first income and 50 percent of all the later increases in his income. Of course, the author of the plan did not foresee years of inflation, and income tax rates that now exceed 50 percent. He indicated that anyone who followed that savings plan all his working life, would have, by retirement age, such a good investment income that he would not feel the loss of his wages. Savings are, of course, the only real source of old age security.

Effect of New Savings

When new capital is invested, the very first thing it does, whether it is invested in a new company or in the expansion of an old company, is to bid up wages and the prices of raw materials. It bids up everything that is needed to expand production, including labor, and you cannot make anything without labor.

Labor is one of the scarcest things in this world. Many mines are not worked because the available supply of labor is worth more in other occupations. The same is true of farm lands. The same is true of every occupation. Every economic endeavor is limited by the high cost of labor. Labor is one of the scarcest things that each of us has, and likewise, that each business or nation has. Many projects are not undertaken because of this shortage of labor.

With new savings, there are employers, people economists call "entrepreneurs," who are constantly trying to employ more workers. They have to bid for limited quantities of labor in the competition of the market place. The factor which helps labor most is the increased savings that permit employers to bid workers away from their previous, lower-paying jobs. After these savings are turned into new or larger factories, workers are then able to produce goods and services previously not available.

In the last lecture we tried to show how the managers of

these new expansions determine what to produce. They try to find out what is not available that is next in importance on the value scales of consumers. They then expand the production of those things not sufficiently available that they think customers want most. They bring more production to the market. Each worker working with more or better tools produces more. If there has been no increase in the quantity of money, as more goods reach the market the result must be lower prices. With lower prices for consumers' goods, everyone can buy more with his or her limited quantity of money. This method, that is, increasing the amount of savings available per worker, is the only one by which a society can raise the real wages of all its workers.

In some industries, such as the steel industry in my country, the companies need an investment of some $20,000 per worker, for workers to get the high wages they are paid. In a market economy these high wages are shared by all. The barber, who has not changed his methods very much in the last one or two hundred years, competes in the labor market with steel workers, each of whom uses $20,000 worth of equipment. Wage rates of all workers are thus set by the average savings available to help workers increase their production. These higher wages and lower prices must appear before the savers can get any of their money back, to say nothing of any interest or profit on their speculative investment.

Profits may come, but they can only come later, if some buyers voluntarily, of their own free will, decide that the new market offerings are better bargains than all other available goods and services. This is the secret of progressively higher living standards in a free market society. The secret of higher wages is more savings per capita, more savings per worker. A man with a modern expensive earth-moving machine can move far more earth than the strongest man using his hands or even a shovel. As more and better tools become available, and as more goods are produced, there will be a higher standard of living for everyone who participates in the market economy.

Effect of Present Union Policies

What are the policies that we find in the market today? The essence of labor union policies is (1) to restrict production and (2) to prevent the unemployed, or those employed at lower wages, from improving their economic situation by underbidding union-imposed wage rates. We cannot improve the general welfare by following union policies that restrict production by making high wages higher for some workers, with the result that low wages are forced lower or become non-existent for those made unemployable.

In my counₜtry there may not be as high a percentage of workers in labor unions as there are in Argentina. However, whenever union workers get a raise above free market wage rates, this increase raises production costs, and as a result prices must be raised to consumers. With higher prices, fewer goods are sold. When fewer goods are sold, some of the workers are laid off, and the laid-off workers must then compete for the lower-paying jobs. Their competition in the next lower-paying jobs drives out some previously employed workers. This forces their wage opportunities still lower. Such policies restrict production and keep men from working where they can produce the goods most wanted by society.

Much of this is, of course, due to economic ignorance. It is due in part to the fallacious idea we discussed in our second lecture, the idea that only an equal exchange is a fair exchange, and that if the employer gains, he must have done so at the expense of the worker. This is responsible for much of the antagonism against the capitalist, against the investor, against the saver – the belief that his gain is unearned, and that the capitalist or saver is getting something at the expense of the worker. This is Karl Marx's exploitation theory. It is the theory of class warfare as opposed to the market theory of voluntary social cooperation.

Marx put great stress on this. He believed that under the natural law of wages, employers worked the workers too long. Workers produced enough to reproduce themselves in, let us say, ten hours per day. Employers worked them eleven or twelve hours. According to this idea, what workers produced in the extra hour or two was taken and kept by the capitalists. So one of the chief policies of labor unions has been to demand shorter hours for the same pay. If you shorten hours for the same pay, you have less production. Less production does not provide a higher standard of living. If widely practiced, it must mean higher prices and a lower standard of living. Of course, throughout history, men like to take some of their increased standard of living in the form of longer hours of leisure. When this is done by market processes, it means that market participants prefer to take some of their potential increased production in the form of more leisure.

Another fallacy in this area is the argument that money wages must be raised in order to provide workers with the purchasing power to buy their production. Actually, higher living standards require more production, not more money. Workers can only buy what is produced. If production is reduced because fewer workers are hired, increasing money wages does not provide any more goods. The idea that raising wages can do this is an old fallacy. There is no way to increase the purchasing power of one worker by increasing his wages, without at the same time decreasing the purchasing power of other workers.

Fallacy of Excessive Employer Power

The employer has no power to set wages. He cannot in the long run pay more than the consumer will repay him. Nor can he long pay less than the market value of labor's contribution. This Marxian idea simply does not stand up. Yet many people, people who have been or who are in high places, quite honestly, quite sincerely, subscribe to this idea that employers have too much power. Their failure to understand free market economics permits them to believe that in a modern industrial society employers have great power, while the poor workers are helpless.

Here are a few quotations from some prominent men of my country who subscribe to this erroneous doctrine. One of these is Donald Richberg. Some of you may have heard of him. He was one of those who felt very sorry for the poor workers back in the days of President Wilson and the New

Freedom. He participated in the political propaganda that brought forth one of the first Federal labor laws in the United States, the Railway Labor Act of 1926. He was later one of the men who headed the National Recovery Administration of our New Deal days. In his later years he learned a few things from experience and changed some of his political interventionist opinions, but he still held the popular fallacy that, in a free market, employers possess what he called "excessive bargaining power." He therefore felt that labor's "resort to political aid" is "a justifiable use of government power in order to establish a fair balance between the conflicting economic powers of property owners and wage earners . . . the logical way to counteract the overwhelming, and often oppressive, power of the managers of large properties." [2]

President Truman, in his last Economic Report to the Congress of the United States of North America in January 1953, said (page 22): "There is the problem of maintaining fair and peaceful bargaining among the powerfully organized private groups. The Government can help in this by protecting and encouraging the maintenance of balanced bargaining power."

Fallacy Almost Universal

Now we need not pick on any one particular political party of my country. Let me read from a pamphlet called *The Worker's Story*, by Martin P. Durkin, a Secretary of Labor under President Eisenhower. This represents the thinking of the Republican Party, a party that many in our country tended to think of, at that time at least, as conservative, or, in European and Latin American termi-

---

2. Donald R. Richberg. *Labor Union Monopoly: A Clear and Present Danger* (Regnery, 1957), pp. 37 and 132. The Supreme Court, in a 1921 decision written by Chief Justice (former President) Wm. H. Taft, stated it this way: "They (the unions) were organized out of the necessity of the situation. A single employee was helpless in dealing with an employer. He was dependent ordinarily on his daily wage for the maintenance of himself and family. If the employer refused to pay him the wages that he thought fair, he was nevertheless unable to leave the employ and to resist arbitrary and unfair trentment. Union was essential to give laborers an opportunity to deal in equality with their employer." (American Steel Foundries Co. v. Tri-City Metal Trades Council, 257 U.S. 184, 204-1921.)

nology, as nineteenth century liberal. This pamphlet states the thinking that is common in many places in the world today. It says:

> Suppose there were no labor unions and no labor laws and you went out to get a job. Unless you had something very special to offer you would be in competition with a lot of other workers trying for the same job. As a result, you would have to accept what the employer offered you, or look for something else to do. You would quickly find that the man who has a job to offer almost always has the advantage over the man looking for work.
>
> Then, supposing that, having got the job and there still being no union or law to support you, you found your wages too small to live on or the working conditions unsatisfactory. You would be only one individual against the employer's strength. You could not successfully insist on his giving you what you ask, if he did not want to do so. As an ordinary individual worker you would have little bargaining strength.
>
> But, suppose that you and several other workers got together and elected some of the group to speak on your behalf with the employer, pointing out that unless he could see his way clear to make such-and-such an improvement in wages or conditions of work, the group would stop work. Either he would have to look for workers elsewhere (and if those other workers also belonged to your group he would not be able to get them), or he would have to come to some kind of agreement regarding your demands, at least to the extent that he still finds it profitable to stay in business.
>
> This second kind of arrangement by which workers, by joining together, get some kind of agreement with their employers is called "collective bargaining.". . . Collective bargaining and labor unions are two sides of the same face . . . .
>
> The job of the government under the Constitution is to maintain a balance among its citizens, and help them resolve their differences. Consequently, during the past forty years [this was written in 1953], and particularly during the past twenty years, legislation has been enacted to bring about a more reasonable balance between employers and organized labor and to provide certain services in helping to settle disputes . . . .
>
> One of the first Federal laws protecting unions was the Railway Labor Act of 1926 . . . . The National Labor Relations Act . . . gave Government protection to the formation of unions . . . . The act did this by prohibiting certain employer practices, and by insuring employees reinstatement in their jobs with back pay if their employers discharged them for union

activities . . . . It . . . required employers to bargain collectively
with the union so certified. [3]

And it is not only in official circles that we find this
fallacy. Here is a quote from one of the last great old-time
liberals of America, who passed away in 1964 at the age of
93. He was one of the most respected men of our legal
profession, Roscoe Pound, the last of the old liberal Deans of
the Harvard Law School. Since his retirement as Dean in
1936, a saying has become popular about people who go to
Harvard: it is that you enter Harvard and then turn left. But
this gentleman was one of the old school. In his little
pamphlet, *Legal Immunities of Labor Unions*, written in
1957 when he was 86, he reiterated this popular error when,
in this otherwise fine work, he said: "In an era of huge
incorporated industrial enterprises there had come to be gross
inequality of bargaining power between the incorporated
employer and the individual workingman . . . . Traditional
sanctity of property restricted effective employment of
collective action in case of strikes . . . . Traditional ultratech-
nical judicial procedure resulted in a legal system which put
the worker in a condition amounting almost to subjection.
Reaction was inevitable."[4]

This general lack of economic understanding extends
throughout the Western world. In the lectures that follow I
shall touch somewhat on this problem in England, and how it
contributes to the financial problem there.

Union Policies Need to be Analyzed

Questioning the virtues of organized labor today is like
questioning or attacking religion, monogamy, motherhood,
or the home. In public opinion, the test of whether one is for
or against labor, the workers, or the poor in general is one's
attitude toward labor unions. One simply cannot argue that
certain union policies hurt labor, and expect to be taken
seriously. The fact is, of course, that union policies *have* hurt

---

3. *The Workers' Story*, 1913-1953 (U.S. Dept. of Labor, 1953), pp. 78, 79, 87 &
90.
4. Published by the American Enterprise Assoc., Inc., p.2.

workers in general, and particularly those at the lower end of the income scale.

The essence of the union wage policies is to reduce production, and to keep the unemployed from finding work and the low-paid from competing for higher-paying jobs. Such policies are not going to raise the nation's standard of living. We can never improve the general welfare by policies that reduce production. Unions make high wages higher for some, but they make costs higher for others, and thus reduce the production of goods and services that consumers, including workers, can buy in the market place.

The unemployed, those at the bottom of the economic ladder, have no voice in union affairs or in setting wage rates. They are completely shut out. Union officers care very little about non-members or beginners trying to get started. We have had cases in New York where you cannot get into a union unless your father was in it before you. The fact that, under the law, only union members can work in certain trades, has hurt Negroes trying to enter trades white unions have monopolized. Since his father was not in the union, how can a Negro ever get into it? This has applied to other low-income minorities in times past. The unions do not help the relatively poor. They help the aristocrats of labor at the expense of low-income workers. They get privileges for their members at the expense of other workers or would-be workers, and they raise prices for all consumers.

Combinations of workers – unions – can raise wages only if they can raise the value or the quantity of the product they produce. Now, as we have mentioned in previous lectures, if the quantity produced is smaller, other things remaining the same, the value per unit is greater. The available quantity will satisfy fewer consumers and thus provide less human satisfaction. So, if they do not increase production, the only way unions can raise the relative value of a unit of labor is to reduce the units of labor employed and the quantity of goods produced in that industry. Without the power to keep out other workers, unions can do little to raise the market value of what their members produce. This does not help either the workers who are excluded, or consumers in general.

We live in an age of mass production for mass consumption. If we do not have mass production, we cannot have mass consumption. So by reducing the amount of production, unions are not helping workers in general. By setting wages at higher than free market wage rates, unions reduce the amount that can be sold. They throw people out of the jobs where they could be most productive. What the unions gain for their own members results in a loss to those who are excluded from cooperating in the task, and it results in a loss to all consumers, since they will have to pay higher prices per unit for a smaller quantity of goods and services. Every consumer who does not share the union's gains will have to go without something he could have bought, if the union gain had not raised prices.

The control of wage rates is also the control of entry into a trade or industry. Such control also determines rates at which a company or industry expands or contracts. In a free society, if the wage rates in an industry were lower than those forced by unions, that industry would expand. When unions raise the wage rates of an industry, that industry either has to contract or, if it stays the same size, is prevented from expanding as it would if it could pay free market wage rates.

Expanding means paying higher wage rates to attract the additional workers needed. It also means producing more goods that consumers want most, and lowering prices so the same wages will buy more. Of course, there is also a tendency toward the elimination of profits. Unions can protect their members from the competition of other workers by merely raising union wage rates, because then the employer cannot afford to employ any more. This is one of the inevitable results of the union seniority principle. Those with high seniority are not worried about those who lose jobs because of higher union wage rates.

Effect of Union Policies on Savings

One of the most important factors in the labor situation is the effect of union policies on employers, savers, and investors. Many think that wages can be raised at the expense of the employer or the investing owners, and thus higher wages need not hurt the consumer. They think you can just reduce profits a little bit more and that will take care of the higher wage costs. As we have tried to make clear, the way to raise the wages of workers is to increase the savings invested in tools that workers can use to increase their production.

We have in Table XIII an example that is based on certain assumptions — all economic problems are based on certain assumptions — in order to give you some idea of the problems faced by workers and by those who try to make a living by employing people. First, we assume a steamship, which cost $2 million to build and which is expected to last 20 years. It has a yearly depreciation and interest charge of $150,000 and an expected market revenue of $14,100 per week. It is expected to operate 50 weeks of the year. The people who are investing this $2 million considered it carefully in advance, as all human beings do, particularly when making a substantial investment of this kind. If their forecast is correct, they expect their weekly costs to be:

Depreciation and interest $3,000
Labor wages   8,000
Other operating costs   2,100

They hope for profits of $1,000 over and above the interest they could get by lending the money out. The total of the items mentioned comes to $14,100.

Of course, if they foresee future developments incorrectly, they will suffer a loss. But if they have foreseen future operations correctly, if they have calculated their labor and other costs correctly, and if they have estimated correctly what the public will pay for the service, then and then only will they earn the estimated profits. Then only will they earn the estimated profit and be able to replace the ship and continue to employ the workers after 20 years.

In order to make this problem easy to understand, we shall assume that this ship is on a lake and cannot be moved to be used any place else. So once this investment is made, those who have turned their savings into a steamship cannot withdraw them. If a labor union has the power, either through public opinion or through the laws of the land, to raise wage rates above those prevailing in the market at the time, the investors will be at the mercy of the unions.

Now, we shall assume here, in the next column, that the union is able to threaten a strike or otherwise use its power to raise wages 10 percent. This increases the cost of labor to $8,800 and reduces the profit over interest to $200. Under such a situation, the owners will continue operating. They will get a small profit, smaller than they had calculated, yet more than they would have gotten if they had lent their money out at market rates of interest. They are still — you might say — ahead of the game.

The union members, having found it easy to use their power to get this 10 percent increase, are still not satisfied. They try it again. Let us assume that this time they increase wages to 25 percent above free market wage rates. You see the results in the next column — a situation in which the workers are then getting a weekly total of $10,000 in wages. There are no longer any profits after interest. In fact, the employers are not even covering their depreciation and interest. They are only getting two-thirds of this expense, or $2,000. Under such circumstances, they will still operate the steamship. If they stopped operating, they would get nothing for depreciation and interest, and $2,000 is better than nothing. As we

---

**EFFECT OF UNION POLICIES ON
INVESTMENT IN AND OPERATION OF STEAMSHIP**

ASSUME: A steamship, cost, $2,000,000; expected life, 20 years. Annual depreciation and interest charge, $150,000. Market revenue, $14,100 per week (50 weeks per year).

Weekly Costs	At Free Market Wages	If Union Forces Wages Up 10%	25%	50%
Depreciation and interest	$3,000	$3,000	$2,000	$ 00
Wages of labor	8,000	8,800	10,000	12,000
Other operating costs	2,100	2,100	2,100	2,100
Profit (over and above interest)	1,000	200	00	00
Totals	$14,100	$14,100	$14,100	$14,100

mentioned in the last lecture, everyone prefers a little something to nothing. At this rate, when the ship is worn out, they will not be able to replace it. They will not have depreciated enough. So, of course, when the ship is worn out, this business will be ended and the men will lose their jobs.

But assume the union workers do not see this. Suppose they go on and ask for a further increase. This time we assume they are able to get a total increase of 50 percent. Then you find the situation in the last column, where you have arrived at the margin. The owners receive nothing for their capital, no allowance at all for depreciation or interest on their capital. The operating income is just covering the wages of the workers and other operating costs. Then, it no longer pays the investors to operate their steamship. They have reached the point where they operate the ship for nothing. This they do not care to do. So the operation comes to an end and the workers lose their jobs. They have killed a good thing.

Savers Can Be Scared Away

All this is not very far from reality. We had a somewhat similar situation in the United States. It was not even on a lake. For many years we had the Old Fall River Line, as they called it in my youth. It was a steamship line that provided overnight boat service between the beautiful harbor of New York and Fall River, Massachusetts, a short train ride from Boston. It was a trip that many of us enjoyed. But the unions kept raising the wage rates of their members until the steamship line was forced out of business.

There are lessons to be learned from this illustration. Businessmen can get caught. Investors can get caught. Savers can get caught. Once they put their money into particular forms of capital they are caught. When unions can raise wage rates to the point where business income covers only part of the depreciation and interest expenses, the investors will still operate their business, because any income is better than writing off the whole 100 percent investment. But what is the effect of this on potential investors? Would you, if you had any savings and saw this happening, try to go into competition or start a similar service elsewhere?

This is the problem that workers face. Yes, unions can temporarily raise some workers' incomes. But they also reduce the competition for workers, and in the long run they reduce the number of high-paying jobs available. In real life, tools, machines, and other capital goods wear out or become obsolete one by one. Everything does not go to pieces at one time. A typewriter wears out and it is replaced. Some small machinery wears out from time to time, but whole factories seldom wear out all at once. Unions push wages up to the point where it pays to replace some parts and continue operations. This keeps businesses already established in operation, but it greatly discourages the starting of new businesses.

These union policies tend to stifle the very thing that encourages competition for workers and raises wages. If we are to have higher real wages, higher real income, that is, more goods and services, we must have more savings and more businesses competing for the workers. This union policy we have been discussing reduces the savings and the number of employers who compete for workers. Under such policies people with savings will tend to put them under the mattress or send them out of the country.

There are many people in many parts of the world who are sending their savings outside of their country, just because of such conditions. They no longer feel that it is safe to invest savings in their own country. Other people stop saving. Why save, if it is going to be confiscated? Why not spend, live high, and have a good time while you are here? Still others will put their savings in government bonds in the belief that they will be safer there than invested in private enterprises. But the money will then be spent to buy votes, and the interest on the government's debt will become an added burden on the taxpayers and on the workers too. So we see that if union wages are forced up above free market wage rates, they end by killing the goose that lays the golden eggs of higher wages for all, that is, the increased invested savings that provide higher and higher standards of living for all.

Only Savings Can Reduce Economic Hardships

The reason why we have so much starvation in so many countries, in India for instance, is because private property is not protected. Investments are not protected. After India became independent of England, Nehru said that India needed and wanted foreign capital. It is true, he admitted, that India is going to be socialist, but, he added, if you will put your capital in India, we will promise not to confiscate it "for at least ten years." How much money would you or any sane person invest in India under such conditions?

If workers want to raise their wages they must adopt policies that will encourage savings. We have had this problem in the Western world for a good many years now, for most of this century. We shall be discussing it more in the lecture on the depression. However, as union wage rates have gone up in the more productive industries, which unions can most easily organize, and in what we call bottleneck industries, like transportation, the unions can shut down other industries. They raise the wages of some, but raising wage rates raises prices, and with higher prices fewer articles are sold, which means fewer men are employed in the organized industries. The workers kept from jobs in these industries must then compete in some other, lower paying industry. This drives those wages down unless they too are organized and held up by politically privileged unions. Then more workers are thrown into competition with still lower-paid workers, until some of them are, by these very "pro-labor" policies, forced to work for wages on which they cannot keep body and soul together. Then, we feel sorry for them.

The popular remedy today for such very low wages is a minimum wage law. The minimum wage law says that you cannot employ a man unless you pay him a specified minimum wage. In my country this is now $1.40 an hour. We still do not have a dictatorship. Until we do, employers will only employ people if they can hope to get the $1.40 back from consumers. If the consumer says a man's contribution is only worth $1.30, the employer is not going to pay him $1.40. The employer is only an agent of the consumer. So the man becomes legally unemployable. It is now illegal for anyone to hire him. He cannot even earn what he could, which is what the consumer *will* pay for his contribution. So we have invented unemployment insurance to take care of these people. When unemployment insurance payments expire, the popular remedy is relief or welfare payments, which become a burden on taxpayers, who are, of course, in the long run, the workers. The only possible outcome of such policies is higher prices, higher taxes, less production, and more poverty.

Good Names for Laws Not Enough

We have had many attempts at intervention in my country, and I presume here also, as in other countries. People with the best intentions and the least economic understanding constantly try to help the people on the bottom of the economic ladder by governmental intervention. In our country we had the National Recovery Act, which was supposed to help both business and labor by letting them organize with government help to set high prices and high wages. We had the Agriculture Adjustment Act. We had the Securities and Exchange Act. We had many such acts with very nice-sounding names.

The question, as I mentioned in the very first lecture, is not good intentions. The question is: Is this a sound means for attaining the desired or specified ends?

The National Recovery Act did not produce national recovery. The Agriculture Adjustment Act did not adjust agriculture to consumers' wishes. We had surplus after surplus. We had to give billions of dollars to the farmers, and still do. After thirty-five years, the program is still floundering around and costing taxpayers billions per year. But there was one of these programs that was correctly named. That was the Unemployment Insurance Act, because it surely did insure, that is, guarantee, unemployment.

Those interventions did not increase production. In a free market society everybody can get a job at the highest wage the consumers will pay for his contribution. No one can long get any higher wage, and nothing that government can do will change this situation or improve it. But many workers and voters believe unions can raise the wages of all workers.

As I said earlier, governments have to do what is popular. They cannot do what is unpopular. Today it is popular to think that no worker's wages should ever be allowed to fluctuate downwards. Wage rates, it is thought, should only move upward.

The market system, whose operations we tried to describe in the last lecture, permits consumers to change their wishes and wants. When these shift, employers have to change the things they produce to satisfy the customers. The way this happens in a free market is that the prices of things no longer wanted in such large quantities go down, while the prices of things for which demand has increased go up. Businessmen switch from producing losing lines of goods to producing goods on which they hope to make a profit. They stop producing goods that can only be sold at a loss. When the demand changes, they do not make as many candles, for instance. They switch to producing electric bulbs and lamps. And so it is with workers in different industries. But we no longer permit any wages to fall. So if employers can no longer pay the union-demanded wages, they must cease operations altogether and fire everybody, including those who might be satisfied with slightly lower wages until they can find better-paying jobs.

Employers and Employees Are Not Enemies

Actually, in real life, workers and investors in the same company are not competitors. Production and marketing are not class warfare. Investors, employers, and employees of the same company are team workers. A demand for a Ford automobile is a demand for a Ford factory and for Ford workers. All those needed to produce the factory and the autos are a team. Anything which helps an automobile company helps all those who are on the team, either as investors or workers. The ultimate demand of consumers is for a team combination, and it is this free combination that is going to help all of us have more of the things we want most.

The demand for workers at higher wages should come from those putting increased investments to work. New investments always seek new workers. Then all other employers have to pay the new higher wages, because no employer can keep workers if a competitor is offering higher wages. Present union policies cannot raise the wages of all workers. They lead only to higher prices and lower production.

If we are going to stop the ever-upward wage-price spiral before there is a complete collapse in the value of the monetary unit, we must create a climate that will demand the repeal of all laws that permit unions to exclude qualified workers from competing for jobs in union-organized industries. We must stop subsidizing unemployment and permit wage rates to be set by free market competition in the service of consumers.

The Keynesian Solution

This is not the policy in most countries of the world. What is happening instead is that workers are getting higher money wages, which are lower real wages because the value of the monetary unit is constantly being diluted. We are going into progressive inflation. Savers are being liquidated. Their property is being confiscated. New savers are scared away. Politicians are constantly afraid, and rightly so, of doing things that are unpopular. They endorse popular spending measures but they shun the resulting costs, and to stay popular they have resorted to inflation. This is the so-called Keynesian policy. It is set forth in Keynes' book, *The General Theory of Employment, Interest and Money*. The key sentence is: "A movement by employers to revise money-wage bargains downward will be more strongly resisted than a gradual and automatic lowering of real wages as a result of rising prices."[5]

This was the policy endorsed by Keynes. It is the policy of most governments in the Western world today. Keynes knew, as every economist does, that the only way that you can employ more people is to lower the wage rate. But ever since World War I this had become politically more difficult in Great Britain. Powerful British labor unions, with the help of the Fabian Socialists, had built up public pressures which

---

5. John Maynard Keynes, *The General Theory of Employment, Interest and Money* (Macmillan & Co., Ltd., London, 1936), p. 264.

opposed any lowering of any money wages. British politicians of all parties were afraid to resist this popular union policy. So in 1931, when the number of unemployed became unbearable, the politicians in office preferred to lower wages by devaluing the British pound. The workers kept their puffed-up pound wages, but their pounds bought less.

In 1936, Keynes gave this political policy academic sanction in the book and sentence just quoted. Since then, most Western nations have adopted this "full employment" policy. In essence, when unemployment is considered too high, wages are lowered by lowering the value of the monetary unit. This is done by increasing the quantity of the monetary units. This will be the subject of the next lectures. We will then discuss money and the government handling of this monetary problem. We have gotten into a situation of ever-rising wages and prices, with more and more workers paid less than they would earn in a free market. It is very difficult to get out of such a situation. The real answer, of course, is economic education.

Present Policies Doomed

Neither union leaders nor union workers are stupid people. Keynes and the British politicians were able to fool the employees in England when they first tried this scheme in 1931. They changed all the index numbers, making it difficult to document the price rises reflecting the lower purchasing power of the pound. But now every union has a statistician. They may call him an economist, but he can see from the official cost of living indices that prices are going up. And when they go up, the unions demand still higher wages. This system of Keynes' has just about reached the end of the road. You can no longer fool the workers by lowering the value of the monetary unit. They are on to what is happening and they are not going to take it much longer. The only final answer to this problem is more economic education, showing that the only way to keep raising wages permanently is to increase production, and the way to do this is to encourage savings. For it is only increased savings that can provide workers with more and better education and

more and better tools, with which they can produce and buy
more and better products that they want most.

QUESTIONS AND ANSWERS

Unions Could Serve Society

Q. Are you against unions per se?

A. I can answer that in Spanish: NO! I am not against unions
per se. Unions could be very beneficial to society. I am
against privileges for anybody, including unions. If unions
were organized on the basis of accepting only the best
workers as members, and if union members performed a full
day's work of high caliber, I, as a prospective employer,
would be happy to hire union men and only union men
rather than untried non-union workers of questionable
ability. When unions serve society as they serve their
members, they operate under the Golden Rule. Then they
can be a force for good. The problem arises when you give
them special privileges, such as the power to shut out other
potentially able workers in their drive to raise wage rates
above those that would prevail in a free market.

Minimum Prices and Wages Restrict Efficiency

Q. What is the difference between minimum prices and
minimum wages?

A. They are both political interferences with the efficiency
of the free market. We have discussed tonight the effects of
minimum wage laws. These laws try to raise workers' wages
above free market wages. This cannot be done in a market
economy without forcing some workers into lower-paid jobs
or unemployment. If you have a complete dictatorship, yes.
But short of a complete dictatorship, an employer will not
long pay a man more than what he hopes to get back from
consumers. Of course, men make mistakes, as we said in the

very first lecture. An employer may do it for a week, a month, or a year, but sooner or later he has got to stop. He cannot do this as a permanent policy. Now, by minimum prices, you mean laws or policies which try to keep prices above free market prices. Some companies try to maintain prices higher than free market retail prices for certain products. This means, of course, that fewer units will be sold and fewer workers employed by that particular company. When such practices are protected by law, they hurt consumers and workers generally. They give some people a special privilege. When such practices are not protected by law, they invite competition.

Government Indoctrination of the Young

Q. Is education a function of government?

A. If we had about two hours, I should like to answer that. My short answer has to be "no," except for those in the Army and Navy. The training of officers for the Army, Navy, and Air Force is a function of the government. Other than that, education is not a governmental function. Anyone who understands the benefits of competition must hold that the system that is best for producing what people want most through the market forces is also the best system for producing the best education. I would not give any corporation, church, or government a monopoly of education. Both goods and education are improved by competition. A short answer will sound like heresy. But let us remember that a person who works for a large corporation or anybody else could not teach publicly that his boss might be wrong and keep his job long. A teacher on the public payroll is not going to advocate a reduction in government expenditures, if his own salary depends on higher government expenditures. As a government employee, a teacher is in an awkward position. The maintenance of freedom depends on eternal vigilance against any encroachments by those in political office. It is very difficult for government-paid teachers to be critical of their employer for any extended period.

The public school system was started by people of good will who were sorry for the children of poor people. They thought these children could not get an education without subsidies from taxpayers. But public education is one of the most expensive ways to do it. In my country, we have palaces for the children of poor people. Many children are in school buildings of far better quality than their homes, and the poor people still pay taxes to build these palaces. We also have graft in putting up school buildings. We do not have competition for the best teachers. In the city of New York we had three teachers' strikes during the last school year. The students got no education whatsoever during those periods, except perhaps the lesson that the way to get things in this world is to join a union and strike against the general welfare. There is much that could be said on this subject, but for a short answer let us say that competition would greatly improve the quality of our education and the ability to spot encroachments on our freedom. There is the problem of the teachers, too. If they had more employer groups competing for their services, they would do a better job and the good ones would be better rewarded.

Sound Economics and Patriotism

Q. Is the man who sends his money outside of his country doing a good job for his country?

A. In general, the answer is probably yes. If he is doing it because his country is not following sound economic policies, he is pointing up one of the inevitable results of such poor policies. Those poor policies are not going to be changed until there is a better public understanding of the bad results that inevitably flow from such policies. If those who set economic policies realize that unsound policies make it impossible to replace the worn-out factories, as in the case of the steamship, and to provide the high-paying jobs that workers want, then the politicians may come to the realization that they must do something to keep investments in the country. Gresham's law still works. So unless people

are encouraged to invest at home by sound economic policies, they will send their savings abroad.

Compulsion Should Be Avoided

Q. What is your opinion about compulsory collective bargaining?

A. I am against all privileges, and the use of compulsion in a
free society is either a privilege or a crime.

Unions Scare Savers

Q. What are the consequences of compulsory collective
bargaining?

A. They are the results that I have tried to portray in this
particular lecture. They raise some wages above those of the
free market. Some workers may get these wages, but the
policies scare capital and savers. In the long run such policies
hurt the workers. Once capital is confiscated, it will not be
voluntarily reproduced. An increased standard of living
comes from increased savings per capita. There is a feeling in
many places that capital increases just as automatically as the
sun rises in the East. Capital does not increase automatically.
Some people have to refrain from spending all their wealth,
to save some of it. Then they must be induced to invest
these additional savings. In a market society this is best done
by providing savers with the hope of improving their
situation by the receipt of interest and possibly profits if
earned.

Inflation Fools Some, But Not All

Q. Does inflation fool workers?

A. Inflation does not fool all the workers. The person who

asked this question apparently thinks that it still does fool them. Certainly it does fool some. Of course, I cannot speak for the workers in your great country. But there are fewer and fewer being fooled in my country, and those that are fooled are certainly not the ones in the big unions – the steel workers, auto workers, and so forth. Their unions have people who understand inflation and they demand ever-higher wages to compensate for the higher prices. Our labor unions have recently awakened to a new point. If the cost of living goes up 7 percent, they are no longer satisfied with an increase of 7 percent, because they realize that out of that 7 percent the state and Federal governments are going to take in taxes some 25 to 35 percent. So in order to get 7 percent more they have to get a raise of 10 or 11 percent. This adds 10 or 11 percent to production costs, and this starts the wage-price spiral going still further. In my country the leading labor unions are in on this. I certainly wouldn't say that all government workers are. Some workers are still buying government bonds that pay only 4½ percent, when the cost of living is going up 7 percent. That does not reflect a high economic awareness of what is going on.

Reason for So Much Violence

Q. Does inflation provoke union violence?

A. Probably every case is a different one. I certainly cannot speak for your country. In my country, violence results from the fact that labor unions have the privilege of getting away with violence. They are not punished for their violence. This is the reason it continues. In fact, today they need only threaten violence to get their way. Man, as we said in the very first lecture, tries to improve his situation from his point of view. If men find that they can improve their situation by violence or the threat of violence, they are going to resort to those policies. The workers have done this in my country, and now the students are doing it in the colleges and even in the high schools. As long as the law is not enforced equally against them, there will be more and more such violence. If people think that they can get away with violence, they will undertake it whenever they are unhappy. Inflation, of course, is one thing that keeps people unhappy and makes them desperate.

Popular Ideology Suppresses Free Market Ideas

Q. Why are there so few people who believe in the free market?

A. Well, we have already answered that in part in answering the question on public education. Public education in itself, being a government enterprise, promotes further political interventions and opposes free market competition. The means of mass communication in my country, the newspaper, the radio and television stations, gather their material for the most part with the help of labor union members. Reporters of the major newspapers and press associations are all labor union members. The radio and television stations get their permission to operate from the government. Like teachers, they too are hesitant about saying things that are not popular with organized labor or the political party in power. In my own country we cannot be regularly employed on a radio or television program if we will not join the union. I am not against unions, but I am against privileges for the unions. As a result of such privileges those who expose the weaknesses of present union policies are not permitted to participate in any regular program. So the basic answer to the question is that for the most part the means of mass communication are in the hands of those who believe honestly and sincerely, but mistakenly, that the answers to all our problems are more government laws hampering free market competition.

Dictators and Majorities Can Both Steal

Q. Last night you said that we steal by majority vote. This expression hurts our democratic feelings in South America, where we fight life-long battles against the demogagic dictators who always have a state-intervention mentality of robbing the rich, of stealing through the bureaucracy. So far no questions. Your words should be, I suggest, "we are permitted to steal by decree," meaning that we are in the hands of dictators.

A. I cannot comment on the situation here as I am certainly no specialist on Argentina, and I shall not be one until I get back in the United States. But for those who may not have been here last night, I commented on the fact that we have changed the commandment, "Thou shall not steal," to "Thou shall not steal *except by majority vote.*" All governments tend to do what they think the majority want, and this includes the appropriation of the wealth of unpopular minorities.

Unemployment in a Free Society

Q. Can there be unemployment in a free market economy?

A. There can be unemployment of everyone who wants to be unemployed. But everyone who wants to work can find a job at a wage that somebody else is willing to pay. Now, we all think that we are worth more than other people think we are worth. But in this world we have to be satisfied with the judgment of others, and in a free market society we can always get that. As I mentioned earlier, there are many natural resources in this world that are not occupied or used because of the scarcity of labor; so labor, being scarce, is always in demand at a price close to the market value of its productivity.

Helping Some by Hurting Others

Q. When wages are held above the free market level by compulsory means and still there is full employment, is this because inflation makes real wages lower?

A. When all wages are higher than the free market level, there is not full employment. When wages go higher than the free market rate, the people cannot buy the same quantity of goods at prices that include these higher wages. However, when some wages are above free market rates, there are also some people who are underpaid. So all could be employed. But for every one who is paid a higher than free market wage, someone else has to be paid a less than free market wage. This is always helping some at the expense of others.

Part II

The Theory
Of Money

The subject of this fifth lecture is the theory of money and its value.

Money is the most important commodity in a market economy. A sum of money is at least one side of every market transaction. Sums of money are both sides of many transactions. In all transactions involving annuities, life insurance, bank accounts, bond buying, and other loans of money, a sum of money is on each side of each transaction. Therefore, anything that affects the value of money affects every market transaction. The value of money affects not only the transactions of the moment but also all transactions over periods of time.

The Function of Money

The role of money is to make trade easier. Without money, there would be the awkwardness of barter. The use of money leaves more time for production and helps to boost the number of transactions which are expected to increase the satisfaction of each participant. Its use thus permits the increased division of labor and mass production for mass consumption. Money helps men to help others as they help themselves. Money might, therefore, be called a catalyst for the Golden Rule. A sound and simple monetary system is probably the greatest material tool available to men for the multiplication of human satisfactions.

In the earliest days of voluntary social cooperation, one man probably hunted while another fished or picked fruit. Then, they exchanged some of the products of their toil. Such simple exchanges were not difficult. However, as the production of wealth and division of labor increased, direct exchanges, or barter, became more complicated. If you were a fisherman and wanted a house, it would be difficult for you to find a carpenter or house builder who would take your fresh-caught fish in payment for a house. Before long, those fish would smell, and the builder would have little use for most of them.

So, before barter became so involved, men decided to exchange something they had for something that was in more popular demand, something that was more acceptable to others. Then, they would take this commodity which was in greater demand and exchange it for the things they wanted. If we raise chickens, we do not drive up to a gasoline station and say: "Here is a chicken. Please give me a gallon of gasoline." We could lose a lot of time finding someone with gasoline who wanted chickens. Long before barter became so awkward, men learned to exchange what they had or produced for a more marketable commodity, a more acceptable commodity, and then to exchange this more marketable commodity for what they wanted. It was traders, not governments, who originated media of exchange.

Diversity in Demand

Every commodity has a different marketability, a different acceptability. Some things have a wider marketability or acceptability than others. For example, there was a classified advertisement in an Ohio paper a few years ago which read:

FOR SALE: Second-Hand Tombstone.
Good buy for a person named Murphy.

Not many people would want that tombstone. Another example appeared in a newspaper clipping a short while ago. It told about an airplane carrier that the British Navy no longer wanted. It had cost millions to build during World War II. In relation to its cost of production, you could get that carrier at a bargain price, because not many people want airplane carriers.

There are many factors which contribute to the different marketabilities of different things. First, there is the number of persons who might want them for their own satisfaction. Many people want bread, but few people want books in Swahili. Many people would like to buy the Mona Lisa, but few people would buy our family photographs.

Next, there is the question of their portability. Some things are heavy and bulky and difficult to move around, like cement and lumber, as compared with diamonds and the precious metals.

There is also a question of the quantity desired. There are some things we want, but we want only one or two units, like a furnace or an air-conditioning machine for a house or a room. We would not normally want many of them, or a new one every day, as in the case of loaves of bread. There are some things, like bananas, that are very perishable. There are clothes that get out of date in a year or two. There are yesterday's newspapers and last week's programs for the theatre or sports events. There are other things you could not sell at any price, such as a used toothbrush or an individual's eyeglasses or dentures.

By trial and error, men soon learned the commodities that were the most marketable in their communities. Over the years, the most marketable commodity has been many different things in many different places. The most marketable commodity for the early Romans was cattle. The Latin word for money is *pecunia,* which comes from *pecus,* Latin for cattle. At times it has been shells. It has been beads. It has been furs. The Aztecs used cocoa beans and cotton handkerchiefs. In World War II, United States troops in Europe used cigarettes. The most acceptable commodity has been many other things at different times and places.

How Money Developed

At first, only a few people in the community saw the advantage of using some specific commodity in a double or indirect exchange rather than putting up with the time-wasting clumsiness of barter or direct exchange. They exchanged their products for a more acceptable "medium of exchange," and then later exchanged this medium of exchange for the things they wanted. Others observed, noted the advantages, and adopted the same procedures. Please note, it was not governments that invented this system. Men did it of their own free will. They found it improved their situation from their point of view.

As economies progressed, the number of generally acceptable media of exchange decreased. And as they did, it became easier to trade, and easier to calculate in advance the expected gains from the contemplated exchanges. It became easier to find out where you could get what you wanted at the lowest cost and easier to exchange what you had for the highest return. This opened the door to a great expansion of trade and division of labor, with the benefits from the increased transactions shared by all who participated. Remember, no one trades unless he expects to improve his situation.

Over the years it was found that the intermediate, more marketable, more acceptable commodity had to be one that didn't spoil, that was easily recognized, that could be divided or combined without loss of value, and that had a high value in small quantities, making it easy to transport without great expense.

Over the years, the media of exchange gradually narrowed down to the metals. At first copper was used. Then came the other metals, and with their use people developed a market system of prices in terms of the locally selected medium of exchange, whatever it was. First a metal was used locally, in one small area. Then its use spread until it included nationwide markets, and finally an international world market. This permitted greater and greater division of labor and greater and greater efficiency in increasing the satisfactions of men through exchanges that benefited all who participated. This is how the use of money developed.

Differences in Economic Goods

Economic goods can be divided into three classes or groups: (1) producers' or production goods, sometimes called capital goods. These are goods used to produce ultimately the second group: (2) consumers' goods and services. The third group comprises: (3) the media of exchange, more popularly known as moneys.

Group 3, the media of exchange, or moneys, are not consumed in their ordinary usage, which is to exchange them for other economic goods. Money is a part of private capital, but an increase in the quantity of money does not help society, only the individuals receiving some of the increase. This is something that we are going to discuss at great length. Money is neither a producers' good nor a consumers' good. It is merely a medium for facilitating exchanges.

Any increase in the available quantities of producers' goods or consumers' goods represents a net gain in human satisfaction. As a result, every market participant can have more. Any loss or destruction of a producers' good or consumers' good results in a loss to mankind. It is not only a loss to the former owner, or the insurance company; it is also a loss to all of us, because there are fewer goods competing for the limited sum of money in the hands of each and every buyer.

More Goods Mean Lower Prices

Let me expand a bit here. The more goods and services there are in the market, the more each of us can buy with his limited supply of money. The competition of more available goods and services results in lower prices. As each of us has only a limited supply of money, this means that any increase in production helps not only the producer but all of us. If Mr. Ford makes more Fords, not only is he richer, but every one of us is also richer, because there are more Fords. With more automobiles, there are more goods in the market competing for our money. Prices will thus be lower. As a result, we can each buy more.

Likewise, when there is an accident and something is destroyed, as when a house burns, or a plane falls to the ground, this is a loss to all of us. Society has to divert the scarce goods (raw materials) and services (labor) needed to reproduce what has been lost or destroyed. The scarce raw materials and scarce labor so used cannot be used to produce the things that could have been produced, if they did not have to be consumed in reproducing the lost or destroyed assets.

This applies not only to the loss of goods but also to the loss of men. In my country, every time a boy is killed in Vietnam, we all feel the loss in our hearts. But we also suffer an economic loss. The nation, and his family in particular, have invested much in bringing that boy to the age where he can make contributions to society. All his potential contributions are lost forever. Besides the fact of his loss, there are the pensions and other funds that have to go to the loved ones he left behind.

Likewise there are great losses to society when people who want to work and produce remain unemployed. The fact that they are not producing means that there are fewer goods competing in the market than there could have been. As a result, prices are higher than they would have been.

So on the one hand, every increase in consumers' goods and producers' goods helps all of us, and on the other hand, every decrease, every loss, in consumers' goods and producers' goods, every potential producer kept unemployed, hurts all of us. There are fewer goods and services available in the market place. Consequently more people have to go without goods and services they could have had if the production available had been greater.

More Money Means Higher Prices

Now, this is not true in regard to money. If the total quantity of money is changed, there is neither a gain nor a loss to mankind. Changes in the quantity of money involve only changes in prices, in the ratios of the various goods and services to the money commodity. The welfare of mankind remains unchanged. It is not money that we want. It is what we can buy with money that we want. Making more money does not create more of the things that men really want. No increase in the quantity of money can increase the welfare of mankind as can the increase in the quantity of any other economic good. An increase in the quantity of money merely helps some people at the expense of others. In this sense, money differs from all other economic goods.

As mentioned before, it is not money that men want; they want what they can buy with money. The only ones who want money *per se*, and as much as they can get, are misers and coin collectors. All other men want purchasing power. If someone were to give you a million dollars tonight, you would get rid of it within forty-eight hours. You would either buy something you wanted or invest the money. It is not the money you want, it is the money's purchasing power. This purchasing power of money is, of course, greatly affected by the quantity of money available and the demand for it.

We should always look at the problem of money from the viewpoint of the individual. Each individual has a demand for a quantity of money, and it is this demand of individuals for money that is the basis of the total demand of the whole community. It is important that we remember that all knowledge of money starts from the view of the individual and not of society. For it is the subjective values of individuals that determine all human actions, and it is their differing subjective values that determine all market transactions.

The demands of individuals for money are the most important factors in determining its value. No matter how unlimited our demand for goods and services may be, we do not demand unlimited quantities of money. Every one of us determines how much money he wants to have in his pockets and in his bank account. When he has too much, he knows how to get rid of it. When he does not have enough, he does what he can to sell his goods or services, until he has what he considers an ideal quantity. No one keeps more money than he wants in his cash holdings.

A consumer uses his cash holdings to bid for one product in competition with other products, and in competition with other persons for that particular good. It is this concatenation, this coming together in the market, that produces market prices, as we tried to explain in Lecture III. These market processes "objectivize" the subjective values of the individual participants, and increase our efficiency in increasing our satisfactions.

An exchange takes place in the market when units of two commodities are placed in different relative orders on the value scales of two different persons. In the market economy, one of those commodity units is always money, a specific quantity of money.

Multiple Moneys Complicate Trade

As economies progressed and as the number of moneys decreased, it became easier for all people to trade and to calculate prospective gains. It became easier for all people to compare prices and find out where it was cheapest to buy what they each wanted, and where they could each get the highest price for what they had to sell. But even in modern times, different countries have had different moneys. However, by the nineteenth century, civilized nations had narrowed down their moneys to the precious metals – gold and silver.

But even then, if one country was on a gold standard, as many countries were, its traders had difficulties in selling their products to a country which was on a silver standard, to India for instance. Between the time the order was placed and the time the payment was received, the market ratios between gold and silver might have changed. This change created an unanticipated loss or gain for the traders involved.

Most businessmen are knowledgeable in their own business, but they do not like to take risks in areas on which they are not informed. To assume these risks of changes in exchange rates or ratios, foreign traders employed specialists, called *arbitrageurs* by the French. Under such conditions these foreign exchange specialists were useful. For a price, they assumed the speculative burden and eliminated exchange losses for businessmen not familiar with foreign exchange problems. However, where there is only one money, these men are not needed, and they would be released to produce goods and services that men want more than they want two different kinds of money.

Problems of Bimetallism

At the end of the eighteenth century, some countries used gold for money, while other countries used silver. Still other countries used both gold and silver as money, with the result that they had two sets of prices, a set of gold prices and a set of silver prices. These two sets of prices caused confusion. Many governments, trying to be helpful, then stepped in and attempted to set a permanent ratio between all gold prices and all silver prices, usually with some point between fifteen and sixteen ounces of silver considered the legal equivalent of one ounce of gold.

Gold and silver could then be exchanged for each other at this officially set ratio at the Treasury or at a bank. It was a form of what we would today call price control for gold in terms of silver, and vice versa, for silver in terms of gold. The purpose was to have the prices in one metal easily convertible to prices in the other metal, and thus eliminate any exchange losses. As with many other interventionist ideas, the sponsors had the best of intentions. Unfortunately, as so often happens, the results were not those anticipated.

This bimetallism, as it was called, started late in the eighteenth century. The world market ratio of silver to gold at that time fluctuated around 15.7 to 1. (See Table XIV.) Spain, Portugal, and most of South America set their official rates at 16 to 1, that is, sixteen ounces of silver and one ounce of gold were always exchangeable for each other at the nation's treasury. Cuba set her official rate at 17 to 1. In the United States of America, Alexander Hamilton, our first Secretary of the Treasury, set the official rate in 1792 at 15 to 1. For every ounce of gold our Treasury offered only 15 ounces of silver, while the world market offered 15.7 ounces of silver. The results were easy to foresee. Gold flowed into world market uses and most Americans used silver for money. Although we were officially on a bimetallic system, in reality we went on the silver standard.

In 1803, France adopted an official rate of 15½ to 1. After the Napoleonic Wars, Great Britain went back on gold in 1816, with subsidiary silver coins valued at 16 to 1. As you can see, all of these countries had different rates. Then, in 1834, the United States changed its official rate from 15 to 1 to 16 to 1. This reversed the previously existing situation, by making it profitable for silver, rather than gold, to flow into world market uses. As a result, we went on a *de facto* gold standard. Then, as you know, in the 1850s and 1860s there were great discoveries of gold on the West Coast in California, and later in Alaska and Australia.

In 1866, at a time when gold production was increasing rapidly, the Latin Monetary Union was formed with a set ratio of 15½ to 1. This Union, spurred on by Napoleon III, included France, Belgium, Switzerland, Italy, and later Greece. Austria, Spain, Portugal, most Balkan nations, and

Table
XIV

GOLD-SILVER RATIOS, 1792-1874

With Spain, Portugal and South America at 16 oz. silver to 1 oz. gold (Cuba 17 to 1) and the world market at about 15.7 to 1 —

1792 — Hamilton set U.S.A. silver-gold ratio at 15 to 1 — on *de facto* silver standard.

1803 — France set ratio at 15½ to 1.

1816 — Great Britain returned to gold standard, with subsidiary silver coins at 16 to 1.

1834 — U.S.A. went to 16 to 1 — on *de facto* gold standard.

1850s and 1860s — Gold discoveries in California, Alaska and Australia.

1866 — Latin Monetary Union formed at 15½ to 1.

1873 — U.S.A. demonetized silver and Germany announced shift from silver to gold.

1874 — Latin Monetary Union restricted silver coinage.

many of the countries of Latin America conformed informally, but never actually joined the Union. Then, in 1873, the United States of America demonetized silver, and Germany, upon receipt of a French war indemnity of five billion gold francs, announced a shift from the silver standard to the gold standard. These events increased world market supplies of silver, reducing its market value, so that in 1874, the Latin

Monetary Union was forced to restrict silver coinage and the free exchange of one ounce of gold for every 15½ ounces of silver presented.

Economic Laws Ignored

Now, these governments had all thought that both metals would continuously circulate as money at the official ratio. They had failed to take the immutable laws of economics into consideration. They had thought, as many people do today, that governmental laws can replace economic laws. Among those who thought along these lines was a recent President of the United States, who officially stated that he had signed into law a statute that had superseded some economic laws he did not like.[1] Such advocates of political intervention do not realize that the laws of human action, economics, are unalterable.

One of the economic laws that advocates of bimetallism did not take into account was the fact that values change. Values are no more constant than the minds of men. They do not stay put. They constantly fluctuate, and no man-made law can keep them constant. The relative values of any two commodities rarely remain constant over any extended period of time. Every change in the demand for, or the supply of, either commodity must change the relative exchange values of one for the other. As the demand for, and the supply of, both gold and silver are constantly changing, the relative values of the two commodities, gold and silver, in terms of each other, are also constantly changing, government's laws notwithstanding. These legal experiments with a bimetallic monetary standard were the first attempts of modern governments to regulate the value of money. They failed miserably.

---

1. "The Employment Act of 1946 is one of the most fundamental compacts in domestic affairs which the people through their Government have made during my tenure as President . . . . It is the purpose of the Employment Act – the one most widely recognized at the time of its passage – to prevent depressions. . . . The Act rejects the idea that we are victims of unchangeable economic laws, that we are powerless to do more than forecast what will happen to us under the operation of such laws." Harry S. Truman, *The Economic Report of the President*, January 14, 1953, pp. 8, 10 & 17.

The other law they ignored is known as Gresham's Law, which is popularly stated as: "Bad money drives out good money." Some now jest that bad politicians, like bad money, are overvalued, and tend to drive out or replace good ones.

Stated more fully, Gresham's Law is a law of human action which holds that in a market economy free men will always tend to allocate the available units of every economic good to those uses where they are expected to perform the most valuable services known to men, and thus to provide the greatest possible human satisfactions. The market never allocates any scarce good to perform a function for which it is known that a cheaper article would serve as well. When a government sets a legal ratio between two monetary metals, men, operating through the market, will always select the cheaper metal for money and release the dearer metal for its more valuable functions. As long as men are free to exchange one metal for the other, they will do so, using the cheaper for the monetary function that either metal can legally serve.

How Bimetallism Works

Let us look for a moment at what happens in such a situation, so that we can better understand how Gresham's Law operates. First, let us assume that Country A establishes a legal ratio of 15 ounces of silver to 1 of gold, while Country B establishes a ratio of 16 to 1, and the world market price or ratio is somewhere between 15 and 16 to 1.

Under these conditions, Country A will use only silver for money, while Country B will use only gold. The treasuries and the taxpayers will lose on all transactions. Under such conditions, human beings who have or can get an ounce of gold will present it to Country B, where they can exchange it for 16 ounces of silver. Then, they can go to Country A and with only 15 ounces of silver replace their ounce of gold, retaining a profit of one ounce of silver on every such transaction. This loss will be borne by the treasury, and ultimately by the taxpayers, of Country A, whose treasury must replenish its supply of silver at world market prices. Likewise, the treasury of Country B must meet the demand for gold by replenishing its supply of gold at world market prices.

Next, let us assume that the world market ratio rises to 16 plus to 1. Then both countries, A and B, will use silver for money. They will both allocate gold to its other more valuable uses. People with gold will not spend it as money. It is worth more in the market place for its other uses.

Lastly, let us assume that the world market ratio falls below 15 to 1. Then we shall have the opposite situation. Both countries will use gold for money, while silver will be allocated to its other uses where it is considered more valuable. People with silver will dispose of it in the world market, where they can get an ounce of gold for less than 15 ounces of silver.

This is not how I say it should be! This is not how I want it to be! This is how men act, when left free. It would take an all-powerful dictatorship to prevent these results.

Left alone, each country uses for money the commodity best suited and least expensive for that purpose. When the government interferes successfully, it diverts goods to uses where they give less satisfaction. Such governmental actions are restrictions on the first choices of men. Men must then be satisfied with their secondary or lesser choices. Only a free and flexible economy permits goods and services to flow unhampered to those persons and places where they can give the highest human satisfactions. This is as true for money as it is for every other economic good.

The Market Chose Gold

About 1900, gold became the universally accepted money for international trade. It is still money for international trade today. It is still the money that every nation in the world wants and values most. Despite what is being said against gold by more and more people, nobody is refusing gold. Under the conditions existing at the end of the nineteenth century, gold was selected by the market as the most suitable commodity to perform the functions of money.

Gold was not selected as money by governments. They had sought bimetallism by every method they knew. Their policies, along with the new gold discoveries, created conditions which, at that time, legally overvalued gold in terms of silver. Market traders, operating in accordance with Gresham's Law, then selected gold as money.

With all world prices quoted in gold, it became easy for traders to calculate all costs, including transportation, and then decide where in the world it was best to buy or sell those things that people were most interested in buying or selling. Under a gold standard, goods move with the greatest dispatch to those areas and persons where they attract the highest prices, and where they are expected to provide the highest relative human satisfactions. Likewise, holders of gold, that is, money, can most easily calculate where in the world they can get the most for their earned or saved money. Since all prices and calculations are in terms of the same commodity, gold, it is immediately evident which of many prices are the cheapest. This is not so with the use of multiple moneys.

In a free market society, everything, including money, tends to flow quickly to those places and persons where each unit is expected to serve the highest human satisfaction that it is capable of serving. Money is the most marketable commodity in a market society. It is the commodity for which, in a market society, there is the greatest demand. Consequently, it tends to move faster than any other commodity. However, people do not want money for consumption. They want it primarily to exchange for other things they do want for consumption. People want money for its purchasing power.

There are, of course, many, many fallacies concerning money. However, most sponsors of popular monetary errors fall into two groups: (1) those who think that money is more than a commodity, and (2) those who think it is less than a commodity. Money is neither more nor less than a commodity. Money is merely the most marketable commodity in a market society.

The use of money presupposes an economic order based on private property, the division of labor, and the exchange of private property for the expected gain of all parties. Its use helps to direct production and consumption into those channels which are expected to furnish the highest possible human satisfaction.

A Socialist Society Is Priceless

In a socialist society, where the government owns or controls all the means of production, there is no need or use for money. Since the government owns all the factors of production, there cannot be any competitive market bidding with money for capital goods, or with capital goods for money. Government officials, not the market, determine what is produced and who gets what. The use of money presupposes that there must be private property being bought and sold in the market. Money must take its value from the valuations of independent economic agents competing with each other in valuing things and exchanging whenever they find it is to their mutual advantage.

This is quite evident when you study what happens in the areas under socialist domination today. Soviet Russia would not be able to function at all, if she could not refer to prices outside her borders. She has no other way of knowing which is the cheapest material to use to make anything. Without a domestic market, she must look beyond her borders to see whether tin, iron, steel, aluminum, or what not is the cheapest metal for a particular use. She must first find out their relative values in the world markets; and it should be remembered that these prices cannot reflect the demand and supply conditions within her country. So the Soviet Union is steering her economy down a road without any helpful signposts. She lacks the price signs that guide all production in a market economy.

Let me refer to a news item in the *New York Times* of April 19, 1966. It reports on an East German trade treaty with the Union of Soviet Socialist Republics. At that time, about 50 percent of East Germany's foreign trade was with the Soviet Union, and only 10 percent with West Germany, which had refused to give her long-term credits. East Germany got 90 percent of its steel and 100 percent of its crude oil and iron ore from Soviet Russia. The gentleman who negotiated this trade treaty for East Germany, a Dr. Erik Apel, committed suicide because of complaints that this trade treaty was not fair to his country. It had been alleged that the treaty was too favorable to the Soviets and too costly to the people of East Germany.

After Dr. Apel had committed suicide, he was succeeded by a Mrs. Elsa Bauer. She defended the trade treaty by saying: "There is no unfairness in the terms of trade with the Soviet Union. The terms are considered correct. Prices have been based on the average world market prices over the last three years."

How would you like to *buy* goods at the average prices of the last three years? How would you like to *sell* goods at the average prices of the last three years? This is how a socialist society has to operate. If the whole world were socialist, there would not be any market prices of either the present or "the last three years" to use in calculating production costs of different things and processes. Without prices, all decisions on what and how to produce must be completely arbitrary.

Money Permits Complicated Calculations

The objective or exchange value, or ratio, of any given commodity may be expressed in units of every other kind of a commodity. Nowadays it is expressed in units of the commodity we call money. The market permits any commodity to be turned into money, and likewise the money commodity may be turned back to its other commodity uses when it is no longer more useful or more valuable as money. We have recently seen this happen in the case of silver. With one commodity used as a medium for expressing the relative values of all market goods and services we can compare our different value scales more easily. This is why and how men operating in the market develop the value of money.

The value of money is subjective. Prices are ratios expressed as quantities of the money commodity. Prices are comparisons. They are for one time and place. They are flexible and subject to instant change. They cannot be added any more than we can add our love for different people. However, it is easier for all of us if the ratios are expressed in just one commodity. It makes comparisons easier and calculations possible.

Goethe, the great German genius, once called double entry bookkeeping one of the greatest inventions of mankind. It permits nationwide and even worldwide division of labor and the use of complicated production processes over long periods of time. With the use of prices, businessmen can calculate the results of completed transactions and the anticipated, but uncertain, results from any future transactions they may be contemplating. They will select for future operation those transactions which their calculations indicate may be most profitable. These are the uses of available labor and capital that are expected to bring the highest prices over costs, from consumers.

On the Value of Money

All consumers' goods and producers' goods have both use values and market values. Their use value is the value they provide the owner in satisfying his own personal wants or needs. Their exchange value is the value they provide others in satisfying their wants or needs, that is, the price that others will offer to pay for them. Thus, these consumers' goods and producers' goods have both subjective use and objective exchange or market values. However, in the case of money, these two values coincide. The expected use of money is the possibility of exchanging it for other economic goods. The value of money always depends on the subjective use value of the economic goods for which it can be exchanged. Its exchange value is, in the end, the anticipated use value of the things that can be obtained for it.

The original value of any money was the use value that commodity had in its other uses before it was first used as a medium of exchange. It then had an objective exchange value based on some other use or uses. This historical link is absolutely necessary, not only for commodity money, but also for every legally sanctioned credit or fiat money. No fiat money ever came into use without first satisfying this requirement. It is absolutely impossible to start a new money without an historical use value, or without its being related to some previous money or commodity with a prior use value. Before an economic good or a "paper money" begins to function as money, it must possess, or be given, an exchange value based on some use or good other than its own monetary value. The legal tender values of paper money are today always tied, or related, to gold, or to another monetary unit that in turn is related to gold.

Thus, there is a continuous historical component in the value, or purchasing power, of every money. We tend to think of the value of any money in terms of what it was worth in the most recent past, yesterday or an hour ago. We start all our valuations of money from its most recent, or current, purchasing power. Then, we try to forecast what may change its purchasing power in the future. Our actions in regard to money are always guided by these appraisals of its past value and its expected future value. So the immediately prior value of a money has an influence on the future market or objective value of that money. People start their present valuations of money from the instant just passed, and then make up their present values by their estimates of what they think is going to be the net effect of expected changes in its market conditions.

If people think that the purchasing power of money is going down, they will tend to spend more of it immediately or in the very near future. On the other hand, if they think its value is going up, they are likely to hold on to more of it than otherwise. So the original starting point of the value of any money is found in the immediate past subjective valuations of the marginal utility of the units under consideration. As in valuing other economic goods, we never consider the value of the total supply of money. We always consider the value of a specific number of units of money, the value of the marginal units. We either want to spend certain units of money, or we want to acquire certain units in exchange for something we have to offer. So at any particular time, the value of money is the result of the coming together in the market of the subjective valuations of all the individual market participants, who each value it according to the use value to them of the marginal units of what they can buy with a unit of money.

Changes in the purchasing power, and thus in the value, of money can arise either from the money side, or from the goods and services side, of market transactions. Such changes can arise from new data or information affecting either (1) the demand for, or (2) the supply of, money, or (3) the demand for, or (4) the supply of, the vendible goods of the market place. However, a general rise or fall in the demand for all goods and services, or for most of them, can only arise from the side of money. When all, or the great majority of, prices are going up or down, we know something is happening to the quantity of money.

On Government and Money

The original aim and intent of government in getting into the money situation was to release individuals from the need to test the weight and fineness of monetary metals. By coining or minting money, governments guaranteed that the metallic coins contained a certain quantity and quality of the monetary metal. Individuals no longer had to employ experts to assay and weigh them. This was a valuable service.

However, the most important function that governments have today concerning money, the one that has to exist in a free market society, is the duty to decide disputes in courts. Governmental courts have to decide the meaning of disputed contracts. When a private contract calls for the payment of a certain amount of money, that money must be paid. Suppose one party offers something he calls money in payment of a debt. The other party disagrees. He claims that what is offered is not money and does not satisfy the contract. They must then take their dispute to the courts of law. Then, the government must decide what was meant by the term "money" as used in that contract. So governments have the legal duty to define what is money. There is no way that this monetary function of government can be eliminated. The peaceful settlement of disputes is one of the primary functions of government. If people quarrel about what is money, the government must settle those disputes if it is to maintain order. So ultimately governments must define the monetary unit.

Money is always scarce. Otherwise it would not be an economic good. It would not have any value. If everyone had all the money he thought he wanted, money would be worthless. There is no need for the government to interfere in the quantity of money. It cannot be helpful. Whenever the government increases the quantity of money it helps some at the expense of others. It cannot be otherwise.

Quantity of Money Must be Limited

The service that money renders to society cannot be improved by changing the quantity. All individuals in a market society need a certain amount of ready purchasing power. They hold it in the form of cash holdings. We never leave the house without some cash holdings. How much cash each person holds depends primarily on its purchasing power. It may appear to an individual that he has an excess or deficiency in his cash holdings. He then quickly takes steps to adjust it. He can either reduce his cash holdings by spending or investing some of his money, or increase his cash holdings by trying to sell his services or some of his goods. However, the quantity of money available in any society is always sufficient to perform for everybody all the functions that money can perform — *i.e.*, the efficient comparison of individual value scales in order to locate and facilitate transactions which may be mutually advantageous.

Under the gold standard, the determination of the quantity and value of money is dependent upon the profitability of gold production. The value of gold as money is not the fact that it glitters. It is the fact that the quantity of gold cannot be easily increased by the arbitrary acts of men. The cost of mining gold keeps it scarce and a valuable "economic good." Gold cannot be printed. It cannot be manufactured, although we hear today of governments creating all the "paper gold" they want. This will be one to watch. The alchemists could not produce gold, and it is doubtful that calling certain pieces of paper "paper gold" will endow them with the value of gold.

The value of gold is affected by the quantity mined. However, the biggest variations in the value of money during the last century have not originated in the area of gold production. They have sprung from the policies of governments and their central banks of issue. Under the gold standard proper, the value of money is independent of the politics of the hour. However, the actions of governments can lower the value of money by political interventions that reduce the human satisfactions that could be obtained by the more efficient operations of a free market.

Some Popular Fallacies

One of the most important popular fallacies concerning money is the spurious idea of the supposed neutrality of money, and the corollary idea that its value can somehow be kept constant by political manipulation. In this world there is no such thing as constancy of values. Change is ever with us, and changes in the values of money will be with us as long as men's minds change their individual value scales. There is no governmental law, edict, or regulation that can make or hold the value of money rigid or settled for all time. Our valuations of the same and differing units of money are constantly changing and always will. Changes in the value of money, far from being neutral, affect every market transaction.

One of the other related fallacies concerning money is the crude quantity of money theory, the idea that there is a constant relationship between the quantity of money and its value in the market exchanges. This idea is that a certain proportional increase in the quantity of money will produce a certain proportional increase either in all prices, or in "average prices." This idea is usually interpreted to mean that an increase in production requires an offsetting increase in the quantity of money. This is not so. An increase in the quantity of money produces different changes in the prices of different goods. The changes are neither proportional nor all at the same time. Such increases are inflation, which we shall discuss in the lectures that follow; so we shall not go off in that direction now.

The purchasing power of money is the same everywhere. The market reflects this purchasing power and market participants soon wipe out any discrepancies that appear. Before the development of the subjective marginal theory of value, not even economists were aware that the value of money is constantly changing. Most of you in this country have learned this lesson. Unfortunately, many in my country still think, with apologies to Gertrude Stein, that a dollar is a dollar is a dollar, always. Variations in the quantity, and thus the value, of money do not affect the market values, or prices, of all economic goods and services in the same way. Some prices change before others, and some prices change more than others.

The value of money is not a legal proposition. Contracts may provide for the payment of certain quantities of money, but they cannot, and do not, provide that any specified sum of money will retain equal value over periods of time. Legal definitions deal with physical quantities and qualities, and not with market values. These physical quantities and qualities of a money can be kept constant, but the value of any money constantly fluctuates, and no government is powerful enough to stop this fluctuation except by making the money worthless.

In a market economy, money is distributed among individuals, and hence among nations, according to the extent and intensity of their respective demands for money. Money, like other goods, flows quickly, when permitted, to those who place the highest value on it. International movements of money are the cause, not the effects, of favorable and unfavorable trade balances. Money moves only when and because both a buyer and a seller want it to move. It moves from person to person, or from nation to nation, because the value scales of the interested parties place higher values on what they get than on what they surrender. People export money because they prefer the imports, or whatever else they buy, to the sums of money exported.

Government controls on the shipments of money are unnecessary, and as inappropriate as controls to insure a sufficiency of coal, iron, or wheat. In a free society, no person, group, or nation need fear the lack of a sufficient money supply. Any quantity of money can be divided and subdivided to reflect the market ratios or prices, which will keep increased supplies of scarce goods and services moving to those who place the higher values on them.

Textbook Fallacies

In many textbooks, the authors speak of three functions of money. They usually mention first that money has the function of a medium of exchange. It does, and this is what we have been discussing. But many textbook authors also think of money as a "measure of value." There is no such thing as a measure of value. Measurement standards, like ounces, pounds, and tons, or yards, meters, and miles, are always constants. Values are in the minds of men and, like the minds of men, they are never constant. There is no standard by which ever-fluctuating values can be measured. There are no constant units, and never can be any, with which to measure values. The same economic good has different values for different people, and different market values at different times.

The third function frequently attributed to money in textbooks is that of a "store of value." Money can be a "store of value," as any other commodity can be, but it is not a store of a *constant* value as is so often implied in these textbooks. If anyone puts a certain sum of money in a sound bank, that sum should be there later, but the value of that sum will not be the same. Its value will always be fluctuating. With governments increasing the quantity of money, the value of that money tends to fall. Many people have learned this the hard way in recent years. So it does not need much emphasis here.

Actually, money is a medium of exchange, and only a medium of exchange. It completely fulfills its function when exchanges of goods and services are carried on more easily with its help than is possible under barter.

Storing or hoarding money is one way of using wealth. If no one wanted to hold money, it would be without value. The uncertainty of the future always makes it advisable for everyone to have some money on hand. How much one has on hand depends on his own estimate or appraisal of future conditions. Urgent demands for money to spend, as well as money to take advantage of profit possibilities that may arise unexpectedly, have to be considered. In deciding how much cash to hold, people must also weigh what they expect to happen to the value of money as the result of deflation or inflation. All these factors contribute to the future purchasing power of money and help explain why people want to hold some money.

Effect of Changes in the Quantity of Money

Changes in the quantity of money affect different people differently. There is just no way in which money can be introduced into, or taken out of, an economy so as to affect all people equally. The injection of new money into a society adds no new wealth. It merely redistributes purchasing power, and thus the titles to existing wealth. Those who receive some of the new money can buy more of the existing goods before prices rise, while others find prices rising before their incomes do. So some can thus take what a free market, with an unmanipulated quantity of money, would allocate to others. Every increase in the quantity of money therefore helps some at the expense of others.

Changes in the quantity of money produce changes in the value of money. An increase in the quantity of money, like an increase in the quantity of any other economic good, causes the value of every existing unit to fall. However, changes in the value or purchasing power of money do not affect all persons and prices evenly or at the same time. Changes in the value of money always start at some given point and then spread gradually through the whole market community.

When the quantity of money is increased, the recipients of the newly created money immediately place a lower subjective value on each unit of money they possess. They are then more apt to spend money than they were before their supply of it was increased. They might even pay higher prices than they previously would. As they spend more money, some of the increased money reaches new recipients, who, in turn, place a lower value on each unit of money. Thus a lower subjective value for money is passed step by step from person to person, and more and more persons become willing to pay higher prices because they have more money. This process continues until the full effect of each increase in the quantity of money is completely dissipated. Those who receive some of the increased money early in the process are benefited, while those who do not receive any of the increased money until the later stages are hurt. It cannot be otherwise.

The economic consequences from changes in the value of money are determined not by what causes the increase in the quantity of money, but by the nature of the slow progress of the new money from person to person, from one commodity price to another commodity price, and from one country to another. Anything that changes the demand for, or supply of, any marketable good or service affects the value of money. Everything that changes the supply of, or demand for, money must also affect the patterns of prices for the various marketable goods and services. Changes in the supply of, or demand for, money also shift wealth among different individuals. Some become richer, while others become poorer.

Despite the teachings of economics, many still think that economic activity can be permanently stimulated by an artificial increase in the quantity of money or credit. An increase in the quantity of money or credit adds no new wealth to a society. It merely redistributes previously existing wealth. Some benefit as the early receivers of the newly created money. With more money, they can buy more of the available supply of goods and services, leaving less for those whose money holdings have not been increased. Thus, some gain at the expense of others.

Such an increase in the quantity of money also misdirects production in a manner that cannot be maintained. People who get the new money become bigger spenders. Businessmen produce for those who spend money. They cannot tell the difference between money spent by workers and savers, and money spent by those who have received some of the newly created money. So production facilities are increasingly shifted to produce more for those who are spending the artificially created increased quantity of money.

Inflation Not Permanent

Sales to these buyers cannot be continued forever. As the quantity of money is increased and prices rise, injections of larger and larger quantities of money are required to produce the same effects. If the quantity of money increases in ever larger quantities, prices will rise faster and faster as the value of each monetary unit falls. Sooner or later, the increases must be stopped. If they are not stopped before the value of the monetary unit falls to zero, people will eventually run away from the money and spend it on anything they can get, because, in their minds, anything will soon be worth more than a constantly depreciating money.

When governments increase the quantity of money, the effects tend to follow a certain pattern. Of course, the inflation can be stopped at any point. The first stage of inflation is when housewives say: "Prices are going up. I think I had better put off buying whatever I can. I need a new vacuum cleaner, but with prices going up, I'll wait until they come down." During this stage, prices do not rise as fast as the quantity of money is being increased. This period in the great German inflation lasted nine years, from the outbreak of war in 1914 until the summer of 1923.

During the second period of inflation, housewives say: "I shall need a vacuum cleaner next year. Prices are going up. I had better get it now before prices go any higher." During this stage, prices rise at a faster rate than the quantity of money is being increased. In Germany this period lasted a couple of months.

If the inflation is not stopped, the third stage follows. In this third stage, housewives say: "I don't like flowers. They bother me. They are a nuisance. But I would rather have even this pot of flowers than hold on to this money a moment longer." People then exchange their money for anything they can get. This period may last from twenty-four hours to forty-eight hours.

Conclusion

As we said earlier, the role of money is to make trade easier. Without money, there would be the awkwardness of barter. The use of money also tends to minimize human errors, and thus unnecessary losses. The use of money makes economic calculation possible. This helps to increase the division of labor and encourages more complicated mass production for mass consumption. It results in increasing the transactions that are expected to increase the satisfaction of each participant. The increased production is distributed by market processes to all who contribute to the joint production, in accordance with what the individual participants value most among all the many alternative purchases open to them.

Money thus helps men to help others as they help themselves. Money might be called a catalyst for the Golden Rule. A sound and simple monetary system is probably the greatest material tool available to man for the multiplication of human satisfactions.

The question that men face today is: Who should choose the money? The government? Or the people buying and selling on the market? It was the market, not governments, that developed the precious metals as money. Few would maintain that present-day government interferences in the field of money have been helpful.

The value of money is always the anticipated use value of what it will buy. Permitting politicians to manipulate the quantity of money permits them to affect indirectly the values involved in every market transaction. In fact, it permits them to disrupt, prevent, and otherwise hamper transactions that would increase the satisfaction of every member of the society. Increasing the quantity of money does not increase the quantity of goods people want to buy. It only helps some at the expense of others.

If men are to remain free and if Western civilization is to continue, people must regain the right to limit the political expansion of the quantity of money and/or credit. We must *never* again permit politicians to print money or get their hands on the money we put in banks and think is always there. A free market economy cannot permanently operate on a politically manipulated paper money standard. Free men need a market-selected money. Under present conditions, this means a gold standard.

QUESTIONS AND ANSWERS

Price Changes Helpful

Q. Will you define the stability of prices?

A. The value of prices, as we tried to show, is that they are ratios expressed in quantities of one commodity. They permit the easy comparison of different values. They reflect the things which are most in demand, and price changes reflect changes in both demand and supply. We as individuals are not interested in all prices, or in low prices, or in high prices. We are interested in individual prices. If prices were constant there would never be any changes in demand and supply, and there are such changes. Prices serve to indicate the changes in production that are desired as the wishes of consumers change. As consumers want more of some good, the price of that good goes up, while the price of the good they switched from goes down. Prices have to move as people's values change. They cannot be stable. If they were stable, they would reflect no change in market conditions. If prices were unchanged from those in the 1870s, we would live and die the same as people did a century ago. We would have both production and population stabilized. As the population is never stabilized and consumers' desires are constantly changing, prices must constantly change. As long as markets exist and men's minds change, stable prices will remain an impossiblity.

Steps to a Gold Standard

Q. What are the fundamental steps that a country must take to go to a gold standard?

A. My great teacher, Ludwig von Mises, wrote a supplement on "Monetary Reconstruction" for the 1953 edition of his *Theory of Money and Credit*. He stated that two things must be done instantly. One is to stop the artificial increase in the quantity of money, and the other is to take the government out of the gold market. Then, we should permit a free market in gold. After a period of time the free market in gold will tend to stabilize at some ratio of the monetary unit to gold. Then that ratio should be adopted into law, and that ratio should be defended from then on out, with all of the paper monetary units convertible into gold upon demand. The paper money would then be interchangeable with the agreed legal quantity of gold.

Gold in One Country

Q. Can you establish a gold standard in just one country?

A. Yes, it would be helpful to that country. That one country would never have to worry about people refusing to take its money. But the more countries the better.

Why Socialists Cannot Calculate

Q. Please explain a little more about economic calculation in a socialist society.

A. We spent an evening on the formation of prices last week. In a socialist society, you cannot have this formation of prices. You do not have private ownership of the means of production. In answer to a question after that lecture, we talked about how one bureau in Moscow built ships to go south on the Volga, while another bureau built a fleet to go north on the Volga, because there was no market, there were no classified ads, to show that one set of ships could have handled the cargoes going in both directions. The Communists have to consider these things. They have to watch the values in the newspapers of other countries. They have no market. They have no competition. In that same lecture we tried to show how iron is allocated by market competition to the highest bidders – those who think that their use of iron in the products they are going to make will bring the highest return from consumers. It is this bidding of businessmen, independent economic agents, from which prices emerge. Where you do not have private ownership of the means of production, there is no competition. There is no way to determine the relative values or the economic allocations of the factors available, because there is no competitive bidding for them. As a result, the socialists have to operate by relying blindly on the whims or values of one man, and these are of no use for calculation. They are just pure guesses, and do not reflect the relative demands of consumers.

Hoarding Helpful to Others

Q. Do you think that if a man keeps money out of circulation it is harmful to his country?

A. No, sir. It is helpful to everybody else, because that money is not bidding for the goods and services available in the market place. As a result, everybody else can buy more with their limited quantity of money.

Milton Friedman, Inflationist

Q. What do you think of Milton Friedman's monetary theories?

A. This would take at least a book. Milton Friedman is an advocate of inflation. Milton Friedman wants the government to increase the quantity of money by some regular percent every year. He changes this percent from time to time. He does not realize that stability in prices or stability of a general average price is neither desirable nor helpful. He holds the fallacy, along with many others, that it is unfair, in the case of long-term borrowings, if the purchasing power of the money changes. In a free market, expected changes in the purchasing power of money are reflected in the market interest rate. The market interest rate is composed of three factors: (1) The first factor is time preference — that is, you will pay 5 percent interest because you prefer to buy something now for $1,000 and pay out $1,050 a year from now. That is your time preference. The person lending the money to you will have a different valuation of money over those two time periods. He will prefer $1,050 a year from now to $1000 now. That would be his time preference. (2) The second factor or component of the market interest rate is the possibility that the loan may not be repaid. This will differ in each case. (3) The third factor is the expected change in the purchasing power of the monetary unit during the time span of the loan. If, when the loan is made, it is thought that the purchasing power of money will go down during the period of the loan, the market interest rate will take this into consideration and thus will be higher. On the other hand, if the production of goods and services is expected to increase, with no foreseen increase in the quantity of money, a rise in the purchasing power of the monetary unit will be reflected in a lower interest rate. This third factor, known as the "price premium," is the attempt of lenders and borrowers to neutralize the effect of expected price changes, that is, changes in the purchasing power of money. The market interest rate is a sum of these three factors. It fully reflects and discounts the effects of any expected inflation or deflation.

The inflation that Milton Friedman advocates is an attempt to prevent a recession that would correct the misdirection of the economy brought about by prior inflation. More inflation is never a cure for prior inflation. It merely delays the correction, misdirects the economy still further, and prevents the benefits of lower prices.

Milton Friedman also ignores the fact that when you increase the quantity of money you hurt some people while helping others. He does not deal with this problem. He ignores it. There are other things. One of the great problems in our country is that Milton Friedman is popularly represented as one of the believers in a free market economy. He is a good economist in many areas, particularly in the field of labor, but in this one area, he does not have a sufficient understanding of the theory of money as I have tried to explain it tonight.

Effects of Gold Production

Q. Under the gold standard system, is a country which produces gold in a better situation than others?

A. Not particularly. Under this situation they are working and producing nothing that satisfies men's wants. When gold was found in California, goods were shipped from the Eastern part of the United States for the consumption of the miners. The Eastern parts of the United States had to get along with less, while those men out in California got these things; and all they did was add to the quantity of money. When you add to the quantity of money, you do not increase the quantity of goods which give human satisfaction. Those people who were mining the gold were contributing nothing that people could use or consume. Therefore, they were not helping the community; they were simply lowering the value of every unit of money that people held. Consumers got less. Of course, to the extent that the newly mined gold went into jewelry and industrial uses, it did represent an increase in the quantity of useful goods.

Values Not Measurable

Q. Is money the measure of value?

A. Money is not a measure of value. There is no possibility of ever having a measure of value. Values are mental concepts incapable of being measured. They can only be compared. There is no standard, or constant, by which values can be measured.

Prices Are Ratios

Q. Can you say that a certain quantity of money, or a price, is an expression of value?

A. A price is only one part of a ratio. There are two things being compared: the money and the goods. This is a ratio. If the quantity of money, or price, is 100 pesos for some particular good, you buy it if it is worth more than 100 pesos to you. If it is worth less, you sell whatever quantity you have. Prices are a means for making easy comparisons.

Papal Encyclicals on Economics

Q. Over the last half century, the Popes have issued Encyclicals dealing with wages. Do you think they are consistent with the theory of how the free market should operate?

A. Up until the last economic one, all of them were open to a free market interpretation. They were also open to other interpretations. In other words, they were not clear. The last Encyclical in the economic area certainly advocated governmental intervention and socialism. It was written for the Pope by a gentleman who had no fundamental understanding of these problems.

On Oligopolies

Q. In your recent lectures you expressed strong views on the way unions interfere with the correct level of wages and upset the free market by imposing the burden of their privileges upon all the consumers, while reducing production. Would you say that in present days oligopolies operate in a somewhat similar way and produce the same effects?

A. If they have privileges from government, yes. However, it isn't a question of oligopoly. In such cases there are two or three companies competing. As long as there is competition, anti-consumer actions are not likely to occur. You do not have competition among labor unions in one area. Where there is a monopoly privilege granted by government, the consumers certainly suffer. The people who might be able to produce the good or service involved better or cheaper are not allowed to compete.

Inflation vs. Imports of Money

Q. What is the difference between inflation and exports?

A. Inflation will be defined in my next lecture as an increase in the quantity of money. Exports are, óf course, the sale of goods abroad.

Q. After an export operation you have more gold and less goods available. Haven't you the same effect as inflation in that you get more gold in from selling exports?

A. You will have the same effect in that you'll get higher domestic prices, yes, but the higher prices are not brought about by a government or a bank increasing the wealth of one person at the expense of others. The increased money goes to the exporter who sold his goods or his services, and who earned the more money he received.

Special Drawing Rights

Q. What is your opinion of SDRs (Special Drawing Rights)?

A. It would seem to be getting close to the end of the inflation line. In our country we started with FDR and now we are up to SDR. There is paper and there is gold, but the two are two different products. The SDRs are apparently an attempt to get all governments to inflate at the same rate. An international body will allocate the increase in the quantity of paper money. In this way, if all countries are inflating at the same rate, it will not be easy for people within one country to see what is happening to their money. This program will be extremely difficult to carry out. I expect that it will fail. Of course, no one knows the future, and I certainly do not. It is largely a question of how long the people can be fooled by the claim that paper has the same value as a commodity which has other uses. The reactions of the people in the different countries are unquestionably going to be different.

The Cause
Of The
1929 Depression

This lecture is long and a little complicated. However, it is very important, because millions of people, who once had great faith in the free market economy, have been led to believe that it was the failure of the free market that produced the depression of 1929. As a result, they have accepted government intervention as necessary to save free enterprise from itself.

The Problem Is Ideological

This is basically a Marxian idea. It holds that the free enterprise system contains within itself the seeds of its own destruction, and that, if allowed free rein, free enterprise will destroy itself, with the rich getting richer and the poor getting poorer until the poor revolt in favor of socialism or communism. In more modern terms, it holds that monopolies will arise and dominate the situation until the time is ripe for a socialist revolution.

One of the great men of my country, Abraham Lincoln, quite early in life said:

At what point·then is the approach of danger to be expected? I answer, if it ever reaches us it must spring up amongst us; it cannot come from abroad. If destruction be our lot, we must ourselves be its author and finisher. As a nation of free men, we must live through all time, or die by suicide.[1]

In these days many people are seriously worried about the economic and military strength of the Soviet Union and its Communist satellites in a war that might end civilization. This is not my worry. When you understand the strength of a free market economy, you know better. What we have to worry about is destroying ourselves by destroying the free market. Only the gradual acceptance of communist ideas can do that. The strongest weapon the communists have is the ability of their ideas to destroy the American dollar. Inflation is their Trojan horse in our midst. The ruination of the dollar by inflation would be the greatest victory the communists could ever win. It is communist ideas, not Communist armies, that we should fear most.

Monetary Problems Are Not New

This problem that we deal with tonight is like a snarled ball of yarn. It takes very little effort to snarl up a ball of yarn, but it takes a great deal of effort, patience, and intelligence to untangle it. This evening we shall try to unsnarl the monetary tangle resulting from years of political manipulations of the money supply.

A gentleman whom I consider the first economist of my country, Pelatiah Webster (1726-1795), a great man of our Revolutionary period, gave our forefathers sound advice on a number of occasions. As an older man during the Revolutionary War, he wrote a series of essays advising the new nation against inflation. He strongly opposed the printing of the Continental currency, which set our country back considerably. In fact, this inflation was the underlying cause of Valley Forge, the very nadir of our war for freedom. In his essays he wrote: "An error in finances, like a leak in a ship, may be obvious in the *fact*, alarming in its *effects*, but difficult *to*

---

1. Speech given at Springfield, Illinois, January 27, 1837.

find." [2] This is the problem that we are probing this evening. We are trying to find the leaks in the ships of "modern" finance. They are rather difficult to locate.

Webster also said: "The first thing necessary to correcting an error is to discover it, the next is to confess it, and the last to avoid it." [3] Another interesting statement of this gentleman was: "Money in a state is like salt in cookery; some of it is very necessary, but too much of it spoils every dish, and renders the whole dinner unsavory to the taste, and hurtful to the health." [4]

The Consequences of Inflation

Next, we shall quote from John Maynard Keynes, a gentleman with whom sound economists disagree on many things. However, all good economists can agree with one statement that he made early in life in his 1919 book, *The Economic Consequences of the Peace*, which helped make him a public figure. Mr. Keynes then wrote, and it is well worth taking the time to read:

> Lenin is said to have declared that the best way to destroy the Capitalist System was to debauch the currency. By a continuing process of inflation, governments can confiscate, secretly and unobserved, an important part of the wealth of their citizens. By this method they not only confiscate, but they confiscate *arbitrarily*; and, while the process impoverishes many, it actually enriches some. The sight of this arbitrary rearrangement of riches strikes not only at security, but at confidence in the equity of the existing distribution of wealth. Those to whom the system brings windfalls . . . become "profiteers," who are the object of hatred of . . . [those] whom the inflationism has impoverished . . . . As the inflation proceeds . . . the process of wealth-getting degenerates into a gamble and a lottery.
>
> Lenin was certainly right. There is no subtler, no surer means of overturning the existing basis of society than to debauch the currency. The process engages all the hidden forces of economic law on the side of destruction, and does it in a manner which not

---

2. Pelatiah Webster, *Political Essays on the Nature and Operation of Money, Public Finances and Other Subjects* (1791), "Third Essay on Free Trade and Finance" (1780), p.51.
3. *Ibid.*
4. *Ibid.*, "Second Essay on Free Trade and Finance" (1779), p. 37.

one man in a million is able to diagnose .... The governments of
Europe ... are fast rendering impossible a continuance of the
social and economic order of the 19th century. [5]

Tonight, we shall try to help some of you qualify for this
"one man in a million" group. It is a complicated subject,
and while it is doubtful that Lenin ever made the quoted
statement, it would seem that Keynes once understood the
problem, if not the answer.

Defining "Inflation"

Before proceeding further, we should first define some of
our terms. "Inflation," as we shall use the term, is any
increase in the quantity of money other than an increase
resulting from a switch of the money commodity, *gold*, from
non-monetary uses to monetary uses. For example, the
melting down of gold ornaments to increase the quantity of
gold coins is not inflation. This is merely a market transaction. Inflation results from (1) new discoveries or mining of
gold, and (2) the artificial creation of additional quantities
of legal media of exchange.

This is the old and, to a large extent, traditional definition
of inflation. However, in our day this definition has been
changed. The popular definition is no longer an increase in
the quantity of money. Today inflation is defined as one of
the results of such an increase – higher prices. Today almost
all radio and TV commentators, as well as newspaper writers,
use "inflation" as meaning higher prices. Higher prices, of
course, are one, but only one, of the important *consequences*
of an increase in the quantity of money.

The Significance of the Altered Definition

In all older books, those written fifty or more years ago,
inflation was always treated as an increase in the quantity of
money. Almost everyone knows who increases the quantity
of money. However, those who increase the quantity of

---

5. J.M. Keynes, *The Economic Consequences of the Peace* (Harcourt, Brace and
Howe, 1920), pp. 235-237.

money do not want the public to know who is responsible for inflation, which everyone admits is bad. So those in high places, and their sycophants, have twisted the definition of inflation around to one of its consequences – higher prices.

Who raises prices? Why, the businessmen, of course. So, if inflation is defined as higher prices, it becomes easy to say that businessmen are responsible for inflation. Today, they are usually blamed for it. In recent years, more and more people have been taught that businessmen are responsible for all the evils and suffering resulting from inflation.

Of course, businessmen raise prices. Every businessman would like to raise his prices every day. Employees would also like to raise their wages and salaries every day. Why don't they do it? Why don't businessmen raise their prices every day? You and I know why. They cannot get the higher prices. However, in times of inflation, when there is more money, when the government has created more money, there is more money in the market place bidding for their goods. Then they can ask for, and get, higher prices. The party responsible for inflation is the party that increases the quantity of money. This party is not the businessmen who ask higher prices, nor even the labor unions who ask for higher wages, and get them when there is more money or when laws no longer protect free competition for jobs.

Defining "Credit Expansion"

There is another subpart of inflation that is called "credit expansion." We shall be dealing with this also. Some economists say inflation is just an increase in the quantity of money. They differentiate inflation from credit expansion. However, they are both a part of the general overall increase in the quantity of legal money available to market participants.

There is a helpful comic strip that appeared in the *Washington Star* some years ago. In the first cartoon, the banker, sitting behind his desk, says: "Jeff, you have overdrawn your checking account three dollars." Little Jeff replies: "Oh – I'll just write you a check." In the second cartoon, the banker, rather alarmed, says: "Just a minute!

You haven't any money in the bank! You overdrew what you had! Now you are using the bank's money!" Little Jeff, not to be taken aback, asks in the third cartoon: "Oh – do you use my money when I have it in the bank?" The banker, astonished, replies: "Er – why, yes, of course!" Jeff then demands: *"Well, why can't I use yours?"*

MUTT AND JEFF

Released by McNaught Syndicate

This is what has been happening for a good many years. You put your money in the bank. You think it is there. Yet the bank has been using it. It has been lending your money to others. This double use of the same money is called "credit expansion."

"Credit expansion" is any increase in the number of monetary units loaned that do not represent an equal number of saved monetary units voluntarily made available for lending. Any increase in the purchasing power units of a borrower not offset by an equal decrease in the purchasing power units of a saver is credit expansion, while an increase in borrowing and lending, which is merely an equal transfer of purchasing power units from a lender to a borrower, is not credit expansion.

If you save some money and lend it to somebody else, this is not credit expansion. But if a bank lends money to someone that no one has saved and deposited for lending, if the bank merely creates money by opening or adding to a depositor's account, no matter what the laws or rules are, it is, of course, expanding credit. The bank has increased the quantity of money, but there has been no increase in vendible goods. This means there is more money bidding for the same previously existing quantity of goods. This leads to the great disarray in the market place that we shall be discussing as we proceed.

Governmental Honesty Important

The first aim of a sound monetary policy must be to prevent governments from embarking on inflation and from creating conditions that encourage banks to expand credit. This is very different from a political program that attempts to stabilize purchasing power. There are in the sphere of human actions no such things as stability or security, and no political endeavors are powerful enough to bring them about. Unfortunately, many people and many governments have tried and failed. They may manipulate the money system to increase the security of some people, but in so doing they not only decrease the security of others, they also undermine the very foundations of society.

One of the better economists of forty years ago was Benjamin M. Anderson, for many years the economist for the Chase National Bank. In his great book, *Economics and the Public Welfare*, he wrote:

> There is no need in human life so great as that men should trust one another and should trust their government, should believe in promises, and should keep promises in order that future promises may be believed in and in order that confident

cooperation may be possible. Good faith — personal, national, and international — is the first prerequisite of decent living, of the steady going on of industry, of governmental financial strength, and of international peace.[6]

As mentioned last night, an increase in the quantity of money does not benefit society, merely those who spend it first at the expense of those who do not. An increase in the quantity of money adds no new wealth. It merely redistributes existing wealth and misdirects production in a manner which cannot be maintained. So when governments increase the quantity of money, they are not helping society; they are just helping those who get the new money first.

The Effects of Inflation and Credit Expansion

Inflation and credit expansion are also the hidden causes of corruption and chicanery. They breed uneconomic spending merely for the sake of spending, and the immoral desire to get something that is not yours by the political process of majority votes and government-granted privileges or subsidies. Inflation and credit expansion, like other forms of political favoritism, foster group hatreds that finally result in civil disorders and even wars. In the end, the mirage of politically created prosperity disintegrates, revealing reality. Production is then found to be out of line with human wants.

When an inflation or credit expansion starts, it is not noticed by many people. As a result, the quantity of money is increased without having its full effect immediately. Many housewives, noting higher prices, tend to hold back their money, waiting for prices to fall. Consequently, prices do not go up as fast as the quantity of money is increased. Then, later as the inflation proceeds, a second stage is reached. Then the housewives begin to think that prices are going to keep on rising. They face a very serious problem. Some then decide to buy things before they really need them, and prices rise faster than the quantity of money is currently increasing.

---

6. B. M. Anderson, *Economics and the Public Welfare* (New York: D. Van Nostrand Co., Inc., 1949), pp. 317-318.

On Borrowing and Lending

As mentioned in the last lecture, money is the most important commodity in the market society. It is at least one side of every market transaction, and sometimes both sides. Lending money is a very helpful and profitable transaction in a free market society. It often happens that savers, saving up to send children to college, for later vacations, or for their old age, want to put their savings to work earning interest until they are needed. There are other people who have an urgent need for money that they have not yet earned or saved. They are willing to pay interest to have it now. They may be people who have just gotten out of school and need a car to take a job, or people who have many different immediate needs for borrowing money. They are happy to pay the market interest rate to have things money can buy when they are most needed. This is just a matter of time preference. They prefer to have these things now, instead of later, and they are willing to pay the price – interest.

Banks perform a very useful service when they act as middlemen between borrowers and savers. The borrowers and savers are both willing to pay a small fee for this service. This is a great service to society, like all transactions by middlemen in a free market society. They help move the savings to where their value is higher. The transaction not only helps borrowers, but it also provides savers with an interest income, which they prefer over letting their savings remain idle, earning nothing. This is a valuable social function of banks – one of two major ones.

On the Safekeeping of Money

The other major function of banks in a free society is to act as warehouses, keeping their customers' cash and making it available to them when they want it. This warehouse function was performed in the early days in Great Britain by goldsmiths and silversmiths. They had two functions. They would lend out their own money, plus any money left with them for lending. They would also receive and keep, as a warehouse, the money that depositors might want at any time, yet did not want to carry on their persons or keep on their premises, because of a fear that it might be stolen. The "smiths" performed a very valuable service for their clients, both those who wanted to borrow or lend money and those for whose money they provided safe storage.

Under this system, when the depositors wanted their money, they presented their receipts and got their money immediately. They would then take the money and transfer it to persons to whom they owed, or wanted to pay, money. But as time went on, depositors found that all this was not necessary. Instead of going to the goldsmith or silversmith and withdrawing their cash in gold or silver coins, they would just endorse the receipt over to the person to whom they wanted to pay the money. So these receipts for specific amounts of money, representing actual gold or silver left on deposit with goldsmiths or silversmiths, became negotiable paper. They would pass from one person to another without being presented for redemption in gold or silver. This was much easier when the amounts were in round numbers.

As this custom grew, the goldsmiths and silversmiths became aware of what was happening. Some of them decided that perhaps they could lend out "receipts" for which they had no gold and silver on hand. Some did just this. At first, they issued just a few extra "receipts" for not more than five or ten percent above the quantity of gold and silver they had on hand. This increased the number of purchasing power units on the market, but not the available quantity of goods. The result was a tendency for prices to rise. The people who borrowed this newly created "money" got the advantage of it. They could buy more things than they could have without the newly created "money." The people who did not get any of these newly created receipts then found fewer goods and services in the market place. Consequently, they had to pay higher prices for the fewer goods that were left.

This also changed the direction of production. Goods and services were produced for those who were spending the new "money" as well as for those who were spending the gold and silver they had earned or saved.

How "Runs" Got Started

As time passed, some depositors got suspicious of what was happening. They presented their receipts for redemption in gold and silver. They started a "run." Some goldsmiths and silversmiths were then in trouble. Those who had overissued their receipts could not meet the demand. They had to close their doors. They had certified to receipt holders that they could deliver on demand more gold or silver than they actually could. They had misrepresented themselves as warehouses whose receipts represented items actually on hand, just as warehouses now give receipts for pieces of furniture stored with them for safekeeping. But they did not have on hand the goods for which they had issued receipts.

As this process progressed, the goldsmiths and silversmiths got together in a sort of trade association. Then when there was a run on one, the others would try to help out their unfortunate colleague. This, of course, raised great difficulties. Instead of just one or two dishonest goldsmiths or silversmiths closing their doors when depositors panicked, none closed their doors until they all did.

Later, the goldsmiths and silversmiths became known as bankers. As bankers, they followed the same procedure. Every once in a while, they would overissue receipts, or open accounts on their books for more gold or silver than they had on hand. This was the start of what is now called "the fractional reserve system." It is a system of telling people that paper receipts or bank accounts are the equivalent of a precious metal, even when the precious metal is not 100 percent readily available. As time passed, the fraction, or reserve, that banks kept on hand kept decreasing, and the overissue, or credit expansion, became a larger and larger percentage of the "money supply."

These policies led to the periodic panics, recessions, and depressions of the nineteenth century. We had them in my country and in every other country where the banks adopted the fractional reserve system. Every once in a while bank depositors would get nervous. They would ask for "their" money and the banks would not have it on hand. The banks would then have to close their doors. We had such panics or recessions in my country in 1873, in 1884, in 1893, and in 1907.

Development of Banknotes

In the early days, most people had little use for banks or paper money, which was only issued in large denominations. Many workers were servants or farm hands, most of whose needs were supplied by their employers. Others were largely self-sufficient, producing most of their necessities on the farm and swapping some of their surplus crops for the goods and services they got from others. For their few market transactions, they used coins — "hard money." Only a few rich and supposedly well-informed persons used banks and carried on their affairs with bank accounts, bank checks, and large-denomination bank-issued paper receipts. They were chiefly the large traders in securities, foreign exchange, and internationally traded commodities. This wealthy minority became known as the "financial community."

At first, it was only these members of the financial community who were seriously affected by the bank closings, first known as money panics and later as financial panics. However, as the division of labor progressed, fewer and fewer families and local communities were self-sufficient. With the growth of trade, there was a greater and greater demand for money and bank services. More and more people bought a larger and larger part of their needs in the market place. Consequently, their need for, and use of, money increased. The money receipts, or "banknotes" as they became known, were issued in smaller denominations, and their use, along with bank accounts and checks, became more popular. So, with each succeeding series of bank closings, a larger and larger percentage of the population was affected by the ensuing hardships that resulted when depositors were not able to withdraw "their" money when they needed it.

When a bank overissues its bank notes, it has to be very careful. The issuing bank must avoid any action that will cause users to lose confidence in the issuer's ability to redeem his banknotes. How far a bank or banking system can go in overissuing banknotes depends on psychological conditions. How long will the people trust them? The increase must not be so fast that the users believe that the resulting rise in prices will continue endlessly at an ever faster pace. Once the people believe this, there will be a flight into "real values" and a crack-up boom. The first manifestation of such a disaster is a loss of confidence in the banks or the paper money.

If the government frees the banks from the necessity of redemption, the banknotes become either credit or fiat money. If there is such a suspension of specie payments, the banks become bureaus of the treasury. All their operations are then subject to special regulations. In effect, the banks have been nationalized.

Inevitable Results of Monetary Expansion

Politically sponsored inflation or credit expansion produces three results, in addition to higher prices:

(1) It must lead to overconsumption and malinvestment. When people get more money, they tend to spend more than they would have if the money had not been created artificially. They thus tend to consume more than they otherwise would, and as they spend the newly created money, they are redirecting business, and this brings about a malinvestment of available savings.

(2) It does not remove the necessity of adjusting production and reallocating resources, that is, the factors of production, to the changing wishes of consumers. It only postpones the date.

(3) It cannot be a permanent policy. If it is not stopped soon enough, it must eventually break down the monetary system. As prices rise, larger and larger increases in the quantity of money are needed to maintain the same kind and amount of activity. Sooner or later, the psychological point is reached where people lose confidence in the future value of the monetary unit. The inflation or credit expansion is then at an end.

What we need, in reality, is an increase in the production of wealth, that is, of goods and services, not an increase in consumption or an increase in spending. It is the production of wealth that helps all people, and not the production of money.

Development of Federal Reserve System

As previously mentioned, we had a great panic in my

country in 1907. It caused many people to stop and reflect about this whole business. Many groups were appointed to study the issues. They studied them at home and they studied them abroad. They went all over the world studying foreign banking systems. Bankers studied them. Politicians studied them. Economists studied them. In the end, most of them came up with pretty much the same answers, with only small differences in details. The result was the formation of the Federal Reserve System of the United States of North America.

Our Federal Reserve System was originally based, to a large extent, on the principles and policies of the German Reichsbank. The German Reichsbank was formed to function only in emergencies, somewhat like a fire department. Whenever there was a panic or a run on the banks, the Reichsbank was to supply the banks that had sound loans outstanding with any money they needed to satisfy their depositors. However, the Reichsbank would do this at a penalty rate; that is, for bailing the banks out of their difficulties, the Reichsbank would charge a higher discount or interest rate than the banks were paid on the loans they cashed or redeemed at the Reichsbank. The extra cost of this higher penalty rate was expected to keep bank credit expansions within reasonable limits. Such provisions for emergencies and the financing of governments were the original purposes of starting a central bank.

My country had an antipathy toward central banks. We had had two of them early in our history. We had learned the hard way that they were detrimental to the welfare of the nation. So, instead of calling the Federal Reserve System a central bank, which it really was, we set up twelve different Federal Reserve Banks in twelve different parts of the country. In the beginning, each was supposed to operate separately.

More Money for More Business

Each of the banks was to provide an "elastic money supply" for its own "District." The "money supply" would expand to meet what was called "the needs of business." It would contract whenever the "needs of business" no longer required such a large quantity of money. The Federal Reserve Banks would be free to create all the money required for the "needs of business," but no more than that amount.

It was felt that, before the creation of the Federal Reserve System, difficulties arose from the ability of the banks to inflate the quantity of money without limit. It was thought they overexpanded beyond the real "needs of business." The new system was going to cure this situation. The banks would no longer be able to lend as much as they might like to lend. They were to be restricted to the "needs of business" by a system of what was called "three-name short-term paper."

The origin of this idea can be traced back to the famous *"note du Havre."* A finance minister of France advised Napoleon I, who sent this note from Le Havre to the Bank of France on May 29, 1810. This idea holds that credit expansion is safe if it is limited to short-term loans, loans for no longer than ninety days, backed by regular business transactions, represented by written promises to pay that have been endorsed by both the buyers and sellers. In the case of the Federal Reserve, the endorsement of a bank was also required. It was felt that these requirements would limit the banks in their expansion of credit to actual business transactions, that is, to the actual "needs of business."

Elastic Money Operations

This is how it was supposed to work: There was to be a flexible or "elastic money supply" that expanded and contracted to meet the "needs of business." These flexible banknotes were to be called Federal Reserve Notes. They were to be backed by short-term business paper, and partly by a reserve of gold. Originally, the gold reserve requirement was 40 percent. During World War II, the gold reserve was reduced to 25 percent. On March 18, 1968, this gold reserve was entirely eliminated. There is no longer any gold reserve requirement for the issuance of Federal Reserve Notes. But originally, the Federal Reserve Notes were backed by 40 percent gold, plus 100 percent in amounts of business transactions represented by three-name short-term paper.

This paper was to be a note signed by (1) a buyer, (2) a seller who discounted the note with a member bank, and (3) the bank, which, when in need of cash, rediscounted it with the Federal Reserve Bank for Federal Reserve Notes. When the note was paid by the buyer, the Federal Reserve Notes originally issued in the amount of the loan were withdrawn from circulation.

It was thought that these requirements would stop any overexpansion because the quantity of Federal Reserve Notes outstanding would always be strictly limited to the "needs of business." At the same time, the banks, by discounting their short-term notes, would always be able to get enough Federal Reserve Notes to meet the demands of their depositors. This, it was thought, would eliminate all "runs" on banks and thus prevent the panics and recessions that followed when large numbers of banks, unable to meet depositors' demands, were forced to close their doors.

A typical transaction might be the Ford Motor Company selling Fords to a dealer in San Francisco. The dealer would sign a note in which he agreed to pay for these cars at the end of ninety days. Then, if the Ford Motor Company did not want to wait ninety days for its money, it would take this note to its bank. It would endorse the note and discount it at the current rate of interest. It would then get the money, less the interest charged. Then, if the bank should need more cash, the bank could take this note to its Federal Reserve Bank and rediscount it, at the Federal Reserve discount rate, for Federal Reserve Notes. Everybody would then be happy, and when the Ford dealer paid off the note, Federal Reserve Notes equal to the amount of the loan would be withdrawn from circulation.

This is how the Federal Reserve System was supposed to provide an elastic currency to meet the "needs of business" and at the same time prevent runs on banks. There were people who saw some dangers in it. Some Senators objected to the proposal on the Senate floor. One, Elihu Root, a prominent American statesman, opposed the Act. He is reported as telling the Senate:

We are all optimists in this country. That means we are all

inflationists. The direction of the Reserve Banks will all be optimists. They will be inflationists.[7]

But the opposition was not heeded, and the Act became law on December 23, 1913.

Changing the "Needs of Business"

In 1922, I was taught in a high school economics course that this was a very good thing. It not only limited the expansion of the quantity of money to the "needs of business," but it would also provide banks with a ready means for getting cash to meet any withdrawal demands of their depositors. This, in return, was expected to prevent the recurrence of depressions. Later, as a college undergraduate, and still later, as a graduate student, I was taught the same reasoning. It was not until about fifteen years ago that my great teacher, Ludwig von Mises, revealed to me the error inherent in the "needs of business" fallacy.

An understanding of this error is fundamental for an intelligent comprehension of modern inflation and depression problems. The fallacy involved is simply this: by lowering the interest rate artificially, the banking systems can increase the so-called "needs of business" at will.

For example, if you are considering a project that requires borrowing money, you call up the bank and ask the terms of a loan. The bank says: "We can let you have the needed amount with interest at 6 percent." So you calculate all your costs, and conclude that with interest at 6 percent there is no chance to make a profit. Accordingly, you decide not to go ahead with the project. Then, the next day the bank calls back and says: "We can now let you have this money for 5 percent." You quickly recalculate your lower costs. You decide a profit is now possible. So you borrow the money and proceed with the project.

There will always be some business transactions that will

---

7. Quoted by Adolph C. Miller, Federal Reserve Board member 1914-1936, in testimony before the Senate Committee on Banking and Currency, May 22, 1935, p. 721. This statement was preceded by: "Senator Root of New York came pretty near the truth when he opposed the Act on the ground that . . . "

seem to be profitable with funds available at 5 percent that will not seem to be profitable with interest at 6 percent. So, by reducing the interest rate, banks can increase the "needs of business." In doing this, banks may spur business activities that misdirect the use of available labor and other resources.

Lower Interest Rates

What caused the bank to call back and offer the loan at 5 percent, one percent lower than the day before? Let us look at two possibilities: (1) a free market drop in interest rates, and (2) a bank-decreed drop in interest rates. If someone had saved that money and could not lend it at a higher rate, and was now willing to take one percent less, the bank would merely be offering a normal middleman free market service. It would merely be an offer to transfer the purchasing power of the saver to the borrower. It would not change the total monetary units available on the market. It would merely transfer them for the period of the loan from one person to another.

But this is not always the way the banks do it. Under the fractional reserve system, they can and do reduce the interest rate even when there has been no increase in savings available for lending. They merely open, or increase the amount of, an account on their books, and allow the borrower to draw checks against this account. Of course, as long as the borrower uses the loan by writing checks; and the checks remain in the banking system, there is no need for more cash. The effect is similar to that of the overissue of money receipts, or banknotes. However, if there is a need for cash, the bank can go through the channels provided by law, and discount some loans at its Federal Reserve Bank in exchange for the "needed" money in the form of newly created Federal Reserve Notes.

This was the system that was supposed to put an end to depressions forever. The proponents of the law thought they had found the solution. Amen! This law was passed in December 1913. War broke out in Europe during the summer of 1914. As a result, the Federal Reserve System was quickly organized and got under way in the fall of 1914, a little earlier than originally planned.

Early Federal Reserve Operations

Before the law went into effect, large New York banks were operating on the basis of a 25 percent reserve for checking accounts. That meant that they could make loans until their deposits, including those created by their loans, rose to four times their cash on hand. The original Federal Reserve Act set the legal reserve for major city banks at 18 percent, thus permitting a credit expansion to more than six times their cash reserves. After we entered World War I, the Federal Reserve Board recommended reduction of this legal reserve to 13 percent, and Congress amended the Act on June 21, 1917, to provide for this reduction, thus permitting a still greater expansion of bank credit.

Here is a quotation from a Princeton University professor, Lester Chandler, the official biographer of Benjamin Strong, the first head of the Federal Reserve Bank of New York. Professor Chandler writes:

> With the entrance of the United States into the war in April 1917, the Federal Reserve entered a new phase. A system originally established to "accommodate commerce and industry" became one to "accommodate the Treasury." Its overriding objective became that of assuring the success of war borrowing. The first important monetary action of the Federal Reserve was to serve as a handmaiden of inflation.[8]

Professor Chandler considers *laissez-faire* economics and the gold standard obsolete. He is the author of a popular textbook on money and banking, widely used for some time in American colleges and universities. He is among those who accept political monetary management as a proper means for promoting the stability of business activity and of "price levels." So he is not trying to testify in favor of a *laissez-faire* free market economy.[9]

---

8. Lester V. Chandler, *Benjamin Strong: Central Banker* (Brookings, 1958), p. 16.
9. *Ibid.* See especially pp. 14 and 477.

World War I Financing

How was the Federal Reserve used during the war? As mentioned, it was originally thought that the Federal Reserve System would charge a penalty rate when discounting "commercial paper" for Federal Reserve Notes. The idea of setting the discount rate below market interest rates came up first, not in connection with business loans, but in connection with financing the war. This is how it was done: High-pressure campaigns were launched to sell war bonds to the public. Bright young fellows in Boy Scout uniforms – I was one of them – went around and rang doorbells. In every movie house they had three-minute speakers. Posters were everywhere, and everyone was urged, as a patriotic duty, to buy Liberty Bonds.

Of course, most people did not have a lot of spare cash in their pockets or bank accounts. How could they buy these Liberty Bonds? They paid 5 to 10 percent down and borrowed the rest from the banks. The interest the bond buyers paid the banks was equal to what the government paid on the amount borrowed, so the loans cost the bond buyers nothing. They kept the interest on that part of the bonds for which they had paid, and reduced the bank loans as fast as they could. In any case, the government got the full 100 percent right away.

How was this possible? This is what happened: There were four Liberty Loan drives during the War, and a fifth drive after the Armistice, called the Victory Loan. The sales totaled about $21 billion. Each bond issue paid interest rates a little higher than the Federal Reserve discount rates. So the government would pay the higher interest rates, and the banks, if they needed cash, could discount the bond buyers' notes at the lower discount rates and make money. The banks made the money immediately available to the Treasury. The "money supply" was thus pumped up as fast as the government wanted more money. The banks made money by making money. On the First Liberty Loan they got 3½ percent for their loan, which, if they needed cash, they could discount at 3 percent at their Federal Reserve Bank, and thus make ½ percent. They did this whenever they did not have enough depositors' money to use as a reserve for their credit expansion.

During this period the bond interest rates and discount rates varied. (See Table XV.) However, the banks were always able to make money on the spread, and the government was

LIBERTY LOANS, 1917-1919			
Bond Drives	**Sales**	**Interest Rates**	**Federal Res. Disc't. Rate**
	Millions	———*Percentages*———	
1st: 5/15 — 6/14/17	$ 1,989	3½	3
2nd: 10/1 10/27/17	3,808	4	3
3rd: 4/6 — 5/4/18	4,177	4¼	4
4th: 9/28 — 10/19/18	6,993	4¼	4
V (Victory): 4/19 — 5/10/19	4,498	4¾ *	4
	$21,465		

Reserve requirements reduced 6/12/17:
   From 18% to 13% for central reserve cities; 15% to 10% for reserve cities; 12% to 7% for country banks; and 5% to 3% for time deposits.

*Tax-exempts, 3¾%.

Table XV

able to draw checks for all the money that it felt it needed to finance the war.

When the Federal Reserve Act was passed, the sponsors had not given any thought to the possibility of credit expansion for the "needs of government." The debt of the Federal government at the time the law was passed was only $1.3 billion. Today, with a debt in excess of $350 billion, we would call that "peanuts." [10]

Effect on "Money Supply"

Now just take a look at Table XVI, which shows what happened during this period. The gold stock went up, of

---

10. The U.S. government's public debt, December 31, 1972 — $449.3 billion.

Table XVI

WORLD WAR I MONETARY TABLEAU, 1914-1920

Date	Gold Stock	Quantity of Money	U.S. Debt Holdings		Interest Rates		
			Fed. Res. Banks	Comm'l. Banks	Fed. Res. Discount	Call Rate*	N.Y.C. Prime Comm'l.
End of	*Billions*	*Billions*	*Millions*			*Percentages*	
6/14	$1.6	$16.1		$818	(11/14) 6	1.8	4.5
12/16	2.6		$55		3	4.4	4.2
12/18	2.9		239		4	5.3	6.0
6/19	2.8	29.7	292	5,147	4	6.6	5.4
6/20	2.6	34.2	341	3,748	(6/1) 7	7.3	7.9

Gold stock as a % of quantity of money: 6/14 – 9.9%; 6/20 – 7.6%
U.S. debt as a % of quantity of money: 6/14 – 5.1%; 6/19 – 18.3%; 6/20 – 12.0%

*1920 call – High, 9.9% in February; Low, 6.96% in December.

course, as the Europeans shipped gold to this country. The "money supply,"[11] which had been $16.1 billion on June 30, 1914, before the Federal Reserve was formed, went up to $29.7 billion by June 30, 1919. By that date the banks were also holding more government bonds. The Federal Reserve Banks owned almost $300 million, while the commercial banks held $5,147 million. These government bonds were all bought with bank depositors' funds, or by means of credit expansion using such deposits as the fractional reserve.

This great expansion of the "money supply" was brought about by the fractional reserve system and holding the Federal Reserve discount rates below the call rates and the prime commercial rates in New York City. The banks lent money out at the higher interest rates and, when they needed cash, discounted their loans with their Federal Reserve Banks at the lower discount rates. This perfectly legal process pyramided the "money supply." The "money supply" went up all through the war and kept booming after the Armistice. This credit expansion was not based on commercial paper. It was based primarily on notes secured by government loans. By 1919, about 95 percent of all Federal Reserve advances were based on government securities.[12]

At that time, there were some people in office who had some idea of the problem. One of these was a member of the Federal Reserve Board to whom I shall be referring frequently, Adolph C. Miller, a former economics professor at

---

11. As used in these lectures and tables, the "money supply" or "quantity of money" includes (1) currency outside of commercial banks, (2) demand deposits or checking accounts of banks, and (3) time deposits of commercial banks. The Federal Reserve System does not include time deposits of commercial banks in its "money supply" figures. It treats such deposits as a "Related Item." However, they have been included in this study, because time deposits of commercial banks are in practice generally withdrawable on demand and, as the Federal Reserve System operates, are subject to an even greater "credit expansion" than demand deposits. Their required reserves are much lower. This is not true in the case of mutual savings banks. They cannot expand credit by lending out more than the funds available from their capital account and cash deposits. Accordingly, their deposits are not included in the "money supply," except for the cash they have on hand, which is included in "currency outside of commercial banks."

All financial figures and statistics for the United States appearing in the text and Tables of this lecture are taken from *Banking and Monetary Statistics* (Board of Governors of the Federal Reserve System, 1943), which includes data through 1941.

12. Chandler, *op. cit.*, p. 118.

the University of California. On February 26, 1919, he wrote
a letter to Benjamin Strong, the Governor of the Federal
Reserve Bank of New York, saying:

> The most serious part of inflation is, after all, the aftermath.
> We sow the wind to reap the whirlwind. Somehow or other we
> have got to come down off the perch. But this is an uncomfort-
> able process for nearly everybody and, for some, a very costly
> and ruinous one. We shall be fortunate in this country if we get
> off without some serious financial troubles and some very serious
> political troubles growing out of the currency and credit
> disorders. That has always been true in the past and I am terribly
> afraid it will be true in the present instance . . . . There has got to
> be liquidation. [13]

Post-War Consequences

So the Federal Reserve System decided upon liquidation.
For millions of poor farmers with heavy mortgages and other
debts acquired in expanding for the war effort, this liquidation was rather hard to take. For many of them liquidation
meant lower prices for farm products, bankruptcy, and loss
of their farms. We do not have time to go into all the details.
There are more important things we must consider.

The "money supply" kept increasing until it reached $34.2
billion on June 30, 1920. This was more than double the
figure before the Federal Reserve System began. We had
loaned the Allies $7 billion during the war. There were more
loans to European countries after the war. Post-war loans to
foreign governments amounted to over $3.8 billion. During
the war, the British pound had been pegged at $4.76 by J.P.
Morgan and Co. In the spring of 1919, the Morgan company
stopped pegging the pound and its value on foreign exchange
markets promptly dropped, hitting a low of $3.19 in
February 1920.

What did the Federal Reserve do to liquidate? They put
the discount rate up. They raised it to 6 percent in January
1920, and then to 7 percent on June 1, 1920. The market
interest rates were just about the same. This resulted in a

13. *Ibid.*, p. 138.

decrease in bank loans that reduced the "money supply" in a period of a year from $34.2 billion to $31.7 billion. (See Table XVII.) In about eighteen months the inflationary condition was largely corrected without much other government interference in the economy. The inflation was stopped, but of course the consequences could not be avoided. The farmers were hurt. In fact, all people in debt were badly hurt.

There were many serious problems, not only at home but also abroad. Our farmers and other exporters could not sell as much abroad, because the European men were back on their farms and in their factories producing many things they had gotten from us while they were busy fighting in uniforms. The railroads, operated by the government during the war, were turned back in poor condition to their private owners. Price controls, rationing, and other war controls had gone off. Many prices were rising; others, largely farm prices, were falling. War production employment and the "money supply" were going down. Many people were hurt.

But by and large the government kept out of it. There were no price and wage controls or other major government interferences with market processes. Wages, prices, and production were permitted to adjust quickly. The economy was able to recover fairly well in from twelve to eighteen months. Of course, many people were hurt. This always happens after an inflation. But the situation settled down, with rising production and little unemployment. Then, the Federal Reserve System dropped its discount rates below market interest rates again. The situation again started to deteriorate.

Post-War Political Changes

There were also many problems developing abroad. We do not have time to go into them in any detail. In 1920, we turned out the Democratic Party, which had been in power during the war. We elected the Republican Party, which was pledged to high tariffs. The Republicans first put in high agricultural tariffs, and then later passed the Fordney-McCumber Act, placing higher tariffs on industrial imports.

**Table
XVII**

POST-WAR DEPRESSION, 1920-1923

Date	Gold Stock	Quantity of Money	U.S. Debt Holdings		Interest Rates		
			Fed. Res. Banks	Comm'l. Banks	Fed. Res. Discount	Call Rate	N.Y.C. Prime Comm'l.
End of	*Billions*	*Billions*	*Millions*		*Percentages*		
6/20	$2.6	$34.2	$ 341	$ 3,748	(6/1)* 7.0	7.3	7.9
6/21	3.0	31.7	259	3,386	(6/16)* 6.0	6.0	6.75
12/21	3.4		234		(11/3)* 4.5	5.1	5.1
6/22	3.5	33.0	555	3,981	(6/20)* 4.0	3.7	4.4
6/23	3.5	36.1	102	4,705	4.5	5.0	5.0

Gold Stock as a % of quantity of money: 6/20 — 7.6%; by 6/22 — over 10%.

*Effective starting date.

These tariffs made it extremely difficult for Europeans to pay their debts to the United States. As a result, the international situation was deteriorating.

There is one other factor that should be mentioned. There had been growing differences between the President of the United States and the Federal Reserve Board. When the Federal Reserve Board Chairman's term expired on August 9, 1922, the President refused to reappoint him. It was nine months before a new man was appointed. This gentleman's name was Daniel R. Crissinger. Nobody had ever heard of him. Prior to the Republican Administration, he had had no experience worth mentioning in banking or economics. Nonetheless, he was appointed to the top position of this important agency.

Who was he? He had been the prosecuting attorney and city solicitor for Marion, Ohio, President Harding's home county and city.

The banking community and many economists were alarmed. Many appealed to the Secretary of the Treasury, Andrew Mellon, who also opposed the appointment. The Secretary went to the White House for a session with the President. The President is reported as having told his Secretary of the Treasury, "This appointment is very dear to my heart."[14] So the man at the head of the Federal Reserve System was a personal political friend of the President with no understanding of financial problems.

A Look at Europe

In the meantime, there were other important developments. On June 19, 1923, the Anglo-American debt settlement was signed, providing for the repayment of the British war loans with reduced interest rates on the amounts outstanding. The German inflation reached its climax later that year when the mark, worth 23.82 cents before the war, went to 16 trillion to the dollar. It was later stabilized at only 4 trillion to the dollar.

By December 1923, Germany was in a state of economic

---

14. Anderson, *op. cit.*, p. 117.

Table
XVIII

MONETARY EXPANSION, 1922-1924

Date	Gold Stock	Quantity of Money	U.S. Debt Fed. Res. Bks.		Fed. Res. Discount	Interest Rates Call Rate	N.Y.C. Prime Comm'l.
End of	*Billions*	*Billions*	*Millions*			*Percentages*	
6/22	$3.5	$ 33.0	$555		4.0	3.7	4.4
6/23	3.8	36.1	102		4.5	5.0	5.0
12/23	4.0	36.7	134		4.5	4.5	5.0
				(5/1)*	4.0		
6/24	4.2	37.6	431	(6/12)*	3.5	2.3	4.1
12/24	4.2	39.9	540	(8/8)*	3.0	3.5	3.6

*Date effective.

collapse, both internally and externally. Her former European enemies wanted reparations, but they did not want German goods or worthless paper marks. In 1924, the Dawes Plan attempted to put Germany back on her feet financially. It granted Germany a foreign loan with which to stabilize the mark and re-establish the gold standard. In return, Germany had to accept foreign supervision of an internal taxation system intended to raise funds for repayment of the loan and reparations payments according to a prescribed "index of prosperity."[15]

Inflation in the United States

Meanwhile, in the United States the "money supply" was again increasing. By holding the discount rate below the call and prime interest rates, the "money supply" had been expanded between June 1922 and the end of 1923 by roughly 10 percent. (See Table XVIII.) As a result of this misdirection of the economy, the free market processes were unable to correct the increasing imbalances, and there was a slowdown in business that worried a number of people.

Moving into 1924, a Presidential election year, those in political office had to have prosperity at any price. So the Federal Reserve System, with its new Chairman taking a leading part, lowered the discount rates three times in 1924 before Election Day: first on May 1, to 4 percent; then on June 12, to 3½ percent; and lastly, on August 8, to 3 percent. This was a deliberate attempt to create enough money and spending to make it look as though the country was very prosperous. It was expected that the voters would then keep the party responsible in power.

The Federal Reserve Banks were also using "their" reserves to buy government securities. Their holdings of government securities, as you can see in Table XVIII, went up $406 million in 1924. Actually, in the twelve months before the election, they increased by $472 million. These funds found their way into the market place, driving up prices and reducing the purchasing power of every dollar.

---

15. B. M. Anderson, "The Report of the Dawes Committee," *Chase Economic Bulletin,* Vol. IV, #1, April 24, 1924, p. 27.

Just before the election President Coolidge, in a campaign speech, said, "It has been the policy of this Administration to reduce discount rates."[16] The party in power was doing everything it could to create "easy money" conditions before the election.

These policies *did* increase the "money supply," which in turn stimulated business activity and security speculations. Prices also started to rise. So right after the election, the Federal Reserve attempted to slow down the economy. In five months, the Reserve Banks sold off $226 million of government securities, and in February 1925 the discount rate was raised to 3½ percent.

Prosperity by Political Promotion

Benjamin Strong, Governor of the Federal Reserve Bank of New York, was really a strong man. He dominated many of the policies of the Federal Reserve System from its early years until his death in 1928. He felt these 1924 policies were necessary to head off "some recession in business." In December 1924, he wrote that they had helped develop "a greater feeling of tranquility and contentment throughout the country."[17] There were some who believed that if Mr. Strong had lived longer, his skill and ability in manipulating monetary policies might have averted the 1929 depression. His official biographer, Professor Chandler, has this to say:

> The easy-money policy of 1924 was of historical importance. It was the first large and aggressive easing action deliberately taken by the Federal Reserve for the purpose of combatting a decline of price levels and business activity and of encouraging international capital loans.[18]

---

16. Cited in B. M. Anderson, *Economics and the Public Welfare*, p. 182. In testimony before the Senate Banking and Currency Committee, May 1935, Professor H. Parker Willis stated: "Coolidge in his radio address on the night before he was re-elected as President said ' . . . that his Administration had always favored low discount rates and it always would do so.' "
17. Memorandum of December 26, 1924, as cited by Chandler, *op. cit.*, pp. 242-246.

So the party in power was returned to office with the help of an inflation deliberately sponsored by the Federal Reserve System, which was supposed to be an independent Supreme Court of monetary policy and economics that was above party politics. Permit me to remind you, as I shall from time to time, that this was not free enterprise operating. It was political intervention manipulating the quantity of money, the most important commodity in a market economy. Every such change in the quantity of money not only affected the value of every dollar, but it also upset the free market price relationship of every transaction. It thereby misdirected business production away from the first choices of consumers.

A Look at England

Meanwhile, there was another important overlapping development. In the spring of 1924, Mr. Strong, the head of the Federal Reserve Bank of New York, wrote to the Secretary of the Treasury, Andrew Mellon:

> At the present time it is probably true that British prices for goods internationally dealt in are as a whole, roughly, in the neighborhood of 10 percent above our prices and one of the preliminaries of the reestablishment of the gold payment by Great Britain will be to facilitate a gradual adjustment of these price levels *before* monetary reform is undertaken .... This ... can be facilitated by cooperation between the Bank of England and the Federal Reserve System in the maintaining of lower interest rates in this country and higher interest rates in England .... It will be difficult politically and socially for the British Government and the Bank of England to force a price liquidation in England .... Their trade is poor and they have over a million unemployed people receiving government aid. [19]

In Sir Henry Clay's official biography of the late Lord Norman (Montagu Norman), head of the Bank of England from 1920 to 1944, we read:

> It did not, however, turn out to be easy to regulate credit in America in such a way as to meet both London's requirements

---

19. Letter of May 27, 1924, to Mellon, cited by Chandler, *op. cit.*, pp. 283-284.

and domestic needs . . . . In January 1924 Strong was again writing that Coolidge's . . . election and European recovery might start a speculative outbreak difficult to control; rates could not be put up . . . . He leaned rather to open market operations. In June New York had put its rate below London with the deliberate intention of helping London back to the Gold Standard, but he still thought higher rates would be needed to check inflation in the New Year. [20]

In the same biography of Montagu Norman, we read an October 16, 1924 letter of Mr. Norman to Mr. Strong. This was a letter from the head of the Bank of England to the head of the New York Federal Reserve Bank, just before our 1924 election. Mr. Norman wrote:

> I agree entirely that we shall need some sort of understanding between us as to the future gold policy. I think you are helping to this end if you keep your rates as low as possible and lend freely to the rest of the world as your Market is now doing. [21]

There were many more letters. I have not time to read them all. But let me remind you, these were not free market operations.

England Asks for Help

On December 28, 1924, right after Christmas, Montagu Norman arrived in New York, where he had a private luncheon with Benjamin Strong and Secretary of the Treasury Andrew Mellon. He was looking for a pledge of $500 million to help England go back on the gold standard. He got a pledge of $200 million, at no cost, from the Federal Reserve Bank of New York, with later Federal Reserve Board approval. Mr. Strong felt "that [central bank] operations for profit of a competitive character in any market are a mistake . . . . Reserve Banks . . . have the power to issue notes and . . . in effect manufacture the credit." [22]

---

20. Sir Henry Clay, *Lord Norman* (London, Macmillan, 1957), pp. 142-143.
21. *Ibid.*, p. 151.
22. Hearing before House Banking and Currency Committee, April 1926, reprinted in *Interpretations of Federal Reserve Policy*, ed. by W. Randolph Burgess (Harper, 1930), p. 265.

This was not free enterprise. Actually this was a pledge of bank depositors' money, or a credit expansion based on their deposits.

For the other $300 million, Mr. Norman went to J.P. Morgan. Being a businessman, Mr. Morgan wanted to charge a fee for such a pledge, whether or not it was drawn upon. Discouraged, Mr. Norman contracted for a pledge of only $100 million from the Morgan company. He returned to Europe to get the rest of the backing.

Mr. Norman and certain Federal Reserve officials had agreed that it was essential to keep the Federal Reserve discount rate down below the bank rate of the Bank of England. Otherwise, gold would flow out of England. Mr. Strong recorded in January, 1925, that the only desire of Mr. Norman concerning Federal Reserve policies

> ... was to understand in a general way what we expected our policy to be, and to express the hope it would be directed toward maintaining as stable a price level as possible in the United States. [23]

Keep Congress in the Dark

Montagu Norman went home, attended to some affairs in London, and then, as all well-to-do Europeans of his time did, took a little vacation. On March 9, 1925, he wrote Benjamin Strong from the Riviera:

> All official consideration of a gold program was deliberately pushed over to this month, so that nothing about it should come out until your Congress should have adjourned.[24]

Before the days of Franklin D. Roosevelt, our Congresses expired on March 4, every second year. The new Congress did not meet until the following December. So Mr. Norman was referring to the fact that our Congress had to go home on March 4. He continued:

> If we begin consideration next week (as I expect), we cannot

23. Chandler, *op. cit.*, p. 315.
24. Montagu Norman's Personal Letters. See Andrew Boyle, *Montagu Norman: A Biography* (London: Cassell), p. 187. See also Chandler, *op. cit.*, p. 316.

**Table
XIX**

			EFFECTS OF HELPING ENGLAND, 1924-1927		Interest Rates	
Date	Gold Stock	Quantity of Money	U.S. Debt Fed. Res. Bks.	Fed. Res. Discount	Call Rate	N.Y.C. Prime Comm'l.
End of	*Billions*	*Billions*	*Millions*	——————————*Percentages*——————————		
12/24	$4.2	$39.9	$540	3.0	3.5	4.1
12/25	4.1	42.6	375	3.5	5.3	4.4
12/26	4.2	43.1	315	4.0	5.2	4.5
6/27	4.3	43.8	370	4.0	4.3	4.25
12/27	4.1	45.4	617	(8/5)* 3.5 (Chicago 9/7)*	4.4	4.0

*Date effective.

expect a final decision before early or middle April – meanwhile I shall *hope* to have it all kept secret, and of course out of Parliament till the end.[25]

Free enterprise? No. This was political manipulation of monetary systems, all with the very best intentions.

On April 2, 1925, the Federal Reserve Bank of New York officially approved the principles of the agreement with the Bank of England. On April 23, the specific details which guaranteed a pledge of $200 million to Great Britain were approved. Then on April 28, 1925, Great Britain announced she would henceforth redeem paper pounds in gold at the pre-war rate of $4.86. At about the same time, the Bank of England raised her bank, or discount, rate from 4 percent to 5 percent. The Federal Reserve discount rate remained at 3½ percent for the rest of 1925.

So England returned to the gold standard, backed by a pledge of money that Americans had put in their bank accounts, and which they thought was there for them to draw out at any time. This was also done with the understanding that our Federal Reserve System would keep our discount rate low, below that of the Bank of England, and, incidentally, below free market interest rates. This resulted, of course, in a great expansion of the "money supply" of the United States. In short, inflation or credit expansion was the avowed policy of our monetary officials.

Manipulating the Quantity of Money

The gold stock stayed about the same from the end of 1924 to the end of 1927. (See Table XIX.) The "money supply" went up from under $40 billion to over $45 billion. The Federal Reserve holdings of government securities fluctuated, but almost doubled during 1927. The discount rate remained much below the call rate. The call rate is the interest rate paid for money borrowed to buy or hold stock exchange securities. Such loans can be called on demand. Then the borrower has to pay his loan on demand, or his

---

25. *Ibid.*

securities are sold and the loan is repaid from the proceeds. In 1926, the banks could lend money on stock at 5 percent plus, and then discount eligible loans at 4 percent at their Federal Reserve Banks. This was a very profitable and an entirely legal business for commercial banks.

As a result, stock market prices started to move up. They moved up faster and faster as time passed. All through 1925, Mr. Strong opposed raising the discount rate, although domestic conditions seemed to call for it. As one Board member expressed it in his diary on October 13, 1925:

> Strong is thinking more of the effect of rate increases on Great Britain than in the United States. Platt and Miller (Board members) believe rates should be increased and I am inclined to the same view, especially in view of the stock speculation movement in New York. [26]

On December 1, 1925, Governor Strong was saying privately that an increase in discount rates might result in drawing gold from Great Britain and further unstabilize her economy, while creating deflation and uncertainty in the domestic business of the United States. The discount rate was finally raised from 3½ percent to 4 percent on January 7, 1926. At the time, one major New York bank was reported as borrowing $115 million from its Federal Reserve Bank on fifteen-day notes and lending it on stock exchange securities at from 6 percent to 7 percent. Nice business, if you can get it, and all perfectly legal.

Whenever business turned down, the Federal Reserve Banks bought government securities. They would buy these governments with a fraction of every bank depositor's money that by law had to be kept with a Federal Reserve Bank, supposedly as a safety measure. So under this system, if you were a bank depositor, a certain percentage of your money was used by the Federal Reserve System to buy government securities. When the sellers of the securities spent their proceeds, the depositors' own money was actually competing in the market against depositors, raising prices higher than

---

26. This and immediately succeeding quotations are taken from Charles S. Hamlin's Diaries in the Manuscript Room of the Library of Congress (Washington, D.C.).

they would have been in a free market. In any case, the Federal Reserve operations were not free market operations.

Mr. Hamlin's Diary

This lecture will run long, I am sorry to say, but there are some important quotations from the diary of Mr. Charles S. Hamlin that just cannot be omitted. Mr. Hamlin was appointed by President Wilson as the original head of the Federal Reserve Board from 1914 to 1916. He remained a member of the Federal Reserve Board until 1936, when the changes signed into law by Franklin Delano Roosevelt became effective. He kept a diary in which he scribbled what happened at every meeting of the Federal Reserve Board and at many of its committee meetings during the twenty-two years he was a Board member.

Herbert Hoover had been Secretary of Commerce from 1921 until 1929 and then President during the early depression years (1929-1933). In the volume of his memoirs devoted to the depression, his account differed somewhat from that in Benjamin Anderson's book, to which I have referred. Benjamin Anderson, whom I had met, had already passed on. As I had had some connections with President Hoover, I wrote him, asking for his explanation of these differences. He referred me to this personal diary of Mr. Hamlin. It was written in ink in Mr. Hamlin's own handwriting with his own abbreviations, some of which were difficult to decipher. I have spent many fascinating days in the Manuscript Room of the Library of Congress in Washington reading this diary with his accounts of what happened behind closed doors at these all important Federal Reserve meetings. The following inside information comes from this diary.

Prevent a Recession: Inflate

From his entry on March 20, 1926:

Strong says a business recession has started. We must be prepared to cope with it. If it continued to increase "we" should ease up the situation by further investments in government securities.

Four days later he noted:

> Strong says New York banks are rediscounting heavily, tending to put pressure for liquidation of customers' loans. Conditions in Europe bad, feared recessions. We should buy government securities to ease the money market; that this money would return in the shape of paid off rediscounts; thus giving greater facility for enlarging customers' loans. He also said "reducing discount rates would only make it easier for member banks to carry their rediscounts." Open Market Committee unanimous it be given permission in case of emergency to buy between now and April 15th not to exceed $90 millions of government securities in addition to replacing maturities.
>
> Miller violently objected. He said "we would be hauled before a Congressional Committee and that talk of depression was rot and that real reason was to help the stock market."

Mr. Hamlin himself "feared increase in recession and that European conditions might become worse at any moment." On March 25, we read:

> [Secretary of the Treasury] Mellon said: "undoubtedly a recession in business." He favored liberality looking towards increased credit.

The motion to buy more government securities was then passed by a vote of 4 to 3. This was under a Republican Administration, and the crucial vote was cast by Mr. Hamlin, a Democrat then seeking reappointment. He thought that if he voted with the Administration he might be reappointed. He was, later.

On April 13, we read:

> Strong told CSH [Hamlin] he was very much aroused by Miller's statements *re* his being influenced by stock market needs and intended to speak of it to [a Congressional] Banking and Currency Committee. Mellon also indignant and had told him. CSH advised against bringing in open, said "Miller, perhaps unconsciously, was a rabid deflationist." He said Miller, Willis, the *Commercial and Financial Chronicle* all heaped together in the interest of radical deflation.

He was referring to H. Parker Willis, one of the young men who helped to write the original Federal Reserve Act in 1913 and then in 1914 became the Board's first Secretary. In 1918, Dr. Willis resigned to become Professor of Banking at Columbia University, where he was later my teacher.

Land and Security Speculations

As some of you may know, we had a land boom in Florida in the mid 1920s. People from all forty-eight states were eager to buy almost any kind of real estate in that sunny state, supposedly ideal for vacations or retirement. Some were even buying lots that were under water at high tide. Banks that had lent money on the boom prices of Florida real estate were in trouble when the high land prices broke early in 1926. We learn from Mr. Hamlin's diary that a man from the Federal Reserve Bank of Atlanta appeared before the Board in Washington on April 21, 1926. He told them the "collapse of the Florida real estate boom would probably involve 50 banks in failure." He said the Governor and other directors of the Atlanta Reserve Bank wanted to assist the banks to the limit "without careful scrutiny of paper offered for rediscount. He and others opposed as banks were in insolvent condition. He urged closing the banks to prevent favoring public [government] deposits at the expense of small depositors."

He feared that Federal Reserve support of these banks might wipe out the capital and surplus of the Atlanta Reserve Bank and leave it insolvent. The Board "agreed with his views but refused to issue any instructions prior to full discussion."

That spring, 1926, there was also a corrective break in the stock market. Prices dropped about 10 percent. On April 22, the Reserve Board approved a lowering of the discount rate from 4 to 3½ percent, for the Reserve Bank of New York only. The cheaper credit helped to send stock prices soaring again. For months, Federal Reserve officials debated whether the law should be amended to permit Reserve Banks to refuse to discount eligible paper offered by member banks making security loans. On August 13, the New York discount rate was raised back to the 4 percent rate of the other eleven Reserve Banks.

This was a manipulated money market, not a free one. Mr. Hamlin, an original Democratic appointee, was nervously awaiting his reappointment by a Republican Administration. On June 13, 1926, he wrote in his diary that the Federal Reserve Board was "pretty well shot to pieces." He felt that the President did not want to reappoint him and would do so only because of "dire necessity," for implied political reasons. Then he noted: "The Federal Reserve Board has degenerated into a political appanage of this Administration."

England's Plight

This was the situation in the United States. Meanwhile, what was happening in England? When England went back on the gold standard in April 1925, with the pound valued at $4.86, she had raised the value of the pound about 10 percent above its average value of about $4.40 on the open market the previous year. This meant that England, which operated largely as a factory, importing raw materials and exporting finished goods, had raised its export prices by roughly 10 percent. For Americans, buying a British product that cost a pound sterling, the price was now $4.86 instead of the earlier $4.40.

Economics teaches that with higher prices you sell smaller quantities. Consequently, you produce less to sell. This means you employ fewer workers. So with the return to the gold convertibility of the British pound at $4.86, unemployment grew in England. This 1925 misadventure of the British was made while Winston Churchill was the Chancellor of the Exchequer. In overvaluing the pound, he was responsible for repeating the same error the British had made a century earlier, after the Napoleonic wars, which had produced great distress. The free market solution for this increased valuation of the pound would be to permit money wages to fall by about 10 percent. Such a drop in money wages would not affect real wages, because the pound was now worth approximately 10 percent more. Unfortunately, organized labor in England would not listen to this solution. Labor leaders and their followers wanted to keep this whole 10 percent gain for union members.

Lionel Robbins, the British economist, in his book, *The Great Depression*, tells us:

> The effects of the over-valued exchange made themselves felt with great severity in the coal trade. Throughout 1926 there raged labour disputes, which were the direct consequences of these troubles — first the general strike. [This lasted from May 3-14, 1926, when all of organized labor stopped work in England.] Then a strike in the coal-fields which dragged out for over six months, still further endangering the trade balance. By 1927 the position was one of great danger. [27]

In addition to the general labor problems, German coal was getting back on the world market, and ships, which had used British coal for centuries, were switching to oil. So Britain's coal exports were rapidly dwindling.

There was another important aspect of this problem. Before World War I, British labor unions had taken care of their own unemployed members by levying assessments on working members. Under this system, if wage rates and unemployment got too high, the assessments on the working union members soared to the point where they were willing to work for a lower wage rate, which, without the assessments for support of so many unemployed, provided a higher net income. But the Fabian Socialists had sold British workers and Parliament the idea of "unemployment insurance." This effectively transferred the burden of supporting the unemployed from the working union members to the taxpayers. As a result, the unions were no longer interested in how much unemployment might result from their demands for higher wages. The British politicians felt themselves unable to oppose the demands and privileges of the entrenched unions. This political fear has been due to the erroneous belief that labor unions obtain "gains" for all workers, whereas in reality such "gains" are at the expense of consumers and other workers. This helps to explain the way England has drifted since World War I.

27. Lionel Robbins, *The Great Depression* (Macmillan, 1934), p. 52

Prosperity by Political Pronouncements

Now, let us return to the United States. On New Year's Day, 1927, our President, as was the custom, issued a very glowing statement about the prospects for the coming year. It was going to "be one of continued healthy business activity and prosperity."[28] In his opinion, the booming stock market merely reflected the growing wealth and power of the United States.

There were some businessmen who did not agree. One in the construction industry, a Mr. Strauss, said that commercial building "had reached the saturation point." [29] He felt there would be a down-turn in business activity. Now politicians in office cannot readily accept such a depressing outlook. The Secretary of the Treasury, Mr. Mellon, came to the rescue. He did not agree with the businessman. He said Mr. Strauss did not know what he was talking about and that the present was a good time to build from the point of view of costs.

Meantime, the stock market dipped down. Every time the market started to correct itself, Washington issued booming statements, and the market reacted by resuming an upward movement. Then it would gradually settle down again until some new statement was issued.

For example, after the market sagged a bit, Secretary of the Treasury Mellon announced on March 7, 1927, that the Treasury was going to refinance the Second Liberty Loan 4½ percent bonds with 3½ percent notes on November 14. This meant that the Federal Reserve would be expected to keep interest rates low until this refinancing was completed some eight months later. This told businessmen and investors they could operate with assurance that low interest rates were here to stay at least that long. Two days later, the *New York Times* report on the stock market stated: "Prices rose with a vigor . . . [there was] frequent comment in Wall Street that the 'main advance' had been resumed." [30]

When the market went down again, Mr. Mellon gave the press another optimistic statement as he sailed for Europe.

---

28. Ralph Robey, "The Capeadores of Wall Street," *Atlantic Monthly*, Sept. 1928.
29. *Ibid.*
30. *Ibid.*

He saw "no evidence of overspeculation . . . an abundant supply of easy money should take care of any contingencies that may arise." The government's budget had a surplus and he saw no reason to raise the discount rate. "All signs and indications at the moment point to the country enjoying a successful business year." As the *New York Times* reported, this "created a cheerful feeling in Wall Street." [31]

French and British Financial Problems

Now, let us turn to some of the developments in Europe. The post-war French inflation had shaken public confidence in the franc. At one time in mid-1926, its value had dropped to just over two cents. For years, Frenchmen, as well as the Bank of France, had bought British pounds with their spare francs. The Bank of France also kept gold in London, where it was free from French laws limiting official transactions to the pre-war parity of 19.3 cents. However, by the end of 1926, a new French government had restored confidence in the franc. During 1927, it was trying to keep the value of the franc from rising above four cents and thus hurting French exports.

Meanwhile, the British situation was becoming increasingly critical. The French became worried about their British pounds. Some hoped the franc would go still higher. There was a flight from the pound to the franc. In May and June 1927, the Bank of France started withdrawing gold from London, sending some to New York. The Bank of France was trying to force the Bank of England to raise its discount rate.

All this worried our Federal Reserve officials. They feared that England's loss of gold might weaken the British pound and interfere with her ability to control the monetary situation.

Here are some interesting entries from Mr. Hamlin's diaries. For May 13, 1927:

> Special meeting. Mellon presided. Miller opposed buying government securities up to $250 million. He claimed this would

---

31. *Ibid.*

help the stock market and that there was no necessity of
purchases now while if [we] waited until later, we might
stimulate business in the Fall .... Platt's motion to approve of
slow buying up to $250 million ... passed 7 to 1.

The June 22, 1927 entry informs us that the Federal
Reserve Bank of New York, in order to help England, had
bought $90 million of gold that France had on hand with the
Bank of England.

$30 million shipped to New York when the Federal Reserve
Bank of New York earmarked the remaining $60 million with
[the] Bank of England .... [This was] later resold to the Bank
of France, accepting as payment a sterling credit with Bank of
England, which is to pay interest on the account or invest it in
sterling bills for the Federal Reserve Bank of New York.

These complicated Federal Reserve moves, using the reserves
of American bank depositors, were designed to permit France
to convert her pounds into gold without any further loss of
gold to England.

The June 23 entry indicated the "Bank of France wanted
$100 million gold in its account" with the Federal Reserve
Bank of New York. The discussion was on a motion to
permit the System to buy more government securities to
offset the transfer of gold to the Bank of France. The motion
carried by a vote of 4 to 2. This meant the gold withdrawal
would not be permitted to have the free market effect of
reducing the "money supply." This was a form of inflation.
The same entry included the sentence:

All agreed [it] would have been inadvisable to put up [the]
discount rate.

Governor Moreau of the Bank of France kept a diary too.
He noted in it a June 20 letter from Governor Strong of the
New York Reserve Bank in which Mr. Strong expressed a
wish for the Bank of France to reduce its rates to take the
pressure off of London. He also told M. Moreau that New
York could neither lower nor raise its discount rate. The
former, he said, would give support to stock exchange
speculations, which were already too active, while the latter

would hurt business and hinder the Treasury's financial operations.

Foreign Bankers Visit United States

For July 1, 1927, we read in the Hamlin diary that Mr. Norman, the head of the Bank of England, Mr. Schacht, the head of the Reichsbank, and Mr. Rist, the Deputy General of the Bank of France,

> . . . called at 1 p.m. The Board gave a luncheon for them at the Willard [a Washington hotel] . Governor Norman called and was with me nearly an hour. He believes present falling prices are due to an appreciation of gold. CSH said that in the United States at least, falling prices were not caused by any lack of credit which was cheap and abundant. He seemed to feel we ought not to keep our rates up to 4% . . . . I suspect they did not want to take the Board into their confidence . . . .
> Under Secretary of the Treasury Mills had met them in New York and the papers said that Governor Crissinger returned to New York with them. I heard the Comptroller tell Strong he would be in New York tomorrow. Evidently there have been a series of conferences carefully kept from the Board . . . . Strong is showing poor judgment and a great lack of tact in this matter! in not discussing with the Board questions which he discussed in New York with Governors Norman, Rist and Schacht.

For July 13, we read:

> Dr. Miller said he had a talk with Governors Norman, Rist and Schacht after the lunch, but found them aloof and evasive, evidently not wanting to discuss matters with him. Miller said if the reason for the Federal Reserve Bank of New York selling the $69 million in gold to France and accepting a Bank of England's sterling credit was to help the gold standard in Great Britain we should get into an awful mess . . . . Miller leaves today for a two months trip in California.

Mr. Hamlin was out of Washington from July 14 to 24. He returned on July 25, when he noted:

> Governor Crissinger tells me that there was a formal conference in New York between Norman, Rist and Schacht and the Governors of the Federal Reserve Banks etc. the day after they

left Washington. Governor Crissinger said all the governors representing the Open Market Committee were there and others, that it was in every sense a formal conference although Governor Crissinger did not know this until he got there. Governor Norman unbosomed himself and told in what a critical position the Bank of England was as regards gold; that it must put up its discount rate to the injury of business, commerce, etc., unless the Federal Reserve Bank of New York should reduce its rate. Governor Strong was very short-sighted in ignoring the Federal Reserve Board (except for Governor Crissinger) in this conference. It will give some of the members, already sour, a reason for continuing so.

The Discount Rate Debate

Two days later, July 27, the Federal Reserve Board met with the System's Open Market Committee. Mr. Hamlin noted:

> Governor Strong spoke briefly — showed conditions in Europe — Great Britain cannot keep her gold unless: (1) she raises [her] bill rate or (2) we lower our rate. If she has to increase her rate it will be hard on her manufacturers and merchants and will interfere with her power to buy liberally our cotton, wheat, etc. Also, other European countries will increase their rates with the same results. He said that by lowering our rates we could do the financing for Great Britain of our exports which would be a great thing for the United States. He pointed out that discounts had fallen off materially at Federal Reserve Banks and that he believed that from the domestic point of view it would certainly be advisable to lower the New York rate, and he believed that it should be made a system matter and that all rates should be reduced and that it should be done now before the crop movement is financed. If we do not do it now, European Central Banks must put up [their] rates to protect their reserves, with the consequent injury to American exports.

There was some discussion.

> Most of those present said that while there was no apparent demand for lower rates in their districts, they felt their directors would join in making it a system matter.

The Governor of the Federal Reserve Bank of Chicago objected.

> [He] said his directors saw no need of rate reduction and intimated they would not be willing to join. CSH then read the

resolution of the Federal Advisory Council in May 1927 that if business recession should continue, rates should *not* be reduced, the purpose of the declaration being to keep existing rates as an irreducible minimum. [Mr. Hamlin] favored a 3½% rate and a cautious buying of securities to make it effective.

All agreed, practically, that the only reason for not doing this would be that it might encourage stock speculation, but it was felt this should not be allowed to prevent doing what was best for commerce and agriculture and that direct action should be used to discourage speculation. [The index indicated that the Chicago Governor] was an exception.

On July 28, the Kansas City Reserve Bank asked the Board for permission to reduce its discount rate to 3½ percent. The official announcement the next day indicated that it was done to help the farmers. Nothing was said about helping England. By August 16, the Federal Reserve Bank of Chicago was the outstanding holdout against lowering the discount rate. After much debate behind closed doors, the Board ordered Chicago to reduce its rate, and it did so on September 7, seven weeks after Kansas City.

The official summary of the July 27 Open Market Investment Committee Meeting, prepared at the time by the Committee's acting secretary, William Randolph Burgess, and made public years later, said:

> The credit policy of the system was fully discussed . . . . It was felt that the only possible adverse development resulting from a general lowering of discount rates would be in the speculative security markets, but that this possibility should not stand in the way of the execution of an otherwise desirable policy.

This was not by any stretch of the imagination free enterprise at work.

Bank of France Not Fooled

M. Moreau, the head of the Bank of France, to whom Mr. Strong had written on June 20 that he could not lower the New York discount rate because such an action would stimulate an "already too active"[32] stock market, was not

---

32. Emile Moreau, *Souvenirs d'un Gouverneur de la Banque de France* (Librairie

fooled by the reason officially given for lowering the discount rate — to help improve conditions in the United States. On August 19, M. Moreau entered in his diary:

> I receive a letter from Mr. Strong asking for information on our financial situation and giving me wrong *[mauvaises]* reasons to justify the recent lowering of the discount rate. I reply assuring him that our situation continues to be good. I add that we in Paris have understood he wanted to help Mr. Norman.[33]

A few days later, on August 24, we read in the same diary:

> I receive Mr. Frank Altschul of the Lazard Bank at New York. He tells me that the reasons given by Mr. Strong for lowering the discount rate are not taken seriously by anyone, and that everybody in the United States is convinced that Mr. Strong wanted to help Mr. Norman support the pound.[34]

Mr. Altschul was speaking for the insiders and not for the general public, which was kept completely in the dark.

Production, Prices and "Money Supply"

We could go on here with many more details, but the time is growing late. Table XX shows what was happening in the United States. Production was going up fast. The right-hand column shows the annual rate of production changes for 1922-1927. Raw materials went up at a rate of 2½ percent a year. Manufactured goods were up 4 percent a year. Ton miles of railroad freight were up 4 percent, petroleum up 12.6 percent, electric power 10.5 percent, and automobile

---

de Medicis), p. 360, "*Une spéculation déjà trop audacieuse.*" For date of letter, see Stephen V.O. Clarke, *Central Bank Cooperation, 1924-1931* (Fed. Res. Bank of N.Y., 1967), p. 127.

33. *Ibid.*, pp. 382-383. Translation from the French is by the author. Original text in French is as follows: "*Je reçois une lettre de M. Strong me demandant quelques renseignements sur notre situation financière, et me donnant de mauvaises raisons pour justifier la baisse du taux d'escompte à laquelle il va procéder. Je lui réponds pour le rassurer sur notre situation qui continue à être bonne. J'ajoute que nous avons parfaitement compris à Paris qu'il voulait venir en aide à M. Norman.*"

34. *Ibid.*, p. 385. "*Je reçois M. Frank Altschul, associé de la Banque Lazard à New-York. Il me dit que les raisons données par M. Strong pour justifier la réduction du taux de l'escompte ne sont prises au sérieux par personne, et que tout le monde, aux États-Unis, est convaincu que M. Strong a voulu aider M. Norman à soutenir la livre.*"

production was up 4.2 percent per year. However, prices were hardly changing. The "money supply" had been increased rapidly, but prices were not going up.

However, the "money supply" was booming. In 1926, it had increased a half billion, to $43.1 billion. In 1927, it jumped $2.3 billion to a record high of $45.4 billion. Most of

AVERAGE ANNUAL RATE OF CHANGE, 1922-1927				
In percentages				
Prices (up or down)		**Production (up)**		
Wholesale commodities	− 0.1	Raw materials	+ 2.5	
Farm products	+ 1.2	Manufactured goods	+ 4.0	
Building materials	− 1.3	Ton miles, freight	+ 4.0	**Table**
Textile products	− 1.5	Automobiles	+ 4.2	**XX**
Raw materials*	+ 0.5	Electric power pdn.	+ 10.5	
Finished products*	− 0.4	Petroleum refining	+ 12.6	
Cost of living	+ 0.7			

Source: *Recent Economic Changes,* Report of President's Committee, 1929, pp. 626-636.

* 1923-1927.

this was in the last five months, after the discount rate was lowered. During the last half of 1927, the Federal Reserve Banks used their reserves to increase their holdings of government securities by two-thirds, reaching a new record high. Most people were not aware of any inflation, because the increase in the "money supply" was being offset by increased production. In a free market, there would have been lower prices. Of course, the stock market was booming.

Prosperity on Credit

On January 4, 1928, an announcement was made public that bank loans on collateral to stock exchange brokers and dealers had increased by $341 million in December, reaching a record height of $4.4 billion. In Table XXI, we see what was happening to such bank loans on stock exchange securities. They had about doubled, from $1.7 billion in 1922 to $3.3 billion by the end of 1926. In the first six months of 1927, they rose by roughly 10 percent. However, by the end of 1927 they had risen by more than a billion, to $4.4 billion. A major part of this increase was in the last half of the year.

Table XXI

	COLLATERAL LOAN DATA, 1922-1932 *In billions*		Up Per Month	
Date	Quantity of Money	Brokers' Loans	Q. of M.	B.L.
6/22	$33.0	$1.7		
12/26	43.1	3.3	$.19	$.03
6/27	43.8	3.6	.12	.05
12/27	45.4	4.4	.27	.13
6/28	45.7	4.9	.05	.06
12/28	46.4	6.4	.12	.25
6/29	45.7	7.1	Down	.12
9/29		8.5		.46
12/29	45.6	4.0	Down	Down
12/32	34.0	.3		

When the news of the rapid rise in security loans was printed, the stock market dropped sharply. It was a corrective move, but the Administration was unhappy. So we had a statement from the White House. The January 6th Associated Press story stated:

> President Coolidge is of the opinion that the record breaking increase in brokers' loans is not large enough to cause any unfavorable comment. [35]

---

35. Robey. *op. cit.*

The next day the *New York Times* reported:

> Although loans to brokers and dealers . . . reached unprecedented heights . . . , President Coolidge does not see any reason for unfavorable comment . . . . The President, it was said at the White House today, believes that the increase represents a natural expansion of business in the securities market and sees nothing unfavorable in it.[36]

Stock market participants reflected overnight on the reassuring statement from a usually taciturn President. They concluded that such an unusual statement of confidence invited heavy buying. So the stock market started up again.

Two Cousins Chat

Well, Columbia University's banking professor, H. Parker Willis, to whom we have previously referred, went down to Washington to testify before the Senate Banking Committee that the brokers' loans were too high. After he testified, he stopped by the White House to have lunch with his cousin, Calvin Coolidge. In the course of his conversation, he told the President why he had come to Washington. William Allen White, in his biography of President Coolidge, quotes Professor Willis as follows:

> President Coolidge, referring to what I had said, remarked that my opinion had seemed to show a great difference from his, but he added: "If I were to give my own personal opinion about it, I should say that any loan made for gambling in stocks was an excessive loan."
>
> I [Willis] replied: "I wish very much, Mr. President, you had been willing to say that instead of the public statement you did."
>
> "Why do you say that?" Mr. Coolidge queried.
>
> "Simply because I think it would have had a tremendous effect in repressing an unwholesome speculation, with which, I now see, you have no sympathy."
>
> Mr. Coolidge thought this over for a moment and then he said: "Well, I regard myself as the representative of the government and not as an individual. When technical matters come up I feel called upon to refer them to the proper department of the government which has some information about them and then,

---

36. See also Wm. Allen White, *A Puritan in Babylon* (Macmillan, 1938), p. 390.

unless there is some good reason, I use this information as a basis for whatever I have to say; but that does not prevent me from thinking what I please as an individual." [37]

Meanwhile, the market was going up and up. People from all over the world were getting into it. We could go on with more details of the situation. Mr. Strong is quoted as saying privately on May 25, 1928: "Very few people indeed realized we were now paying the penalty for the decision reached early in 1924 to help the rest of the world back to a sound financial and monetary basis." [38]

Proposed Remedy: More Money

Here is another quotation from Mr. Strong, one of the last before his death. On August 3, 1928, he wrote:

> A gradual unwinding of the situation is quite possible and is the best bet . . . . The problem now is so to shape our policy as to avoid a calamitous break in the stock market, a panicky feeling about money, a setback to business because of the change in psychology . . . . I certainly think it can be done . . . . The very existence of the Federal Reserve System is a safeguard against anything like a calamity growing out of money rates. Not only have we the power to deal with such an emergency instantly by flooding the street with money, but I think the country is well aware of this. In former days the psychology was different because the facts of the banking situation were different. Mob panic, and consequently mob disaster, is less likely to arise. [39]

Mr. Strong thought that a calamity could be avoided by a "rational Federal Reserve Policy. Such a policy means anticipating the approach of the 'breaking point' by any one, or a combination of four possible methods: (a) discount rate reduction; (b) extensive purchases of bills from dealers; (c) purchases of governments; (d) purchases of foreign exchange and the accumulation of a foreign portfolio." [40]

---

37. *Ibid.*, pp. 390-391.
38. Chandler, *op. cit.*, p. 281.
39. *Ibid.*, p. 461.
40. *Ibid.*, p. 460.

Conditions Created by Credit Expansion

Years later, Mr. Miller described the situation:

> The speculator did not ask what was the cost of money, but whether he could get it at any price . . . . In brief, a method of exercising a discriminating control over the extension of the Federal Reserve credit such as the purely technical and impersonal method of bank rate could not do . . . . To put it bluntly, though not elegantly, control by rate action in a speculative gale of such fury as swept the United States in 1929 is a good deal like spitting against the wind. [41]

The fury went on all through 1928. People sent money from abroad to get in on the stock market. Business firms floated new issues, putting the money back in the stock market with the call rate rising to 10 percent and more.

1928 was an election year. We had to have "easy money" and prosperous conditions in an election year. So the "money supply" kept going up. By the end of 1928, brokers' bank loans had gone up to $6.4 billion. By June 30, 1929, they reached $7.1 billion. Before the crisis, they soared to $8.4 billion, more than twice the amount before the reduction of the discount rate in the middle of 1927.

In Table XXII we have the figures for the crisis. The "money supply" had gone up to a point where officialdom began to worry about it. However, the Federal Reserve System held the discount rate below the call and market rates, although the Reserve Banks did sell off some government securities. The call rate fluctuated violently. At one time it went to 20 percent. It was very difficult in an election year for political appointees to do anything to slow down the situation. The speculator did not ask the cost of money. He was trying to get it at any cost and often did not even ask or know the call rate he had to pay.

However, the Federal Reserve stopped pumping up the "money supply" after the end of 1928. They tried to put the brakes on, but they could not. After the discount rate was reduced to 3½ percent in 1927 to help England, it was raised three times in the election year of 1928. Finally, in August, it reached 5 percent, which was still below call and prime

---

41. Adolph C. Miller, "Responsibility for Federal Reserve Policies, 1927-1929," *American Economic Review*, September 1935, pp. 455-456.

Table XXII

DEVELOPMENT OF THE CRISIS, 1927-1929

Date	Gold Stock	Quantity of Money	U.S. Debt Fed. Res. Bks.	Interest Rates		
				Fed. Res. Discount	Call Rate	N.Y.C. Prime Comm'l.
End of	*Billions*	*Billions*	*Millions*	*Percentages*		
12/27	$4.1	$45.4	$617	3.5	4.4	4.0
				(2/3)* 4.0		
6/28	3.3	45.7	235	(5/18)* 4.5	6.2	4.75
12/28	3.9†	46.4	228	(7/13)* 5.0	8.6	5.4
6/29	4.0	45.7	216	5.0	7.7	6.0
				(8/9)* 6.0		
12/29	4.0	45.6	511	(11/1)* 5.0	4.8	5.0
				(11/15)* 4.5		

*Date effective.
†8.3% of the total quantity of money.

commercial rates. At the end of 1928, the call rate was fluctuating about 8.6 percent, while prime business borrowers were paying 5.4 percent.

In 1929, after the election, there was a long and bitter debate between the officials of the Federal Reserve Board in Washington and those of the Federal Reserve Bank of New York. Unfortunately there is not time to give you the details for the period from Mr. Hamlin's diary. The New York Bank wanted Washington to approve a raise in the discount rate to 6 per cent. They asked them to do so ten times. The Federal Reserve Board in Washington refused to do so ten times. They said it would hurt business. If business had to pay such high rates there would be a recession. Stock market activities were not their prime concern. However, the Washington Board did send out a letter on February 2, 1929, to the twelve Federal Reserve Banks, warning them to use "direct pressure" on their member banks and "to take such measures as may be deemed suitable and effective . . . to restrain the use, either directly or indirectly, of Federal Reserve credit facilities in aid of the growth of speculative credit."[42]

But it was perfectly legal to make brokers' loans, and there was a great profit in them. So the commercial banks continued to make more such loans all through the first nine months of 1929, as Table XXI shows. Finally, on August 9, the discount rate was permitted to go up to 6 percent. But it was too little, too late. The crash came in late October. Call loans were called, and borrowers, not able to hold on to their securities, were sold out. The market plummeted. *It was not free enterprise that produced this outcome.*

Conclusion

Let me give you the judgment of Professor Lester Chandler, a staunch defender of governmental manipulations of the quantity of money. He states:

> There can be no doubt that the international situation was the major reason for the 1927 easy-money policy, that Strong was

---

42. Quoted by Adolph C. Miller, *op. cit.*, p. 454.

motivated by an altruistic concern for European countries, especially Britain, and that at least the timing of the policy was related to the conferences with foreign central bankers in early July.[43]

Professor Miller, who, like Mr. Hamlin, was a member of the Federal Reserve Board from its beginning in 1914 up to 1936, had this to say in his 1931 testimony two years after the crash:

> We had something of an obsession for easy money in the system, a feeling that it makes the atmosphere of business, that it can stop a recession of business and turn a period of depression into one of recovery.[44]

Still later he testified before the Senate Banking and Currency Committee on May 22, 1935, in my presence:

> The gold standard ended in 1914 in an economic sense, not the legal sense. Since then it has been managed .... The gold standard, in an economic sense, is a device ... for maintaining a condition of balance among the countries of the world, and among industries within any country, by accurately and quickly detecting and registering the slightest departure from that balance and setting in motion at once corrective forces .... It tells you when something is getting out of joint .... [45]

In a 1935 magazine article, Mr. Miller is quoted as saying that:

> The easy-going credit policy of 1927, which was father and mother to the subsequent 1929 collapse, was originated by Governor Strong, of the New York Federal Reserve Bank, and it did not represent a policy either developed or imposed by the Board on the Reserve Banks against their will.
> The policy was the result of a visit of the Governors of foreign central banks, who unequivocally stated in New York that unless the United States did adopt it there would be a collapse in

43. Chandler, *op. cit.*, p. 440.

44. Adolph C. Miller in 1931 testimony before the Senate Committee on Banking and Currency, as quoted by Professor Edwin W. Kemmerer (Princeton University) in the May 1935 Hearings of the Senate Committee on Banking and Currency, p. 339.

45. *Ibid.*, May 22, 1935, pp. 675, 680 and 683.

Europe. It was a European policy, adopted by the United States to prevent a world calamity. [46]

It was not free enterprise that failed in 1929. It was political intervention. It was the political manipulation of the quantity of money by well-meaning politicians attempting to produce permanent prosperity. They thought that an increase in the quantity of money would solve all economic problems and make everybody happy. Instead, it misdirected investments and production, helping a few temporarily while eventually creating misery for millions of innocent people throughout the civilized world.

Unfortunately, that lesson has not yet been learned. As the Federal Reserve Board member, Adolph Miller, testified in 1935:

Up to this day it has never yet been demonstrated that any agency can be invented to which power to govern the currency could be entrusted without ultimately disastrous consequences.[47]

---

46. *Sphere*, July 1935. Substantially this same statement appears in *Memoirs of Herbert Hoover: The Great Depression*, 1929-1941 (Macmillan, 1952), p. 13.
47. Hearings before the Senate Committee on Banking and Currency, May 1935, p. 745.

The Evolution Of The Present Monetary Crisis

Since 1929, there have been many important monetary developments all over the world. However, most of the emphasis tonight will be on those in my country – the United States. Its monetary and economic situation is extremely important for other countries, because capitalism reached its highest development there, and the values of so many other currencies depend upon the value of the dollar. When anything happens to the value of the dollar, it affects both the trade and the currencies, and therefore the people, of the entire Western world. So we are all vitally interested in what happens to the dollar.

Before proceeding beyond 1929, let us review some of the important figures as they developed. In Table XXI, page 224, we showed the brokers' loans.[1] These are loans made on stock exchange securities. We spoke last night of how they

---

1. Data through 1941 are taken from *Banking and Monetary Statistics* (Board of Governors of the Federal Reserve System, 1943). Figures from 1941-1960 were taken from the pertinent sections of *Supplements to Banking and Monetary Statistics*. Still later figures have appeared in monthly issues of the *Federal Reserve Bulletin*, also published by the Board of Governors of the Federal Reserve System.

went up in 1927 and alarmed some people. However, the politicians in office felt that this merely indicated that prosperity was here forever. By the end of June 1929, these loans, with the help of Federal Reserve policies, had risen to $7.1 billion, almost double what they had been in June 1927. The high point was reached at the end of September when they reached $8.5 billion. The crash very shortly reduced this figure − to $4 billion by the end of 1929. By the end of 1932, such loans were down to $300 million.

This drastic drop was largely due to the fact that many people had bought their stocks with a high percentage of borrowed money. They had put up only 15 or 20 percent of the price and borrowed the rest. When the market prices of their stocks dropped rapidly, the lending banks and brokers had to sell their customers' stocks to protect their own loans. Many investors lost everything they had. Large numbers lost the savings of a lifetime. Many were also to lose their jobs in the depression period that followed.

In Table XXII, Page 228, we find the "money supply" figures. As you see, the "money supply" reached a peak of $46.4 billion by the end of 1928. Although the crash was still months away, it had receded somewhat by June 1929. The Federal Reserve officials were trying hard to slow down the credit expansion. However, the discount rate of 5 percent remained below both the call and the prime commercial interest rates. When the discount rate was finally raised to 6 percent on August 9, 1929, it put an end to credit expansion for business loans. However, it was still below the fluctuating call rates of more than 9 percent. Consequently, there was a rapid increase in security loans until the actual crash. By the end of 1929, the Federal Reserve had reduced the discount rate twice, down to 4½ percent. Of course, market interest rates were also falling fast, and commodity prices had begun to drop.

Deflation Followed Inflation

After the stock market crash, we experienced a period of great deflation. This seriously affected most business firms in the United States. Many consumers were no longer able to spend as much money as they had previously been spending. When the income tax figures were released for the year 1928, the last calendar year before the crash, they showed that 11 percent of the taxpayers' incomes were realized from sales of securities or real estate that they had held for two or more years. This speculation, which had been so rife, had created many millionaires. But the paper profits crashed with the stock market and so did much of the luxury spending.

During the post-crash period, the "money supply" was rapidly contracted. (See Table XXIII.) The "money supply," which had reached $46.4 billion by the end of 1928, had contracted by the end of 1932 to $34 billion, and by June 1933 to $30.8 billion. This was a drop of roughly one-third in the number of dollars available to market participants.

The Federal Reserve officials did not like this contraction. They tried every policy they knew to keep the "money supply" up. However, loans were called, banks were failing, and business activity was slowing down. Prices and wages fell somewhat, but there was considerable propaganda behind a strong movement attempting to keep them as high as possible. So they were held higher than free market forces could or would support. Actually, consumers, with their contracted savings and a much lower "money supply," could not buy as much as they did before the crash unless prices and wages were allowed to drop in accordance with free market principles.

The Federal Reserve lowered the discount rate, as you can see, moving it down to 2 percent for a second time in 1933. The call rate went to less than 1 percent. People were not borrowing money to go into the stock market. The prime commercial interest rate went down below 1½ percent. Business firms were not borrowing either. Wage rates were too high to permit any general business expansion. This 2 percent discount rate was actually a penalty rate and, for the time being, it effectively ended any further credit expansion.

In an attempt to keep the "money supply" up, the Federal Reserve Banks were buying government securities. Their holdings had gone up from $228 million at the end of 1928 to almost $2.5 billion by the end of 1933. These government securities were largely bought with idle Federal Reserve Bank

Table XXIII

DEFLATION, 1928-1933

Date	Gold Stock	Quantity of Money	U.S. Debt Fed. Res. Bks.	Interest Rates		
				Fed. Res. Discount	Call	N.Y.C. Prime Comm'l.
	Billions	*Billions*	*Millions*	*Percentages*		
End of						
12/28	$3.9*	$46.4	$228	5.0	8.6	5.4
12/29	4.0	45.6	511	4.5	4.8	5.0
12/30	4.3	43.6	729	2.0	2.2	2.9
12/31	4.2	37.2	817	3.5	2.7	3.9
12/32	4.2	34.0	1,855	2.5	1.0	1.5
Low point: 6/33		30.0				
12/33	4.0†	30.8	2,437	2.0	.9	1.4

*8.3% of total quantity of money.
†13.0 of total quantity of money.

reserves. These were reserves accumulated by setting aside a part of the money that depositors kept in their bank accounts and felt they could withdraw at any time. The commercial banks were required by law, under the fractional reserve system, to keep a set percentage of all deposits with their Federal Reserve Banks. The Reserve Banks could then use these reserves to buy government securities. They did just this during the period under review, to the tune of more than $2 billion.

A New Administration

A new President, Franklin D. Roosevelt, took office on March 4, 1933. He inaugurated a vigorous program in an attempt to increase the "money supply." He felt that if he could only get the "money supply" back up to where it had been, everybody would be prosperous. Both outgoing President Hoover and incoming President Roosevelt advocated keeping wages and prices high. They sincerely thought that high dollar incomes would produce prosperity. Unfortunately, with such high wage costs and a lower "money supply," this theory could not and did not work. As a result of such policies, about ten million workers joined the ranks of the unemployed. This was the problem that Mr. Roosevelt faced when he came into office.

President Roosevelt, known popularly as FDR, tried a year of pump-priming in 1933. Here are his words from a Fireside Radio Chat on October 22, 1933, entitled "We Are on Our Way, and We Are Headed in the Right Direction":

> I repeat what I have said on many occasions, that ever since last March the definite policy of the Government has been to restore commodity price levels. The object has been the attainment of such a level as will enable agriculture and industry once more to give work to the unemployed. It has been to make possible the payment of public and private debts more nearly at the price level at which they were incurred .... It is the Government's policy to restore the price level first .... When we have restored the price level, we shall seek to establish and maintain a dollar which will not change its purchasing and debt-paying power during succeeding generations .... I am going to establish a Government market for gold in the United

States . . . . We are thus continuing to move toward a managed currency.[2]

"Managed" Money

This, of course, was not a free and unhampered market at work. It was a deliberate attempt of the Government to interfere with free market processes in an attempt to create a prosperity the program's sponsors thought was no longer possible in a free market society. In so acting, the political managers of the economy ignored the fundamental eternal principles of economics outlined in our earlier lectures. Anyone who understood these principles could have foreseen that such interventions would only make matters worse, even from the viewpoint of those advocating them.

Roosevelt's first scheme failed completely. Although he and a cooperative Federal Reserve System did everything they could with low discount rates and pump-priming purchases of an ever-increasing Government debt, their efforts only raised the "money supply" from $30 billion to $30.8 billion.

So at the end of January 1934, Roosevelt decided to devalue the dollar abruptly in terms of gold. In devaluing the dollar by 41 percent, he gave us what we in the United States called the 59¢ dollar. This automatically revalued the banking system's gold stock of $4 billion at $6.8 billion. (See Table XXIV.) It also immediately lowered the prices of American goods to foreigners, but not to Americans. Foreigners started pouring in gold and the $6.8 billion at the end of January became $8.2 billion by the end of 1934. This helped create an upsurge in exports for a while, but it also increased the "money supply" to $35 billion. Meanwhile, the Federal Reserve had lowered the discount rate to 1½ percent in an attempt to expand credit and business activity.

Making a Market for Government Bonds

With the advent of the New Deal, a new factor appeared in the financial picture. The Government began buying its own

---

2. F.D. Roosevelt, *The Public Papers and Addresses*, Vol. II, 1933, pp. 425-427.

bonds in large amounts. This was a nice new way to raise money for spending programs. Just force people to entrust their savings and retirement funds to the Government, replace these funds with Government bonds, and spend the proceeds. If *you* can do it, let me know how. The Government set up trust funds for the safekeeping of social security funds and pension funds for its own employees and then sold its bonds to the trust funds.

The Social Security Act was originally passed in 1935. During the 1936 Presidential election campaign, we were told how social security was going to eliminate poverty forevermore in the United States. It was going to take care of all the old folks, all the widows, all the orphans, and all the unemployed. These unfortunate groups were never going to be in need again. That was in 1936, after the law had been passed, but before it went into effect. The taxes did not start until January 1, 1937, after these promises had helped to win the November 1936 election. No benefits were paid before 1940, the next Presidential election year.

You will note in Table XXIV that the Government's purchases of its own securities started upward with the New Deal. They went from less than a billion dollars at the end of 1933 to more than $5 billion by the end of 1938. You will also note that the pump-priming was successful in getting the "money supply" back up to the $46 billion figure which it had reached in 1928.

High Wage Rates as a Solution

As a result of the devaluation, large quantities of gold had come in from abroad. These gold imports increased our exports, and under our fractional reserve system also served as a base for puffing up our "money supply" still further. The Federal Reserve was holding the discount rate down to 1 percent. So the Federal Reserve System was doing everything it could to pump the "money supply" up. Their policies succeeded in doing this, but the larger "money supply" did not produce the prosperity the Administration had promised.

Now, as mentioned earlier, a major unemployment problem had developed in our country in the 1930s, a period we

Table
XXIV

NEW DEAL PUMP PRIMING, 1933-1938

Date	Gold Stock	Quantity of Money	U.S. Debt Holdings			Federal Reserve Discount Rate
			Federal Reserve Banks	Commercial Banks	U.S. Gov't.	
End of	*Billions*	*Billions*	*Billions*			*Percentages*
12/33	$ 4.0	$ 30.8	$ 2.4	$ 7.5*	$ .7*	2.0
		1/31/34 – $4 billions in gold revalued as $6.8 billions				
12/34	8.2	35.3	2.4	10.3*	1.4*	1.5
12/35	10.1	40.2	2.4	12.7*	2.0*	1.5
12/36	11.3	45.0	2.4	15.3	2.4	1.5
12/37	12.8	44.4	2.6	14.2	4.3	1.0
12/38	14.5	46.5	2.6	14.0	5.3	1.0

*June figures.

refer to as "the depression period." Our labor, business, and political leaders had tried to keep both wage rates and prices up. This was the avowed policy of both the Hoover and Roosevelt Administrations. It was thought that if this were done, we should have prosperity once more. The well-meaning sponsors of this policy thought that, with a pre-crash "money supply," high pre-crash wage rates would revive the purchasing power of the people.

Table XXV shows some economic facts that tell the sad story of this attempt to keep wage rates above those that would have prevailed in a free market. During 1933, we had 11,800,000 men unemployed. Our iron and steel production index was only 54 as compared with an average of 100 for the later 1935-1949 period. Other production indices were also low, including auto production and railroad freight movements.

Prosperity by Law

Roosevelt persuaded Congress to pass the National Recovery Act, popularly called the NRA, and he signed it on June 16, 1933. This National Recovery Act took prices and wages out of market competition. Production and employment were no longer to be guided and shifted in accordance with consumers' wishes as revealed by market forces, according to the principles presented in Lecture III. The Act enabled, even ordered, businessmen to get together and set high prices. It also permitted labor unions to get together and set high wages, which their employers would legally be compelled to pay. President Roosevelt and his supporters felt this would be helpful in pumping up purchasing power and prosperity. The NRA preamble stated that it would produce "national recovery." Those who questioned the economic theory behind the Act were smeared as spokesmen for selfish interests more concerned with their own bank accounts than with "national recovery."

Actually, as soon as the Act was passed, many business firms speeded up their production to beat the date when these new high industry-wide wage and price codes would become the law of the land. Consequently, production leaped up right away. But as soon as the codes went into operation, production slumped. Many small businessmen could no longer compete with the big ones. If they cut their prices, they were charged with a violation of the law. One small local tailor, who cleaned and pressed suits and trousers, tried to stay in business by cutting his prices below those set by the industry's code. He was then prosecuted in the courts and put out of business. There was also the "sick chicken case," involving a small company that tried to sell chickens for less than the NRA code's prescribed prices.

Finally, the Supreme Court, on May 27, 1935, declared this National Recovery Act to be unconstitutional. You can see in Table XXV what happened after this Act had been declared unconstitutional in 1935. Unemployment dropped considerably. Employment increased and all basic production indices surged upward.

The Effect of Free Market Wage Rates

The New Deal Administration did not like the Supreme Court's attempt to maintain traditional American freedom for market prices and wage rates. So the political party in power re-enacted Section 7A, the labor clause of the unconstitutional NRA. This new Act, officially the National Labor Relations Act, became known popularly as the Wagner Act. The country's leading constitutional lawyers advised their clients, the nation's largest employers, that this Act was just as unconstitutional as the National Recovery Act.

As a result, most big businesses simply ignored the Act and went merrily on their way, resorting to free market wage rates and prices to increase employment and production. Table XXV shows how unemployment went down from more than 11 million in 1933 to 6.4 million in 1937. Note also that the 1937 production of iron and steel was more than twice what it was in 1933 and 1934. Auto production for 1936 and 1937 was more than double that for 1933. Railroad freight loadings had gone up considerably, too.

The Effect of a Politically Controlled Labor Market

Then in 1937, the Supreme Court, in a series of 5 to 4 decisions, reversed its reasoning in the NRA case and upheld the Wagner Act as constitutional. Employers were then forced to deal with politically privileged labor unions and were no longer free to hire whomever they chose at free market wage rates.

One of the Wagner Act cases involved the Associated Press, a worldwide news service. This particular 5-4 decision was a body blow to the freedom of the press. The AP had fired a man who was very active in the Newspaper Guild, a union organized by Communists. This former employee rewrote news items from abroad for dispatches to our domestic papers. When the Court ruled that he had been fired for union activity, the AP was forced to re-hire him and pay him two years' back pay. Since then, labor unions and their interventionist ideology have pretty well controlled employment on all major newspapers and news services.

With this Act declared constitutional, the labor unions were able to ask for, and get, higher than free market wages. You can see in Table XXV what then happened to unemployment. In one year, from 1937 to 1938, the number unemployed went from 6.4 million to 9.8 million. You can also see what happened to iron and steel production, auto production, and railroad freight tonnage. These production indices all dropped fast.

World War II Ends Unemployment

This was the situation when war broke out in Europe in the summer of 1939. It was this war, not New Deal interventionism, that put the American unemployed back to work. The French and the British sent their gold to the United States and started putting American men back to work in the fall of 1939. You can note the results in Table XXV. As more men went to work providing the sinews of war, every production index leaped upward. We were supplying France and England. Their desperate purchasing agents were willing to pay higher prices than American consumers could or would pay.

Table XXV

UNEMPLOYMENT AND PRODUCTION, 1933-1942

Date	U.S. Population	No. of Unemployed	Iron & Steel Prdn. Index	Auto Production	R.R. Freight Originated
	Millions	*Millions*	*1935-1939 = 100*	*Millions*	*Millions of Tons*
1933	125.6	11.8	54	1.6	699
1934	126.4	9.8	61	2.2	765
1935	127.3	9.1	81	3.3	790
1936	128.1	7.4	114	3.7	959
1937	128.8	6.4	123	3.9	1,016
1938	129.8	9.8	68	2.0	772
1939	130.8	8.8	114	2.9	902
1940	132.0	7.0	147	3.7	1,009
1941	133.2	2.7	186	3.8	1,228
1942	134.7	-.9	199	.2	1,421

Note: According to a letter to the editor published in *Life* magazine, 6/26/70, the Dow Jones average dropped from 194.40 on 3/10/37 to 98.95 on 3/31/38 – a 49% drop.
Sources: Unemployment figures – *The Economic Almanac for 1950* (N.Y.: Nat'l. Conference Board), p. 164. Production figures – *Historical Statistics of the United States, 1789-1945* (U.S. Department of Commerce), pp. 180, 203, 223.

At the end of 1941, we got into the war. The official statistics show minus unemployment for 1942, because many women and children, not considered part of the regular working force, were going to work. This is how our mass unemployment of the depression period was ended. It was ended by a World War.

Politics in the Saddle

Here is a very interesting quotation from the diary of Henry Morgenthau, Jr., our Secretary of the Treasury at that time. On March 12, 1940, he attended a White House conference to discuss the French and British demands for war material. His diary quotes President Roosevelt as saying:

> These foreign orders mean prosperity in this country and we can't elect the Democratic Party unless we get prosperity and these orders are of the greatest importance . . . . let us be perfectly frank. [3]

Secretary Morgenthau, who quoted this statement of the President's in his diary, added his own opinion: "And he is right!"

We could speak many hours on how the war ended the depression by putting men back to work. Let us merely note in passing that in 1940, FDR ran for an unprecedented third term. Ever since our first President, George Washington, declined a third term, no other President in over 150 years had ever dared to run for a third term. Roosevelt took some members of the opposition party into his Cabinet, and he promised the American public all through the 1940 election campaign that our boys were not going to fight in any foreign wars. Just before Election Day his words in Boston were:

> And while I am talking to you mothers and fathers, I give you one more assurance. I have said this before, but I shall say it again and again and again. Your boys are not going to be sent into any foreign wars. [4]

---

3. *From the Morgenthau Diaries: Years of Urgency, 1938-1941*, edited by John Morton Blum (Houghton Mifflin, 1965), p. 118.
4. F.D. Roosevelt, *op. cit.*, Vol. IX, p. 517.

This and other similar statements, along with high employment and business activity, helped him to win a landslide victory. Behind the scenes he was promising Britain that he would give them what they wanted after the election. Shortly after his re-election, he held a press conference and announced a program that later became known, when passed by Congress, as the Lend-Lease Program. Needless to say, the Lend-Lease Program was financed by inflation.

The Lend-Lease Solution

Table XXVI presents some of the pertinent monetary figures of the World War II situation. At the end of 1938, the money supply was $46.5 billion. By the end of 1941, it had risen to $64.5 billion. During the early war years, gold had flowed in from France and England. But France fell in June 1940, and could no longer send more gold. The United States was not able to capture what was left of the French gold, although it tried. By the summer of 1940, the British had pledged almost all their gold. Since the United States was then on a "cash-and-carry" basis, they could not place many more orders. However, to keep men working and the United States "prosperous," Roosevelt asked for and got the Lend-Lease Act, which he financed by inflation.

Lend-Lease kept American workers working, producing for England and later for a growing "defense" program of the United States. The "money supply" figures for the end of 1941 reflect primarily the inflation due to Lend-Lease costs before the United States got into the war on December 7 of that year. Our "money supply" went up by more than a third from 1938 to the end of 1941, when it reached $64.5 billion. The discount rate was still at 1 percent, and the gold stock, which increased $4.4 billion in 1940, rose by less than a billion in 1941.

More Money in a Hurry

Then, the United States got into war. With four years of wartime inflation, the "money supply" more than doubled. It shot up to $132.5 billion. By the end of 1945, the Federal

Reserve Banks held more than ten times the amount of Government securities they had held at the time of Pearl Harbor. The commercial banks held almost $91 billion, whereas they had held only $21 billion on December 31, 1941, and only $14 billion at the end of 1938. All through the war, the United States Government bought large quantities of its own bonds with Social Security and other trust funds, holding $27 billion of them at the end of 1945, compared with only $5.3 billion at the end of 1938. During all this time the discount rate remained at 1 percent. *This was not free enterprise at work. It was a politically manipulated inflation with a vengeance.*

Now, how did all this happen? Actually, it was very simple. When you have a fractional reserve system, you can very easily create "money" without anyone's having to mine, earn, or save it. The Federal Reserve just opens, or adds to, accounts on the books of the commercial banks. The process was discussed in Lecture V. But don't take my word for how this enormous inflation was created. Read the testimony of William McChesney Martin Jr., Chairman of the Federal Reserve Board, or of the Board of Governors of the Federal Reserve System, as it is now officially known. Mr. Martin testified before the Joint Economic Committee of Congress on March 7, 1961. This is his description of how World War II was financed:

> Immediately upon the United States' entry into World War II in December 1941, the Board of Governors announced that the Federal Reserve was prepared –
>
> (1) "To use its powers to assure that an ample supply of funds is available at all times for the war effort, and
>
> (2) "To exert its influence toward maintaining conditions in the U.S. Government security market that are satisfactory from the standpoint of the Government's requirements."
>
> Making good on its words, the Federal Reserve saw to it that the banking system was supplied with ample lendable reserves to provide the Government with all the war-financing funds that it could not raise through taxation and through borrowing people's savings.
>
> It did so by buying outstanding Government securities on a huge scale. The Federal Reserve's payments for these securities wound up in bank reserves. In turn, the banking system used these additional reserves to purchase new securities that the

Table
XXVI

WORLD WAR II MONETARY TABLEAU, 1938-1945

Date	Gold Stock	Quantity of Money	U.S. Debt Holdings			Fed. Reserve Discount Rate
			Fed. Res. Banks	Comm'l. Banks	U.S. Gov't.	
End of	*Billions*	*Billions*	*Billions*			*Percentages*
12/38	$ 14.5	$ 46.5	$ 2.6	$ 14.0	$ 5.3	1
12/39	17.6	51.5	2.5	16.3	6.5	1
12/40	22.0[1]	58.0	2.2	17.6	7.6	1
12/41	22.7	64.5	2.3	21.4	9.5	1
12/45	20.1[1]	132.5[2]	24.3	90.8	27.0	1

1. Gold stock as a % of total quantity of money: 12/40 – 37.9%; 12/45 – 15.2%.
2. U.S. Gov't. deposits $24.6 billion, a record; 12/40, they had been $753 million.

Treasury was issuing to obtain further funds to finance the war effort.

To keep the process going the Federal Reserve in effect maintained a standing offer to buy Government securities in unlimited amount at relatively fixed prices, set high enough to assure that their interest rates or yields would be pegged at predetermined low levels. When no one else would accept those yields and pay those prices, the Federal Reserve did so. And in so doing, it helped to finance the war.

The process was successful for its emergency purpose. But the procedure of pegging Government securities at high prices and low yields entailed a price of its own that the economy – the people and the Government alike – would later have to pay. The results were twofold:

(1) During wartime, money was created rapidly and continually, in effect setting a time bomb for an ultimate inflationary explosion – even though the immediate inflationary consequences were held more or less in check by a system of direct controls over prices, wages, materials, manpower, and consumer goods.

(2) The market for Government securities became artificial. The price risks normally borne by participants in that market were eliminated: bonds not payable for 20 years or more became the equivalent of interest-bearing cash since they could be turned into cash immediately at par value or better – at the option of the owners, at any time.[5]

Inflation – A Harmful Illusion

Now, of course, all of this new money, all of this great increase in the quantity of money, meant that everybody who had earned or saved dollars beforehand held dollars that were losing value with every increase in the "money supply." This inflation and credit expansion was also directing the economy in a direction quite different from the way the free market would have directed it. It was a manipulated and not a free economy.

Actually you do not need inflation in wartime any more than in peacetime. It merely helps to hide reality. If the politicians had felt that our people really wanted the war,

---

5. This testimony appeared in the *Commercial and Financial Chronicle*, March 16, 1961, and the *Federal Reserve Bulletin* for March 1961. It was reprinted separately by the Board of Governors of the Federal Reserve System under the title, "Federal Reserve Operations in Perspective."

Table XXVII

POST-WAR – MARSHALL PLAN, 1945-1950

Date	Gold Stock	Quantity of Money	U.S. Debt Holdings			Fed. Reserve Discount Rate
			Fed. Res. Banks	Comm'l. Banks	U.S. Gov't.	
End of	*Billions*	*Billions*	*Billions*			*Percentages*
12/45	$ 20.1	$ 132.5	$ 24.3	$ 90.8	$ 27.0	1.0
12/47	22.8	148.8	22.6	68.7	34.4	1.0
6/48	23.5	144.1	21.4	64.6	35.8	1.25
12/48	24.2	147.4	23.3	62.5	37.3	1.5
12/49	24.4*	147.3	18.9	66.8	39.4	1.5
6/50	24.2	146.9	18.3	65.6	37.8	1.5

*Gold stock as a % of quantity of money: 16.6%, post-war year-end high.

they would have had no qualms about asking us to pay for it in the form of sufficiently higher taxes. In life, you do not really want anything unless you are willing to pay for it. But the Administration was afraid the American people did not want the war. So President Roosevelt and his subservient Congresses did not tax us sufficiently to pay the full costs of the war. Consequently, the Federal Reserve resorted to inflation, doubling the "money supply" during the period the United States was in the war. The quantity of money was now many times what it had been back in the 1920s, and *free enterprise had had nothing to do with this increase*, whereby some were helped at the expense of others.

Helping Our Allies

We faced another critical situation during the war period. As in World War I, we had to take care of our allies' economic needs. Their able-bodied men were in uniform. They could neither tend their farms nor produce in factories the many things they needed for survival and the efficient waging of war. So we gave them many of the things they needed. This helped to win the war.

When the war ended, they still had a vital need for many of the things that we provided. So we continued to send them things free for another year or two. Much of this was paid for by inflating the "money supply." You can see in Table XXVII that the "money supply" continued to rise from 1945 through 1947. Although the banks had started to unload some of their government securities, the Government itself had increased its holdings, which rose from $27 to $34.4 billions during these first two post-war years.

As you may remember, our farmers suffered considerably after World War I. During the war, they went heavily into debt in order to expand rapidly to help feed Europe. After the war, their markets and the prices for their products collapsed. So many, unable to maintain payments on their debts, lost their farms during the post-war deflation. This time they were more cautious. In order to persuade them to expand rapidly again, the Government passed a law that promised to support high farm prices for two years after

World War II ended. This period turned out to be 1946 and 1947.

Helping Foreign Politicians

The next year, 1948, was a Presidential election year. The political party in power, foreseeing a collapse in farm prices, was very much worried that such a drop in prices might lead to its defeat. So, well in advance of the election, it came up with a plan to keep farm prices high until after the election. General George C. Marshall, a popular hero, was appointed Secretary of State. On June 5, 1947, in a Harvard University Commencement address, he proclaimed to the whole world that "Europe's requirements for the next three or four years of foreign food and other essential products – principally from America – are so much greater than her present ability to pay that she must have substantial additional help."[6] A week later, he explained that he "had in mind the entire continent west of Asia – and including both the United Kingdom and the Soviet Union."[7] In short, he asked all European nations to get together and submit a list of their needs.

His proposal, first known as the European Recovery Program and later as the Marshall Plan, would be costly. However, the party in power did not plan to raise taxes. This plan could be, and was, financed by an inflation that kept farm prices high.

On September 27, 1947, the Bevin Report of the European governments found that during World War II:

> Industrial production in Belgium, France and the Netherlands was reduced to 30-40 percent of pre-war, and in Italy to only 20 percent, production of bread grains fell to only two-thirds of pre-war . . . .
> Nevertheless recovery proceeded well – indeed much faster than after the end of the first World War. Eighteen months after the end of the fighting in Europe, industry and transport were

---

6. This speech was widely reprinted. This sentence can be found in the *General Report* of the Committee of European Economic Cooperation, Department of State, Vol. I, pp. 9-10.
7. *Ibid.,* p. 10.

moving again vigorously . . . . By the end of 1946 industrial production in Belgium, France and the Netherlands had recovered to 85-95 per cent of the pre-war level, whilst Italian industrial production was back to 60 percent of pre-war level. In the United Kingdom the process of demobilisation of the war economy had been accomplished smoothly and the pre-war level of national output had been fully restored . . . .

In the case of agricultural production, which, though hard hit by the war, had not declined to the same extent as industrial production, the beginning of recovery was evident in all countries in 1946 . . . . The devastated areas of France, Belgium and Western Germany have largely been put back into production; and even in the Netherlands, where inundation was added to physical destruction, land is quickly being restored to use . . . . The countries' own efforts were supported by considerable assistance from the rest of the world.[8]

All of this meant that the European nations no longer needed as much American food and other things as they had previously. They were actually getting back on their own feet. Then, due to "unfavourable weather" and "comprehensive legislation,"[9] the ever-present scapegoats of socialism and interventionism, "this improvement was not maintained."[10] Consequently the European politicians indicated that they would be happy to receive some free gifts of American goods that they could sell cheaply to their citizens.

Helping the Domestic Situation

Now, what was the situation in the United States? The 1948 Presidential election was approaching. The Administration's Secretary of the Interior, a Mr. Krug, reported on October 9, 1947:

Tobacco exports and shipments in 1946-47 were over 500 million pounds, twice as high as during the war years and about a third higher than the average for the 1930's . . . . Tobacco production in 1947 is estimated at 2.2 billion pounds, nearly 50 percent above prewar and second only to the record crop of 2.3 billion pounds in 1946. Domestic consumption . . . is expected to continue at about present levels . . . . Exports, however, are ex-

---

8. *Ibid.*, Vol. I, p. 7 and Vol. II, p. 25.
9. *Ibid.*, Vol. II, p. 25.
10. *Ibid.*, Vol. I, p. 7.

pected to decline from the current high rate toward the level of
the 1930's . . . . The present rate of production could be maintained, however, if sufficient outlets were found. [11]

The "sufficient outlets" were found in the greatest
giveaway program the world has ever known. The Administration resorted to inflation to keep up agricultural "prosperity" by paying high prices for American farm products,
particularly cotton and tobacco raised in those states that
were most crucial to the winning of a Presidential election.
These products were given to the politicians in power in the
European countries. These politicians in turn sold the
products to their own people in their local currencies. Large
parts of the proceeds were used to nationalize a number of
their industries, thus hurting European free enterprise.

Here is a part of the testimony of the Under Secretary of
Agriculture before a Congressional Committee. It may help
you understand why we undertook this supposedly very
generous act.

> *The Under Secretary*: If we lose our export markets, the prices
> are going to come down. . . .
> *Member of the Congressional Committee*: I am a grain and
> cotton farmer. What will the effect of this program be on the
> price I am to get for my crop?
> *The Under Secretary*: I think that any program of the
> magnitude of this with respect to food will assure you of getting a
> pretty fair price for your crops. Without such a program or
> something comparable, I think you could be fairly sure of a much
> lower price in this country. . . .
> I have all the money I have invested in farming, and if you are
> going to cut down my production on the farm it means that I
> would have less income. [12]

That was an American politician "worrying" about the poor
people in Europe.

In 1946, about 40 percent of our exports "were financed
directly or indirectly by loans and grants-in-aid by the United

---

11. Report of J.A. Krug, Secretary of the Interior, *Natural Resources and Foreign
Aid*, October 9, 1947, p. 39.
12. Hearings before the Committee on Appropriations, House of Representatives
(80th Congress) on the Foreign Aid Appropriation Bill for 1949. Part 1, pp. 323,
326 and 329, April 23, 1948.

States Government."[13] Without a continuation of such subsidies, our farmers and others interested in exports were bound to be hurt. In such an event the party in power might well lose the election. Domestic politics played a very big role in this so-called act of charity.

Effects of "Foreign Aid"

Even before the Marshall Plan, our giveaway policy had brought great distress to Greece and Turkey, normally large producers and exporters of wheat and tobacco. They could not sell their wheat and tobacco in competition with the United States giveaway. Their "surpluses" were piled up in warehouses. What was the result? The Communists had a heyday. The impoverished Greeks and Turks were ripe for Communist infiltration and promotion of social unrest. So we had previously had to make loans to help the Greek and Turkish governments combat the Communists. Note how one intervention only makes matters worse and creates a demand for further intervention.

This governmental "foreign aid" giveaway program also upset free enterprise. Remember, free enterprise, with its division of labor and specialization, tends to develop mass production for mass consumption. In a Europe divided into many small countries, you cannot have mass production unless you can sell beyond the borders of one country. This program of intergovernment subsidies made European mass production very difficult. Few privately owned European companies could sell their products in other countries in competition with gifts from the United States Government.

The "foreign aid" gifts also added to the difficulties of privately owned businesses by providing European politicians with funds to nationalize many industries and run them at a deficit. In England, for instance, the British government received free American tobacco and sold it to her citizens in the form of cigarettes, for British money, at something like 75 cents a pack, several times what our domestic smokers then paid. The government then used a good deal of the

13. From an October 10, 1947 statement of Benjamin W. Cohen, Counsellor, Department of State.

money from such sales to nationalize the medical profession. Thus, American taxpayers helped to underwrite socialized medicine in England.

Effects of Monetary Manipulation

Well, the Marshall Plan was passed, and it went into effect on July 1, 1948. During the first half of 1948, the "money supply" had been decreasing. We were having domestic difficulties. Farms and industries previously supported by newly created money were losing customers. So business activity started to slow down. With this new spending program, the "money supply" started moving up again. The commercial banks started buying government securities again, that is, the banks were buying them with their depositors' money or with an expansion based on either their money or the government securities that were bought by increasing the Government's bank accounts. The United States Government was also buying its own securities. All this inflation and government spending helped President Truman and his party win one of the closest elections in American history.

All this spending of newly created money was secretly but steadily taking wealth from one part of the population and giving it to another part. The spending also bought political popularity and thus helped win elections. It was probably the deciding factor in the 1948 election.

By the end of 1949, the effect of the Marshall Plan spending was beginning to wear off. Our politicians had to look elsewhere for a new spending program that would continue the illusion of prosperity promoted by inflation. Business conditions were getting worse. Production was falling while unemployment was rising. The inflated "money supply" was bringing higher prices and a demand from labor unions for higher wages. So, early in 1950, the President asked Congress for price and wage controls. This was the only way he knew to stop rising prices. After considerable public discussion, Congress defeated the proposal in the form of the "Spence Bill." Congress would not endorse price and wage controls during peacetime.

Military Action to the Rescue

Well, if the Congress will not permit price and wage controls during peacetime, what can a President, who does not understand free market economics, do to remedy the situation? He can go to war. So we went into Korea. With unemployment at a post-war high and the "money supply" decreasing even with a discount rate of only 1¼ percent, the President ordered our Army into Korea.

This was not considered an act of war. The President called it a "police action." War was never declared by Congress, but that did not stop the President. For "prosperity," the President needed a spending program the people would accept. He had no power under the Constitution or even under the United Nations Charter to go to war. Nevertheless, in June 1950, we went into Korea.

Table XXVIII shows what happened to our "money supply" after June 1950. It went up again very rapidly. Many people were getting and spending some of the newly created "money supply." Other people were getting less for the dollars they had earned or saved. At the same time our boys were getting maimed and killed on Korean battlefields thousands of miles away from home.

Labor Union Loophole

The President asked for price and wage controls. His proposal was quickly passed by the Congress that summer. However, there was a little loophole in the law to make it palatable to labor unions. While the law placed wage controls on labor, it provided that the controls apply only to current wages. Thus the law permitted employers to increase what we now call "fringe benefits." These are largely retirement benefits. Organized labor could not strike for higher current wages, but union workers could demand and get extra allowances for hospitalization, pensions, and other such benefits that raised the labor costs of business firms. Yet many businesses could not ask for higher selling prices. This is part of the popular anticapitalistic mentality that seeks to soak savers and investors.

While union members could not spend pay raises put into

Table
XXVIII

KOREA AND 1952

Date	Gold Stock	Quantity of Money	U.S. Debt Holdings			Fed. Reserve Discount Rate
			Fed. Res. Banks	Comm'l. Banks	U.S. Gov't.	
End of	*Billions*	*Billions*	*Billions*			*Percentages*
12/49	$ 24.4	$ 147.3	$ 18.9	$ 66.8	$ 39.4	1.5
6/50	24.2	146.9	18.3	65.6	37.8	1.5
12/50	22.7	154.0	20.8	61.8	39.2	1.75
12/51	22.7	162.4	23.8	61.6	46.3	1.75
6/52	23.3	160.5	22.9	61.1	44.3	1.75.
12/52	23.2	169.7	24.7	63.4	45.9	1.75

pension funds, the Government could, because such funds were largely invested in government bonds. Of course, the future value of these bonds would depend on the purchasing power of the dollar at the time the individual workers retired. But most union members were not then aware of the ravages of inflation. So they were happy with this arrangement. With the Korean "police action" pumping up the "money supply" once more, business started up again. Many companies were doing fairly well with increased government orders for a war that was not a war. Of course, in addition to the battlefield casualties, many other people were hurt financially.

By the end of 1951, the "money supply" was up to $162.4 billion. The increased "money supply" built up a pressure on prices that the Government's limited controls could not contain. The effects of Korea and the inflation gradually became apparent to more and more people. As a result, more and more Americans were becoming dissatisfied with the political situation.

The 1952 Election Situation

During the first half of 1952, the dollar supply had begun to contract, since the first stimulating effects of the Korean spending were wearing off. The Administration asked for still higher "defense" expenditures. A Presidential election was in the offing. The Democrats had been in power since 1933. Prices were going up. Social Security benefits were raised again, just before the November election. This added to the pressure on prices and government financing. Taxes were going up.

By this time the American people were a little fed up with the party in power. They did not like the rising prices resulting from the Government's inflation of the "money supply." The Korean incident, on which the inflation was blamed, was no longer popular, if it ever had been. The firing of General MacArthur, a popular hero, had not helped. With growing casualty lists and the limitations placed on our fighting forces, more and more Americans were demanding an end to the Korean "police action."

Although the Administration succeeded in increasing the "money supply" considerably during the last half of 1952, in a last-ditch effort to win the election, it failed, and a new political party, the Republican Party, was brought to power. Many people thought the Republicans would return the nation to our more traditional policies of pre-Roosevelt, pre-New Deal days. This, however, was not to be the case.

"Natural Economic Forces" Repealed

After the election, President Truman, on January 14, 1953, during his last week in office, issued his final annual *Economic Report.* In it he said:

> The Employment Act of 1946 is one of the most fundamental compacts in domestic affairs which the people through their Government have made during my tenure as President. It represents the refusal of Americans in all pursuits – in business, labor, agriculture and Government – to accept recurrent depression as a way of life . . . .
>
> The Act is more than an essay in wishful thinking . . . . It is the purpose of the Employment Act – the one most widely recognized at the time of its passage – to prevent depressions . . . . The Employment Act stands as a pledge on the part of the people voiced through their laws that never again shall any such sacrifice be laid on the altar of "natural economic forces". . . .
>
> Thus . . . the Act rejects the idea that we are the victims of unchangeable economic laws, that we are powerless to do more than forecast what will happen to us under the operation of such laws.
>
> Immediately after the Korean outbreak . . . the work under the Employment Act was fundamental to the program of over-all economic expansion which the Government adopted . . . . Our national output has risen from 285 billion dollars in 1948 (the peak before Korea) to an annual rate in excess of 350 billion dollars at the end of 1952. [14]

President Truman thought this was a remarkable record and that it represented the application of this Employment Act, popularly called the "Full Employment Act." One of the better newspapermen called it the "Fool Employment Act."

---

14. President Truman's *The Economic Report of The President, 1953,* pp. 8, 10, 13 and 17.

The Keynesian Revolution

This "Full Employment Act" was based on the Keynesian principle that when there is large unemployment the best way to reduce wages is to reduce the value of the monetary unit. This is done by increasing the "money supply" – inflation. Acting under the influence of the professed ideas of the late Lord Keynes, our politicians have been doing this ever since. Keynes' theory, as we have mentioned, was written by Keynes in 1935 and published in 1936. It provided an academic justification for the policies which England had followed for years, and which had led to the devaluation of the British pound five years earlier, in 1931. This 1931 *de jure* devaluation was an official recognition of the *de facto* devaluation that had resulted from years of a politically manipulated increase in the "money supply."

At the time of the 1931 devaluation, the British Government changed all its official index numbers. There was no way anyone could compare British prices after the 1931 devaluation with those before that date. The people, including union members, had to wait until a new set of statistics could be developed over a period of years before they, or the statisticians of the British labor unions, could find out what had been happening to prices. In this way, British wage rates were, for a few years, reduced without the workers' knowledge or objection. However, as time passed the union statisticians learned from the new index numbers that prices were rising. Since then, organized labor has demanded higher money wages as the purchasing power of the pound has fallen. Union leaders in the United States have seldom permitted this method of devaluing the purchasing power of the dollar to fool them very long. As a matter of fact, most of our strong unions have pushed up the wages of their working members faster than the value of the dollar has fallen, with the effects mentioned in Lecture IV.

Change in Inflation Theory

In 1953, we had a new President in the United States. We also had a change in the philosophy of those directing financial policy. We could go into more details, but time does not permit. There was a shift away from the philosophy of President Truman and his political party, which held that higher national income and GNP (Gross National Product) dollar figures were signs of prosperity, neglecting for the most part the fact that the purchasing power of the dollar was falling. The new political leaders wanted to reduce the inflation. They wanted to reduce the increases in the "money supply." They did not want the "money supply" to increase so much that it might raise prices. They intended to increase the "money supply" only enough to offset the effects of increased production.

In a free market, as production goes up, prices go down. The leaders of the new Administration wanted production to go up, but they did not want prices to go down. To prevent this, they intended to inflate the "money supply" only enough to prevent a drop in the so-called "price level." The benefits of increased production, which a free market would allocate to consumers, was to be allocated by the Administration as it deemed best for the nation and its chances to remain in office. So when increased investments resulted in increased production, the Administration attempted to increase the "money supply" only to the extent that would maintain what was called a "stable price level."

Inflation Continues — Gold Flight Starts

This effort failed. During the eight years of the Eisenhower Administration, from 1952 through 1960, the consumer price index rose by about 10 percent. Table XXIX shows how much the "money supply" was increased for each of these eight years, rising from $169.7 billion at the end of 1952 to $215.8 billion by the end of 1960. This was an increase of $46.1 billion, or more than 27 percent. While this was a slower rate of growth than under the Truman Administration, it was a great burden on those who had had to earn or save the dollars they spent.

Another item worth noting in Table XXIX is the drop in the gold stocks behind the nation's "money supply." Citizens of other countries were starting to lose some, but not all, of their confidence in the dollar. Although the discount rate

			EISENHOWER ADMINISTRATION, 1953-1960		
				Federal Reserve	
Date	Gold Stock	Quantity of Money	Gold Backing	Discount Rate	U.S. Debt Holdings
	Billions	*Billions*	*Percent*	*Percent*	*Billions*
12/52	$23.2	$169.7	13.7	1.75	$24.7
12/53	22.0	174.2	13.3	2.0	25.9
12/54	21.7	181.2	12.2	1.5	24.9
12/55	21.7	186.6	11.6	2.5	24.8
12/56	21.9	190.3	11.5	3.0	24.9
				8/23* 3.5	
12/57	22.8	194.7	11.7	3.0	24.2
12/58	20.5	207.4	9.9	2.0	26.3
12/59	19.5	210.7	9.2	4.0	26.6
12/60	17.8	215.8	8.2	6/10* 3.5 8/12* 3.0	27.4
Change:	−$5.4	+ 46.1	− 5.5		+ 2.7

*Date effective.

Table XXIX

wavered between 1½ and 4 percent, note that it was reduced twice during the 1960 Presidential election year. That has now become almost a normal procedure. The last column of figures shows the U.S. debt holdings of the United States Government. They went up slightly, about 10 percent, during the eight Eisenhower years.

Reducing the Fractional Reserve

The Eisenhower Administration was less inflationary than the previous Administration. However, the effects of its inflation were felt, even though little understood. One of the main ways the Republicans managed their inflation was a method we have not mentioned since discussing the fractional reserve system in connection with the early days of the Federal Reserve System. The Eisenhower Administration did not launch any new large spending programs.[15] In fact it

15. The only new major spending program, Federal government road building, was financed by taxes imposed on the supposed beneficiaries. PLG.

**Table
XXX**

SOME KEY MONETARY DATA, 1953-1960

| | Reserve Requirements | | | | Gold | Short-Term |
| | *Percentages* | | | | Stock | Foreign Liabilities |
Date	Central Res. Cities	Res. Cities	Country Banks	Time Deposits	*Billions*	*Billions*
End of						
12/52	24	20	14	6	$23.2	$10.5
12/54	20	18	12	5	21.7	12.9
12/56	20	18	12	5	21.9	14.9
12/58	18	16.5	11	5	20.5	16.2
12/60	16.5	16.5	12	5	17.8	21.3
25% Gold reserve	4.125%		3%	1.25%		
$100 of Gold supported:						
1952	$1,667	$2,000	$2,857	$6,667		
1960	2,424	2,424	3,300	8,000		

reduced the expenditures in Korea considerably. The Republicans inflated primarily by reducing the percentage of reserves that banks were required to keep against their deposits. In 1952, before Eisenhower assumed office, commercial banks in the large reserve cities were required to keep 24 percent of their demand deposits, or checking accounts, with the Federal Reserve System. Table XXX shows that this requirement was reduced by the end of the Eisenhower Administration to 16½ percent.

The significance of this is that in 1952 the actual money on hand in the banking system could be expanded, under the fractional reserve system, by roughly four times, whereas by 1960, at the end of the Eisenhower Administration, the actual cash in the reserves could be expanded more than six times. The required reserve for time deposits was also reduced by Federal Reserve regulations from 6 to 5 percent. This permitted quite an expansion of the "money supply" for the Administration to allocate as it approved.

Gold Liabilities to Foreigners

As mentioned previously, the gold stock had gone down by $5.4 billion. Table XXX includes a new column, not previously presented in these lectures — short-term foreign liabilities. These are the obligations of American banks to foreigners that are payable either on demand or within periods of less than a year. The amount of such liabilities more than doubled during Eisenhower's Administration. They rose from $10.5 billion at the end of 1952 to $21.3 billion before Eisenhower left office. These short-term foreign liabilities represented a potential demand on the gold stock of our banking system. The foreign owners of these claims could legally turn them into gold by operating through their country's central bank. Although Americans are not allowed to own monetary gold, a serious violation of free market principles, foreigners holding such liabilities could demand gold from our Federal Reserve System whenever their government or its central bank permitted them to do so.

In 1952, the gold stock of our banking system totalled $23.2 billion. This provided more than 200 percent coverage for the $10.5 billion of foreign short-term liabilities. But by the time Eisenhower left office, the gold stock was actually less than the short-term claim that foreigners could have presented for redemption in gold. This represented a serious deterioration in the monetary situation.

All of the $46 billion increase in the "money supply" during Eisenhower's eight years was an artificial increase. The gold stock went down, not up. This inflation was helping some people and hurting others. It was affecting business, re-directing it in a way that was difficult to maintain without still more inflation at an ever-growing rate. *It was not free enterprise.*

Prosperity by Spending Newly Created Money

After Eisenhower, we had still another political Administration — an Administration that hoped to go far and do spectacular things, with a very young and attractive President, John F. Kennedy, the first President born in this century. It was a Democratic Administration. After Kennedy's assassination in 1963, Lyndon B. Johnson, from Texas, became President.

The top line of figures in Table XXXI shows the averages under the Eisenhower Administration for the annual increases in the "money supply," the annual losses of gold, and the annual increases in short-term liabilities to foreigners. The figures for 1961-1968, the Kennedy and Johnson Administration years, follow.

During the first year of the new Democratic Administration, we were told that prosperity was back to stay. Actually, on the surface, large corporations and their employees seemed to be enjoying prosperous times. In 1961, the "money supply" was increased by $16.9 billion. The following year, 1962, it took an increase that was larger by an additional billion, or $17.9 billion, to keep this apparent "prosperity" going. This was money artificially created by a Government-dominated banking system and spent in the market by persons who obtained it through special privileges. The new funds were first allocated to certain people, as directed by Governmental policies. When they spent the new money they reduced the purchasing power of all other people, who faced higher prices and thus a lower return for the dollars they had earned or saved. The next year, 1963, the increase in the quantity of money was $18.3 billion, or nearly a half billion greater than in 1962.

Now we come to 1964, a crucial Presidential election year. During this particular election year, the Administration, with

YEARLY CHANGES, 1961-1968			
(In billions of dollars)			
Year	Quantity of Money [1]	Gold Stock	Short-term Foreign Liabilities
1953-60 [2]	+ $5.8	− $.7	+ $1.35
1961	+ 16.9	− .9	+ 1.2
1962	+ 17.9	− .9	+ 2.5
1963	+ 18.3	− .45	+ .95
1964	+ 24.7	− .125	+ 2.9
1965	+ 28.1	− 1.7	+ 1.5
1966	+ 15.2	− .5	+ 2.0
1967	+ 36.6	− 1.2	+ 3.0
1968	+ 36.7	− 1.6	+ .3

Table XXXI

1. Includes (1) currency outside of banks; (2) demand deposits; and (3) time deposits of commercial banks.
2. Average under Eisenhower Administrations.

the help of the Federal Reserve System, increased the "money supply" by $24.7 billion. That quantity of money could be used to buy a lot of votes. That, of course, is what most welfare state programs are − vote-buying programs. In any case, President Johnson won an overwhelming victory at the polls.

The following year, 1965, the Administration's fiscal and monetary policies resulted in adding $28.1 billion to the "money supply." This, of course, kept many things humming. We were constantly reading in the newspapers about how each month set an ever-increasing record for continuous "prosperity" under the new Democratic Administration. This newly created money was all being pumped out in special privileges, helping some people at the expense of others. The politicians were appropriating and distributing more than the increase in production, because prices were actually rising, although only slowly during these first five years. The last column of Table XXXI shows, as you can see, that a significant portion of the increase in the "money supply" was going into short-term liabilities owned abroad, where much of it, combined with the gold outflow, was being used as a reserve for the inflation of foreign currencies.

Results Not All Desirable

We had a reaction in 1966. The Administration got scared. Prices were going up faster than the 2 percent those in office considered acceptable. So they cut back the increases in the "money supply." They said they were going to stop inflation, by which they meant higher prices. So they increased the "money supply" less in 1966 than in any of their previous years. That year they increased the "money supply" by only $15.2 billion. This great decrease in the increase created a serious reaction in the country. The Administration's favored people were getting less new money than previously. Hence they were no longer able to spend as much as they had been spending. This led to a slight recession that threatened to get worse. The reaction was actually a movement toward a free market adjustment or correction.

A recession occurs whenever free market forces are permitted to reassert themselves and correct the malproduction brought about by the inflation. The market forces, described in Lecture III, then redirect the economy away from producing so much for the spenders of newly created money and toward producing more for those spending money they have earned or saved. The recession is merely this readjustment period. It can be short or long, depending on how quickly prices, wage rates, and interest rates are able to shift so that they reflect the wishes of consumers.

The Administration did not feel it could politically withstand the rigors of such a free market correction. It would have required politically unpopular higher interest rates, and lower wage rates for many labor union members. So the Administration again resorted to inflation, increasing the "money supply" by almost $37 billion in 1967. In 1968, the Administration inflated the "money supply" at an even faster rate during the first part of the year. However, towards the end of the year, with prices starting to leap upward, the Administration got nervous and cut down the rate of increase in the "money supply." As a result, the total increase for the full year of 1968 was just about the same as in 1967, which was more than twice that in 1966.

Moving on to another phase of the Administration's monetary activities, Table XXXII reveals a drop of $7.4 billion in the gold stock during the eight years of the Kennedy-Johnson Administrations. By the end of 1968, the "money supply" had been increased by $194 billion, rising from $215 billion to $410 billion. The gold stock reserve had dropped from 8.2 percent of the "money supply" in 1952 to only 2½ percent by the end of 1968. Of course, the discount

DEMOCRATIC ADMINISTRATIONS, 1961-1968					
				Federal Reserve	
Date	Gold Stock	Quantity of Money	Gold Backing	Discount Rate	U.S. Debt Holdings
	Billions	*Billions*	*Percent*	*Percent*	*Billions*
12/60	$17.8	$215.8	8.2	3.0	$27.4
——— Kennedy ———					
12/61	16.9	232.7			28.9
12/62	16.0	250.6			30.8
12/63	15.6	268.9		3.5	33.6
——— Johnson ———					
12/64	15.4	293.6		4.0	37.0
12/65	13.7	321.7	4.3	4.5	40.8
12/66	13.2	336.9	4.0 –	4.5	44.3
12/67	12.0	373.5	3.0	4.5	49.1
12/68	10.4	410.1	2.5+	5.5	52.9
Change:	−7.4	+ 194.3	− 5.7	+ 2.5	+ 25.5

Table XXXII

rate was kept low in comparison with market interest rates, permitting the expansion to go on almost as rapidly as the Administration desired. The Federal Reserve holdings of the United States Government debt almost doubled under the Kennedy-Johnson Administrations, rising from $27 billion to $53 billion. This meant bank depositors' funds were being used to support the Government's deficit spending.

Who Buys Government Bonds

The problem of financing the Government's debt is becoming a more and more serious question in the United States. It is a problem that is rapidly coming to a head. Table XXXIII presents four columns of figures. The first shows the ownership of the United States Government's debt on December 31, 1960, at the end of Eisenhower's Administra-

Table XXXIII

			OWNERSHIP OF U.S. GOVERNMENT DEBT, 1953-1968 *In Billions*	
			8-yr. Change under	
			Eisenhower	Democrats
Owner	12/60	12/68	1953-1960	1961-1968
U.S. Government	55.1	76.6	+ 9.2	+ 21.5
State & Local	18.7	24.4	+ 7.6	+ 5.7
Total Governments	73.8	101.0	+ 16.8	+ 27.2
Fed. Reserve Banks	27.4	52.9	+ 2.7	+ 25.5
Commercial Banks	62.1	66.0	− 1.3	+ 3.9
Total Bks. & Gov'ts.	163.3	219.9	+ 18.1	+ 56.6
Savings Banks	6.3	3.6	− 3.2	− 2.7
Insurance Companies	11.9	8.0	− 4.1	− 3.9
Other Corporations	18.7	14.2	− 1.2	− 4.5
Individuals	66.1	75.8	+ .9	+ 9.7
Foreign	13.0	14.3 }	+ 12.5	+ 1.3
Miscellaneous*	11.2	22.4 }		+ 11.2
Total	$290.4	$ 358.0	+$23.0	+$67.6

* Savings & Loan, Foundations, Pension Funds, Brokers and Dealers.

tion. The second column shows the ownership of the United States Government's debt on December 31, 1968, after eight years of the Kennedy-Johnson Administrations. The third column shows the net changes during the eight Eisenhower years, while the fourth and last column shows the net changes in the eight Democratic years.

During the eight Eisenhower years, the debt rose by $23 billion. Of that total, the Government itself took more than $9 billion of its own bonds. In short, the Government was "borrowing" this amount from moneys collected and held in trust for future pension and Social Security payments. State and local governments had special funds that took $7.6 billion of the increase. So that all governments took almost $17 billion of the $23 billion increase in the Federal Government's debt. If you add to that the $2.9 billion the Federal Reserve Banks bought, the total comes pretty close to $20 billion out of the $23 billion total.

The commercial banks were actually selling off government securities during this period, because the interest rate paid on governments was not as attractive as those they could get from commercial loans. The same was true for savings banks, insurance companies, and "other corporations." Individuals actually took less than $1 billion of the $23 billion increase. Foreigners and such miscellaneous buyers as savings and loan associations, foundations, private pension funds, brokers, and dealers, altogether, took more than half of the total increase.

Looking at the eight years of the Democratic Administrations, we find the total increase in the Federal Government's debt came to $67.6 billion – almost three times that of the Eisenhower eight years. Of this total, our Federal, state, and local governments had taken close to $30 billion. That is almost half of the total. The Federal Reserve Banks took another $25.5 billion, while the commercial banks were again using depositors' funds to add to their holdings of government securities. Thus, during these eight years of inflation, the various American governments and our politically regulated banks took $58.6 billion of the $67.6 billion increase in the Federal Government's debt.

Supporting the Bond Market

In short, private buyers were not willing to lend their money to the Government on the terms offered. So the Treasury was forced to unload its debt in large measure on purchasers who did not represent private market forces. The Government, to a considerable extent, had to create a market for its own bonds and force the Federal Reserve and its member banks to make large parts of depositors' funds available for government spending. The savings banks sold off more government securities than they bought, even though their deposits were increasing. Both insurance companies and "other corporations" also reduced their holdings of government securities.

Our Treasury was able to persuade individuals to buy only $9 billion of the $67.6 billion total. A large part of this was due to a campaign directed at large corporations, particularly those with government contracts, requesting them to pressure their employees to permit sums to be deducted from their paychecks for the purchase of these bonds. Government employees were also pressured to buy these bonds on the payroll deduction plan. The pressure at one time became so great that it produced a kick-back against the high-handed tactics used. There has been a falling off in such purchases recently, as the interest rate on the small denomination bonds has been below what can be obtained from savings banks. The increase in the government securities held abroad was only $1.8 billion.

What will happen to future increases in the Government's debts? No one knows. In leaving office, President Johnson predicted a balanced budget for Mr. Nixon and left him the task of balancing it. So far, it is not in balance.

The columns in Table XXXIV show the yearly changes in the holding of the Federal Government's debt by (a) the United States Government, (b) the Federal Reserve Banks, (c) the commercial banks, and (d) the total for all three of these sources, as compared with (e) the annual increases in the total debt. In 1967, these three sources, the Federal Government and the two groups of "fractional reserve" banks took more than the total increase in the debt. That meant, in effect, that other holders were dumping some of their previous holdings. This situation improved somewhat in 1968, when these three sources took only $8.8 billion out of a total of a little more than $13 billion. This is still a large part of the total. It essentially represents government spending over and beyond what taxpayers and the financial markets will support.

Cal. Year	U.S. Gov't.	Fed. Res. Banks	Comm'l. Banks	All 3	Total Debt
1961	− $ .6	+ $1.5	+ $5.1	+ $6.0	+ $6.1
1962	+ 1.1	+ 1.9	.0	+ 3.0	+ 7.5
1963	+ 2.4	+ 2.8	− 2.9	+ 2.3·	+ 6.1
1964	+ 2.6	+ 3.4	− .3	+ 5.7	+ 8.6
1965	+ 1.3	+ 3.8	− 3.2	+ 1.9	+ 2.7
1966	+ 6.9	+ 3.5	− 3.3	+ 7.1	+ 8.4
1967	+ 7.2	+ 4.8	+ 5.5	+ 17.5	+ 15.4
1968	+ 3.3	+ 3.8	+ 1.7	+ 8.8	+ 13.3

U.S. GOVERNMENT DEBT YEARLY CHANGES

Part Held By

In Billions

$5.1

$10.4

Table XXXIV

So the Treasury's problem of placing the debt is an increasing one in the United States. Whether or not the debt increases, there remains the serious problem of persuading the public to keep their funds in the government securities they now hold. These securities pay very low rates of interest. These low rates are not high enough to attract private savings at a time when the dollar is losing 5 or 6 percent of its purchasing power each year.

Another part of the problem is that most of the United States Government's debt is in very short-term paper. Congress has put a restriction on the rate of interest the Treasury can pay on long-term bonds. Since that limit is no longer realistic, a large part of the Government's debt today is in short-term issues that must be constantly refinanced. The small savings bonds held by individuals can be redeemed at any time after they have been outstanding six months.

Consequently, close to half of the Government's debt could become due and payable in less than a year's time.

More Money Not a Permanent Solution

In closing, I want to repeat the main thesis of this series of lectures. The recurring economic crises that we have been experiencing are nothing but the consequences of political attempts to stimulate economic activity by means of inflation and credit expansion — despite the warnings of economists. To paraphrase a quotation from Mises' book on money, a passage he wrote in 1934:

> Despite all the teachings of experience and all the warnings of economists, many still think that economic activity can be permanently stimulated by an artificial increase in the supply of money or credit. Most of our economic crises are merely the inevitable result of such politically directed attempts.[16]

In a market economy, a social order entirely founded on the use of money, in which all the accounting is done in terms of the monetary unit, the destruction of the monetary system means nothing less than the destruction of the basis of all exchange. How long could you exist without exchange?

The Economic Solution — *Laissez Faire*

Our modern high standard of living is based on the market system of voluntary social cooperation for the expected mutual benefit of all participants. The unhampered market system is a development of the Golden Rule that leads to a high degree of the division of labor and the investment of accumulated private savings in highly complicated production facilities. This capitalistic system provides workers with expensive, efficient equipment for the mass production of myriads of goods and services, which must be constantly moved to millions of consumers. This can be done satisfactorily only by the mutually profitable exchanges of the market place. Such exchanges require the use of a sound money in which the market participants have considerable

16. Ludwig von Mises, *The Theory of Money And Credit* (Yale, 1953), p. 21.

confidence. Without such a sound money, the market system and the civilization it has built must collapse.

How long could you and your family exist on what you can produce? Not long. We are all dependent on each other. Without a market system of exchanges, millions will be doomed to the poverty, disease, starvation, and short lives of pre-capitalistic times. If we are to prevent such a catastrophe, we must stop inflation, that is, large increases in the quantity of money that eventually undermine public confidence in the monetary unit – the very keystone of the market system.

Illusions Cannot Last

Now we face great difficulties in solving this monetary problem. We have a two-price gold system. There are people in high political positions who think they can create "paper gold" with the value of gold. Possibly they believe politicians can also create glass diamonds if they want to. John Law tried something similar with his "Mississippi bubble." His bubble collapsed. So will our present monetary programs. They are based on actions which are contrary to purpose. They do not properly or intelligently make use of the unalterable principles of human action, as outlined in the first three lectures.

Political Solutions

As a human being, I cannot know the future. No one can. But it would be my judgment, certainly not speaking as an economist or as a scientist, but rather as a pretty well-informed person, that there is a huge possibility that the United States may try to solve the problems resulting from inflation by going to war again. This is what many political leaders of the past have done. When those in high political positions are faced with difficult domestic economic conditions they cannot solve, they tend to look abroad for some foreign devil. They then blame their domestic troubles or their need for higher taxes or more controls on the policies of some foreign power. This is what Hitler did. This is what many political leaders have done in the past, even in my country.

Eventually such policies must lead to war. Politicians in difficulty seldom admit their own errors. It is easier to blame their problems on foreigners. Today our leaders believe the American people will accept wage and price controls in wartime. So if they feel controls are necessary, they may well go to war.

If the United States should go to war in the near future, it would, of course, turn the country into a totalitarian society. Price, wage, and production controls of the type Hitler attempted would undoubtedly be enacted. In such a situation, the market would soon be in shackles. The present population could not then be supported at anywhere near its present standard of living. During peacetime, the people in my country would not peacefully accept a lower standard of living. During a war they might. But freedom would be dead and high living standards would be history.

If there is no war, a continuation of present interventionist policies, financed by inflation, will sooner or later lead to a breakdown in both the domestic and international monetary systems. This would greatly reduce both domestic and international trade. It would mean a great reduction in the division of labor and mass production for mass consumption. Economic conditions would deteriorate to the point at which it would be impossible to support the present population of the United States with anything like our present standard of living.

Present-Day Trends

Without the acceptance and adoption of free market principles, the outlook for western civilization is dark. Special subsidies and political privileges are now the order of the day. The poor, the sick, the young, the colleges, their students, the farmers, the small businessmen, the large corporations, the unemployed, the union members, government employees, the senior citizens, and every minority group, including those who want to go to Mars, want their "fair share" of government spending and special privileges. None are satisfied with what they now get, and everyone knows taxes are too high.

We have already experienced riots on city streets and college campuses. Such violence and disrespect for law and private property may well be a forerunner of what is to come. When people see no peaceful way out of their difficulties, they do not lie down and starve quietly. Unfortunately, the persons who are likely to suffer most are those in the lower income brackets. They are usually the most ignorant and the least capable of adjusting to new and less favorable conditions, so they are the ones most likely to resort to force, violence, and the destruction of private property.

The only satisfactory solution to the present economic and monetary problems is a rebirth of the free market ideology. This is always a possibility. Trends can and do change. They change more quickly and frequently than we think.

Let me cite two examples in my country. President Hoover went into office in 1928 as one of the most popular Presidents we had ever had. Four years later, after the depression had started with the stock market crash, he went out of office the most unpopular man in the land. During World War II, our political leaders did everything they could to help our "peace-loving ally," the Soviet Union, through Lend-Lease and other programs, including favorable propaganda for their way of life. Yet after President Truman met the Russians at Potsdam in July 1945, American public opinion very quickly turned against the Soviet Union. So trends can and do change, and quickly.

At present, however, there is very little indication of any trend toward free market principles. In the United States all the media of mass communication and education are manned by persons with a statist ideology. They see the answer to every social problem, and I mean *every* social problem, in still larger government expenditures and, of course, no higher taxes. They thus furnish the fuel for further inflation.

Free Enterprise Has Never Failed

The popular opinion makers consider free market ideas simplistic, old-fashioned, and doomed to fail, because, in their minds, the free market failed in 1929. This is why it is so important for people to realize that *it was political manipulation of the quantity of money, not free enterprise, that failed in 1929.*

QUESTIONS AND ANSWERS

Setting Up a Gold Standard

Q. What are the steps that you would advocate to have the banking system go back to 100 percent gold reserve?

A. First, it would not be going *back*, because we have never really had such a system in modern times. Second, the problem is primarily one of education. We could very easily move toward a free economy if we had a sufficient popular understanding and acceptance of the free market ideology. The need is for an educational program. You cannot impose an ideology by force. You cannot just pass laws that the people do not understand and do not accept. For example, in my country and, I understand, in this country, the government insures bank deposits against losses. So long as such programs exist, people do not consider or question banking policies. They act as though their deposits are safe and do not watch them or question what their bank does with them. In a free market society, you would not put your money in a bank unless you trusted that bank. You would watch the bank's operations very carefully. So the chances of establishing a gold standard depend largely on education. The mechanics would be simple, but the education is not.

Why Central Banks

Q. Should the central banks exist?

A. In general, the short answer is that they serve very little useful purpose. There could be some kind of an association of banks on a private basis to take care of exchange operations and check-clearing costs within a country. This is the one useful service that central banks now provide. In most countries a check from one part of the country can be cashed for the full amount in any part of the country. You do not have to pay any collection costs, as was the case in the United States before the formation of the Federal Reserve System. These costs, small for each check, could involve considerable bookkeeping, if you had to figure the collection cost for each individual out-of-town check, such as a New York check cashed or deposited in San Francisco. However, the main purpose of most modern central banks is to provide a centralization of cash reserves for the greater expansion of credit. Their sponsors believe such a centralization makes it safe to operate with a lower fractional reserve. This, in their opinion, is a more efficient use of the available "money supply." Of course, central banks also serve as a convenient device for financing a government's debt at lower than free market interest rates. Incidentally, our Federal Reserve Banks once a year return to the Treasury a good part of the interest they receive on the government securities they hold.

Gold and the Depression

Q. How did the 1929 depression take place if you had the gold standard? Or did you really have the gold standard?

A. Well, we did not have a sound 100 percent gold standard. Basically, this was the problem. We had a system which permitted, in fact encouraged, the credit expansion that we discussed in some detail in last night's lecture. This inflated the "money supply," making it impossible for the banking system to maintain specie payments at all times. Then, when the crash came the system had to contract. This crash was really precipitated by a movement back toward a gold standard. The demand of depositors for gold helped to touch off the depression and limit any further expansion at that time. Today, in my country, there is no such limitation on the expansion. There does not legally have to be any gold behind any dollar issued by either the United States Government or the Federal Reserve System. The Federal Reserve System is now free to print as many dollars as its Board wants to. This was not true before. Up until 1968, there was a legal limit on the credit expansion possible in the United States. However, in 1929, when the credit expansion reached the psychological breaking point, the Federal Reserve had to stop it and go into reverse with a credit deflation.

On Velocity of Circulation

Q. Does the velocity of the circulation of money have something to do with inflation?

A. Not directly, no. If anything, it is the other way around. An awareness of inflation encourages people to reduce their cash holdings. This means many will then spend their money faster than they would if they were not aware of the inflation.

On a Dollar Crisis

Q. What would happen if the dollar went into a crisis?

A. Of course, I do not know. However, as I mentioned earlier, in my opinion, there is a good chance that if those in political power saw this coming, they would involve us in a war. In any case, given the present ideology, they would ask for controls. Since a controlled economy is not as productive as a free economy, serious economic difficulties would soon reduce production and living standards as mentioned a few minutes ago.

Effect of Hoarding Money

Q. If people keep money out of circulation, is that a cause or an effect of the depression?

A. It has nothing to do with the depression. People save in the form of money when they think the value, or purchasing power, of the monetary unit is going to go up. The more money people hold out of circulation, including out of banks, the more prices will tend to be lower than they otherwise would have been. Thus such withholding may reduce or offset the effects of an increase in the "money supply." But when people become aware of an inflation, and expect prices to rise, they are not likely to hold on to more money than is needed for expected cash transactions. If they *do* increase their cash holdings during an inflation, this permits an equal amount of inflation to continue unnoticed. However, such increases in cash holdings tend to build up when a deflation seems inevitable. During a depression period, when many people believe prices will go still lower, there is a tendency for such people to increase their cash holdings.

The IMF

Q. What is your opinion of the International Monetary Fund?

A. Well, the IMF is less useful than a fifth wheel on an automobile. It is no real help at all. It is an international attempt to maintain inflation on a basis whereby a number of countries try to bail each other out when market forces reveal their financial difficulties. During the early part of 1945, I spent considerable time analyzing the Bretton Woods Agreement and preparing testimony against it. I know no reason to change my opinion of 24 years ago. The IMF provides nice trips and expense accounts for some gentlemen. But so far, all it has really accomplished is to make it easier for inflation to continue unchecked on a worldwide basis. This will make the inevitable readjustment problems all the greater.

The Fractional Reserve System

Q. Would you please explain the fractional reserve system?

A. Supposing you put $100 cash in a bank that belonged to a banking system operating with 20 percent reserve. If your bank deposited this $100 cash with the central bank, then the bank in which you deposited your $100 would be allowed to have liabilities up to $500. In addition to the $100 account against which you can draw checks, it can also lend out up to $400 to others in the form of bank accounts. It would hold, as assets against these loans, the promissory notes of the people who borrowed the $400. In this way, the bank can increase the $100 cash to $500 of bank accounts. The bank's books would balance at $500 with assets of $100 cash plus notes for $400 and liabilities of $100 to the original depositor and $400 in the accounts of the borrowers.

A fractional reserve system develops very slowly over a long period of time. Banks get to rely on people using checks and rarely withdrawing cash from the banking system. Under this system, the title to cash is merely transferred from one bank depositor to another on the bank's books, or from the books of one bank to the books of another bank. As long as this continues, the banks do not need cash. In my country today this expansion could happen as quickly as I have described it only if someone brought gold into the bank and the gold was immediately deposited, as required by law, as part of that bank's reserve with its Federal Reserve Bank.

Quantity Theory of Money

Q. What do you think of the quantity theory of money?

A. I subscribe to the Mises theory, which is a form of the Quantity Theory. However, it is not the Simple Quantity Theory. The Mises theory holds that any increase in the quantity of monetary units tends to reduce the purchasing power of each unit. Likewise any decrease in the supply of monetary units tends to increase the purchasing power of each unit. However, in the Mises theory there is no proportional relationship. The immediate change in the monetary unit's purchasing power depends on the individual actions of the market participants, how they spend it and how they change their cash holdings. If the quantity of money is increased 5 percent and production remains unchanged – that is, if you could freeze production, which you cannot – all prices would not go up by 5 percent. How much they would go up, no one can tell.

Economics is not a science of measurement. It is a science of human tendencies, of what human beings tend to do under given situations, of how they tend to act to improve their situations. If the "money supply" increases, there is a tendency for prices to be higher than they would have been if the "money supply" had not been increased. Any person who has more money tends to spend more, and in so doing he drives prices higher than they would otherwise have been. Of course, if production increases considerably, a small increase in the "money supply" may not result in higher prices, but prices will be higher than they would have been if the "money supply" had not been increased.

In this connection, the increase in the "money supply" in my country in recent years has not had anywhere near a corresponding effect on prices, because (1) production has increased enormously. Our people have continued to save and invest in expanding business operations. Consequently most Americans have not fully realized how much of the value of the additional production has been politically confiscated and redistributed. And (2) large quantities of the increased "money supply" have been either transferred to foreign ownership or actually exported to other countries. Such funds have either been hoarded or used as a fractional reserve for the inflation of foreign currencies. One of the things to which Mr. Rueff[17] so wisely objects is the so-called gold exchange standard, whereby foreign central banks consider every dollar in their reserves as the equivalent of 1/35th of an ounce of gold. So under the fractional reserve system, each dollar they hold permits them to increase their credit expansion to the extent permitted by their laws.

---

17. M. Jacques Rueff, eminent French statesman and economist, who played a major role in re-establishing the French franc after the inflations of both World Wars; author of *The Age of Inflation, The Monetary Law of the West,* and others.

On Wage Rates and Inflation

Q. In order to reduce inflation, is it necessary to have flexibility in wages, that is, a free market for labor?

A. No, but there is no doubt that such flexibility would help reduce one of the pressures for inflation. One of the great modern problems that I have tried to make clear in these lectures is the fact when organized labor is able to ask for, and get, higher than free market wages, it displaces labor. It leads to either more unemployment or more misemployment of available labor. When the result is more unemployment, this creates, under present-day ideologies, a demand for governmental action that politicians now meet by a "full employment" policy, which, according to the Keynes formula, is to increase the "money supply." This lowers the prevailing real wage and permits more people to be hired at the wage rate they have demanded. People are unemployed for only one reason – they will not take a job at wages that consumers will pay (through their purchases) for their contributions to society. The Government tries to meet this situation by lowering the value of the monetary unit. Then union members can be paid the money wage rates they demand, but the increased "money supply" tends to reduce the purchasing power of each monetary unit and thus results in a lower real wage than the higher wage rate would have represented before this inflation. In short, the higher money wages no longer provide workers the standard of living that they would have provided had there been no inflation of the "money supply."

Mises: The Monetary Theorist

Q. Is the original explanation of the monetary theory of the trade cycle from Mises or from Hayek?

A. It is from Mises, and Mises alone. This is one of the many great contributions that Mises has made. He extended the subjective theory, the marginal theory of value, to the monetary field; carrying it to its highest stage. Hayek was Mises' assistant for many years in Austria. Then Hayek went to the London School of Economics. His book, published while he was in England, was the first one on this monetary theory to appear in English. So the first presentation of the Mises theory in English was by Hayek. Unfortunately the Hayek presentation had some errors in it. This was undoubtedly one reason why the theory has not been received as well as it deserves to be, or even as well as it has been received in German-speaking countries.[18]

On SDRs

Q. What is the SDR?

A. Well, it is actually a bookkeeping entry by which the International Monetary Fund seeks to allocate a certain bookkeeping item. The SDR stands for "Special Drawing Right." Supposedly it will have a value tied to gold. It is something that will exist only on the books of the central banks and the International Monetary Fund. No individual person, customer, or commercial bank will get an SDR or ever see one. It is just something that will appear as a bookkeeping entry on the books of central banks according to the distribution set up and approved by the IMF. The central banks are expected to transfer SDRs as a means of settling balances with each other. There is likely to be great friction over their allotment. However, no one can foresee the future. How they will work remains largely a psychological question. Most people today, particularly in my country where we have not been allowed to own monetary gold since 1933, do not see or understand the significance of gold. Most people do not realize there is an inflation problem

---

18. The first German edition of Mises' *The Theory of Money and Credit* appeared in 1912; second German edition, 1924; first English edition, 1934; first Spanish edition, 1936; and first Japanese edition, 1949. Mises' *Geldwertstabilisierung und Konjunkturpolitik,* which dealt specifically with "monetary stabilization and cyclical policy," was published in 1928; Italian translation, 1935. Hayek's *Monetary Theory and the Trade Cycle,* an expansion of a September 1928 paper, first appeared in German in 1929; English edition, 1933.

until they are faced with higher prices. So the SDRs, a fictitious money, *may*, like the fictitious new clothes of Hans Christian Anderson's emperor, go undetected for a while.

Relationship of Fractional Reserve and Deficit Spending

Q. Do you think that the fractional reserve banking system is more dangerous than deficit spending or inflation?

A. Deficit spending would not be a serious problem if it were not for the fractional reserve credit expansion system. The governments would then have to finance their deficits by selling their securities to private investors in the open market at market rates of interest, unreduced by any special discount rates of their central banks. This means they would have to sell their securities on terms that people would voluntarily buy. Under today's conditions, that interest rate would be much higher than governments are now paying. How high it would be, I do not know. Of course, if you had free market conditions, there would be no politically manipulated inflation. Consequently, there would be no need to include the expected inflation factor in the market interest rate.

You cannot compare the difficulties of the fractional reserve system with those of deficit spending, because deficit spending creates a difficult economic situation only when it is financed through a credit expansion made possible by the fractional reserve system. If there were no fractional reserve system, there would be no credit expansion and the market would handle government deficits satisfactorily. There *are* cases where deficit spending may be helpful to a nation. If a country is attacked, it needs to increase its military expenditures immediately. It cannot raise the necessary funds by taxation immediately. So it must then resort to the loan market for the needed funds. If it sells securities in the market, paying market interest rates, and then raises taxes as soon as possible to balance the budget and pay off the debt, the nation's freedom might be saved by such temporary deficit financing. Of course, if the nation's citizens were patriotic and considered the war a just one for the defense of their freedom, they would be glad to help their country in its time of need in any way they could. This would include buying its securities bearing low interest rates, and paying taxes to retire the debt as soon as possible.

Ignorance of Significance of Fractional Reserve System

Q. Do people realize what is happening under the fractional reserve system?

A. Unfortunately, few do. The dangers are not generally taught or understood. As we tried to show in Lecture VI, this is a sort of semi-hidden technique that developed slowly within the banking profession over a period of 250 years or more. The reserve fraction dropped so slowly that most people were not aware of what was happening. At one time, a 90 percent reserve was considered sufficient to be safe from runs. Years later, 80 percent was considered safe. Then it was 70 percent, and so on down, until now, with reserves almost completely centralized and available to all member banks in need, the legal reserve for demand deposits in large city banks is down to 16½ percent in the United States. The people have not been aware of the significance of what was happening. It is somewhat like the question of the significance of gold in my country. The longer people are prohibited from owning monetary gold, the fewer people there are likely to be who understand the importance of the right of people to redeem their paper money in gold. There are millions of people alive today who have never held gold certificates or seen gold money outside of a museum. Such people have little realization of gold's important monetary role. The longer this goes on, the fewer people there will be who understand the principles involved. The fractional reserve system has now been accepted for a century or more, without a moment's thought, by 99.99 percent of the people. That does not make it right or helpful.

Deficit Spending

Q. Is selling bonds deficit spending?

A. Yes, unless the Treasury is just issuing new bonds to replace outstanding bonds coming due. Such a refinancing does not increase the debt. Deficit spending results in an increase in the amount of outstanding government securities. Of course, as mentioned earlier, so much of the United States Government debt is short-term that the Treasury is refinancing a part of it every week. Only that part which represents an increase in the total debt outstanding constitutes deficit spending.

The Gist of Marxism

Q. What would you say is the essence of the Marxian theory?

A. Well, we could have another series of lectures on that. The essence of Marxian theory, of course, is ignorance of the principles of human action and the erroneous belief that in a free market society the rich necessarily get richer while the poor become poorer. Marxists thus believe there is no hope of improving conditions for working people in a free market society. They seek the salvation of the poor in socialism. They then claim that socialism is bound to come eventually and demand it now.

Parallel Inflation

Q. How is it that we can keep the peso at 350 to the dollar while we still have a fractional reserve banking system and deficit spending?

A. Please remember that the dollar is depreciating too. While I am not equipped to speak about the Argentine monetary problem, let me say that the inflation in the United States is pushing up the dollar prices of consumers' goods now at an annual rate of close to 7 percent. That means that the purchasing power of the dollar is going down by about 7 percent a year. Under the purchasing power parity theory, this also means that when the ratio of pesos to the dollar remains unchanged, the purchasing power of 350 pesos is going down by about 7 percent too. So the drop in the value of the peso is hidden from you by the drop in the value of the dollar. This is one thing the international monetary people are attempting to do — have every nation inflate its currency evenly. Then they hope people will say: "Look, we have no inflation! There is no deterioration in foreign exchange rates when 350 pesos will still buy a U.S. dollar!" However, remember the value of the dollar is going down.

Methodology

Q. As neither austerity nor deflation is a solution for an inflation-ridden country, what principal measures would you apply if you were in charge, with full powers?

A. I would have to follow the teachings of my great teacher, Ludwig von Mises, and resign. No one man can control or change these things by himself. Changes can only be made with the approval and acceptance of the majority of the actively interested people. Many people are apathetic. They neither endorse nor oppose changes until they believe they are affected. However, to make changes you have to have the backing of the majority of the people who concern themselves with the matters under consideration. Therefore, I consider the most valuable contribution I can make is to become a teacher and do what I can to give more people a better understanding of free market economics. The politicians in power will always do what they think the majority of concerned people want. In fact, our last President in the United States, President Johnson, was a good example of this. He operated almost entirely with the help of public opinion polls. He first found out where the public stood on an issue. Then he took steps, as he saw fit, either to change their opinions or follow their wishes. The problem is one of changing public opinion, and obtaining the acceptance of sound economic ideas. This is the task of an educator, not of a dictator. A dictator is strong only so long as he is popular. Once he loses his popularity, he soon loses his power and sometimes his head, if he does not go into exile.

Program for Argentina

Q. I imagine you have collected much information about Argentina's inflation during your stay in this country. According to this information, what steps should be taken to control this inflation?

A. My answer must be to follow the general policies outlined in these lectures. The first step is always to stop increasing the quantity of money artificially. This is a very simple statement to make, but it is an extremely difficult thing for those in power to do. Let us remember that politicians are human beings. They are in the same position as all other human beings. They are trying to improve their respective situations, each from his own point of view. The politician's point of view is that he can best improve his personal situation by winning the next election or staying in power. Today, this means he must advocate spending programs and oppose unpopular taxes, while asking the Treasury to provide the needed sums. This means inflation. Your problem in Argentina, like ours in the United States, is to promulgate sound free market ideas – promote sound economic education.

On Need for More Bank Reserves

Q. What do you think of the statement frequently made that the present level of international reserves is insufficient to finance an increase in international trade?

A. People who say such things could not have graduated from the high school I attended back in 1919-1923. We were then taught that you do not need any more money to increase trade. If market participants are left free to adjust prices, all trades that benefit both parties will be made. In international trade, the payment for exports is imports. If they both increase equally, you would not even need any change in prices. Only the balance needs to be settled in cash. If the balance remains the same, the same amount of money will settle the balance. For example, if you increase your exports by a billion dollars and increase your imports by a billion dollars, the balance that needs to be settled remains the same.

The important thing to remember is that prices do not have to remain the same. Prices can go down. What we are interested in as individuals is not whether all prices are high or low. We are interested in the relative differences in prices. We are particularly interested in the relationship between the prices that contribute to our income and the prices of what we want to buy. The man who makes shirts is primarily interested in the relationship of the price of cotton cloth to the price of shirts. If one goes up, market competition tends to send the other up. If they go up or down together, it does not affect him. If, after he has manufactured shirts with, say, 25 cent cotton, the price of shirts goes down because a decrease in the "money supply" has raised the purchasing power of money, he need not lose any of his business capital, because he can replace his raw material at a lower price. However, if the price of shirts goes down and the price of cotton cloth goes up, he is hurt. On the other hand, if the price of shirts goes up and the price of cotton cloth goes down, he may temporarily make a high profit.

It is the relationship between different prices that interests us. We do not need any more money to determine the relative values of various goods and services. As was said in Lecture V (especially pages 147 and 160-161), any quantity of money is sufficient to do for society all that any other quantity of money can do – facilitate mutually advantageous transactions. When you increase the quantity of money, you only help those who receive it first at the expense of those who do not. An increase in the quantity of money does not help society. Those who advocate an increase in international reserves, such as the SDRs, are merely trying to get something for politicians at the expense of others — the producers and savers upon whom our civilization rests.

Credit Expansion Without Central Banks

Q. Do you think you could prevent the banks from creating money by expanding credit even if there were no central banks? If so, how?

A. Well, the question is, do you think *you* could prevent credit expansion in the absence of central banks? With all modesty, I must say I could not. No one person could. This is an educational problem. It requires general acceptance. Unfortunately, some people may have to lose their savings before they learn the lesson. If their bank deposits were not insured by the government and depositors suffered losses from putting their money in banks that expanded credit, they would soon learn. In a free economy, people would soon learn not to put their money in banks that cannot be trusted. There would be competition among banks for deposits based on the soundness of each bank's policies. This would require a considerable change in present-day thinking. Some people now profiting from political privilege would undoubtedly suffer, as they must temporarily in any move toward a free society, because a free society means the elimination of special privileges. In the end, and it would not take long, the failure of a few banks would soon reveal credit expansion as the reason why the depositors in such banks had lost their money. People would soon learn not to put their money in banks that expanded credit.

When I was a youngster, people in my country were very careful about putting their money in banks. In the early days, few working men used banks. This was largely due to the fact that they did not understand them. People should not use things they do not understand. Before the New Deal, we had in our country double liability for bank stockholders. If a bank failed, the stockholders were called upon to put up additional sums equal to the amount of money they had previously invested in bank stock. For example, if they held a

$100 par share and the bank failed, they could be assessed another $100. This made them watch the bank's operations carefully. Depositors also watched the banks carefully. Under such free market conditions, the consumers are sovereign. Bank failures will then be limited, because bad bankers will attract neither investors nor depositors.

On Safe Savings

Q. In your opinion what is today the safest way to save in the long run?

A. That is a question people ask me very regularly. As mentioned in answer to an earlier question, everyone is interested in trying to improve his situation. For most of us, this means trying to remove our uneasiness about inflation. This is a part of everyone's problems. I face it personally just as each one of you does.

Perhaps one of the most important conclusions to be drawn from these lectures is that *you cannot save yourself if the society goes down*. The problem is primarily one of saving the free market society – the capitalistic system. If the system fails, we shall all flounder.

Let me give you a quick and simple illustration. For centuries Christians were taught by their churches that lending money at interest was an immoral, unchristian action. So the money-lending business was left to the Jews. A number of them became the chief money experts of the world. Many of them realized what was happening in Germany in 1920, 1921, and 1922. They went into Germany and bought everything they could, paying 10, 15 or 20 percent down, and assuming mortgages or other debts for the balance. In 1923, when the mark went to zero, their debts were wiped out. These financially intelligent Jews then became the sole owners of most of the business enterprises and investments in Germany. They found a solution – a personal solution – for the inflation.

The Jews had not caused the inflation. It was not a Jewish plot. The inflation was produced by the German politicians in power after the war. They were trying to get out of what they considered the onerous terms of the Versailles Treaty. However, some intelligent Jews who understood what was happening sought to improve their situation financially. They were merely acting as all human beings do. They were using their knowledge and understanding to improve their situation from their viewpoint. In our first lecture, it was pointed out that this is the a priori reason for every human action.

Most Germans had thought they were improving their situation by placing their savings in banks, bonds, insurance annuities, mortgages, and other assets with fixed values in marks. When the mark collapsed, these innocent but financially ignorant German people lost all of their savings. The value of their life insurance policies was wiped out. Their government bonds were worthless. All their savings in German marks had evaporated. The savings of generations of thrift were wiped out. Then, all around them, they saw Jews profiting, getting rich, seemingly at their expense. Envy and resentment soon gave way to a strong tide of anti-Semitism. This in turn led to the election of Adolf Hitler and all the ugly results that flowed out of his dictatorship. A few fortunate Jews escaped from Germany, with or without their wealth, but many did not.

So if you find a way to profit from this inflation, or even to save what wealth you have, you can be sure you will be considered a public enemy by all the suffering people around you. If you have wealth while those around you are starving, your life will not be worth much. It will not be worth any more than the lives of the Jews in Germany during the final days of Hitler.

There are, of course, some things that are a better form of savings than others. I would have to say paper money is not one of them. Some people say buy stocks. Others say buy real estate. However, let us remember that you cannot just buy stocks. You have to buy particular stocks. Some may go up. Some may go down. The same is true of real estate. If I were to get facetious, I would advise you to buy 100 shares of the "Cost of Living Index." We can be sure *that* will go up!

The problem is one of saving the system. We are all in it

together. It is as though we were all out in a life boat in the middle of the ocean. If the boat goes down, being the richest man in the lifeboat will not save your life. It will not do you any good to own great wealth if the society is not saved. If one of you, or a few of you, could own or get title to all of Buenos Aires, it would be worthless to you without the co-operation of your fellowmen. The lights would go out. The gasoline pumps would not work. Your physical wealth would be completely without value without the social cooperation of your fellowmen. It is the free market society that must be saved.

Index Of Persons Cited

Altschul, Frank, 222
Anderson, Benjamin M., 181-182, 201 n., 203 n., 204n., 211
Aquinas, (Saint) Thomas, 29
Aristotle, 28
Benegas Lynch, Alberto, viii, xi, 1, 16
Böhm Bawerk, Eugen von, 16, 35-38, 41, 45, 75-86
Burgess, William Randolph, 221
Chandler, Lester V., 193, 197n., 204, 207n., 229-230
Churchill, Winston, 214
Coolidge, Calvin, 204, 206, 214, 216, 224-226
Crissinger, Daniel R., 201, 219-220
Durkin, Martin P., 118-120
Eisenhower, Dwight, 261-266, 270-271
Engels, Friedrich, 34
Ford, Henry, 57-58, 95-96, 145
Friedman, Milton, x, 170-171
Goethe, Johann Wolfgang, 156
Gossen, Hermann Heinrich, 39, 40
Hamlin, Charles S., 211-214, 217-221, 230
Harding, Warren G., 201
Hayek, Friedrich A. von, 284-285
Hazlitt, Henry, 20
Heller, Walter, x
Hoover, Herbert, 211, 231n., 237, 241, 277
Jevons, William Stanley, 40,41
Johnson, Lyndon B., 266-271, 289
Kennedy, John F., 266-271

Kemmerer, Edwin W., 230n.
Keynes, John Maynard, 18-19, 21-22, 130-131, 177-178, 261, 284
Krug, J.A., 253-254
Lenin, Nikolai, 67, 177-178
Lincoln, Abraham, 175-176
Locke, John, 16
Malthus, Thomas R., 31
Marshall, George C., 251
Martin, William McChesney, 247-249
Marx, Karl, 19, 22, 33-39, 49, 67, 101, 109, 116-117
Mellon, Andrew, 201, 205, 206, 212, 216-217
Menger, Carl, 40, 41
Mill, John Stuart, 25
Miller, Adolph C., 191n., 197-198, 212, 217, 219, 227, 229n., 230-231
Mills, Ogden, 219
Mises, Ludwig von, i-iii, viii-xi, 1, 2, 7, 10, 16, 22, 28, 35, 39, 41, 75, 102, 191, 284-285, 289
Montaigne, Michel E. de, 28, 29
Moreau, Emile, 218, 221-222
Morgan, J.P., 198, 207
Morgenthau, Henry Jr., 245
Mutt & Jeff, 180
Napoleon I, 189
Napoleon III, 150
Norman, Montagu, 205-209, 219-220
Pound, Roscoe, 120
Read, Leonard E., 23
Ricardo, David, 29-30

Rist, Charles, 219
Richberg, Donald, 117-118
Robbins, Lionel, 215
Robey, Ralph, 216n., 217n., 224n.
Rogge, Benjamin A., 59n.
Roosevelt, Franklin Delano, 211, 237-246, 250
Root, Elihu, 190-191
Rueff, Jacques, 283
Schacht, Hjalmar, 219
Smith, Adam, 11, 29, 66, 111
Strong, Benjamin, 193, 198, 204-207, 210-213, 218, 220-222, 226
Truman, Harry S, 118, 251-260, 277
Voltaire, François M.A. de, 28-29
Walras, Léon, 40, 41
Washington, George, 14
Webster, Pelatiah, 176-177
White, William Allen, 225
Willis, H. Parker, 212-213, 225-226
Wilson, Woodrow, 211

Index Of Subjects

Advertising, 24-25
Agriculture, 199, 251-255
A priori postulates, 10-13
Argentina, 288-289, 290
Austrian school of economics, 40-41, 76
Banks/banking: central, 188, 278-279, 292-293; development of, 183-187, 278-279, 281-282, 286-287. *See also* Federal Reserve System
Barter. *See* Exchange, direct
Bimetallism, 149-153
Capitalism, development of, ii
Change, 28, 48-49, 54, 145-146, 151, 158-159, 161-165
Classical school of economics, 29-31, 35, 66, 76
Communism, 60-61, 65, 89, 96-97. *See also* Marxism; USSR
Competition, 76-88, 94-96, 99-100, 111-112
Consumer sovereignty, 76, 81-86, 90-91, 94, 103-104, 109-111, 114-115, 129
Cooperation, social, ii, 66-68, 129-130, 274-275
Credit expansion, 179-182, 187-195, 227-231. *See also* Banks/banking; Speculation
Deduced postulates, 13-18, 42-52
Deficit spending, 270-274, 286, 287, 288. *See also* Monetary history, U.S. (govt. securities)
Deflation, 234-237

Depressions/recessions, iv-vi, 175-231, 234-237, 239-243, 268-270, 279-281
Devaluation, 238
Economic calculation, 67, 88-91, 96-97, 155-157
Economic fallacies: "Mathematical economics," 42, 46-47, 61, 261; "Stability," 168, 170-171, 181, 262
Economic goods, 40-52, 68-69, 145-148, 157-159. *See also* Money.
Economic laws, 75-76, 151-154, 260. *See also* Postulates, economic; Price, law of
Economic power, 117-118. *See also* Consumer sovereignty
Economic problem, 15-16, 68-69
Economics, 1-20, 23
Economics, defined, 6-10, 283
Education: public, 133-134, 137; role of, 23-24, 276-278, 289-290; textbook fallacies, 163-164
Employment Act of 1946, 151n., 260-261
Encyclicals, Papal — on economics, 173
England, vi, 205-210, 214-215, 217-220
Entrepreneurs/businessmen, role of, 67, 114-115
Exchange: direct (barter), 33, 72-75, 141-142; indirect (monetary), 33, 76-86, 144,

157-158, 274-275; voluntary, 49-52, 54, 66-86

Federal Reserve System: fractional reserves, 187-198, 233-241, 246-247, 263-265, 278-279, 281-282, 286-287; gold reserve requirements, 189, 263-265; history of, 187-231, 233-274; "needs of business," flexible "money supply," 188-193; Open Market Committee, 212, 220-221

Foreign aid, 201-202, 246, 250-256

France, vi, 149-150, 189, 217-219, 221-222

Free market economy, 4-5, 19-20, 21, 49-52, 54, 66-71, 100-101, 103, 106-108, 112, 274-278, 294-295

Freedom, 17-18, 21-25, 107-108

Germany, vi, 166, 188, 201-203, 219, 291-292

Gold exchange standard, 283

Gold movements, 152-154, 174, 217-218, 220, 238, 246, 262-263, 265-268, 269

Gold production, 150, 160-161, 172

Gold standard, ii-iii, 148, 153-154, 160-161, 167, 168-169, 209, 278, 279-280

Golden rule, 50, 62, 94, 106-108, 132, 142, 167, 274

Government, role of, 53, 56, 66, 108, 133, 159

Government intervention, vi-vii, 52-54, 56-57, 94-96, 98-101, 127-129; price and wage controls, 100, 102-103, 132-133, 256-257, 275-276; pro-labor, 105-132. *See also* entries referring to specific forms of government intervention

Gresham's law, 152-154

Hampered market economy. *See* Government intervention

Ideas/ideologies, importance of, 2-4, 16-19, 24, 68, 175-176, 289-290

India, 127

Inflation defined, 174, 178-181

Inflation, effects of: artificial prosperity, 191-192, 197, 210-211, 217, 222-226, 229-231, 266-270; destruction of savings and market economy, 130-131, 274-278, 290-292; higher prices and wages, 130-132, 146-148, 164-165, 170-171, 187, 210-211, 261; malinvestment, 164-166, 182, 187, 198-199, 205, 249-250; social unrest, 135-137, 176-178, 275-277

Inflation, politics and, 167, 204-205, 207-209, 216-217, 256-260, 266-268

Inflation, stages of, 165-166, 182. *See also* Monetary history, U.S.

Interest: rates/discounts, "manipulation" of, 190-193, 197, 203, 209-210, 213-214, 216, 219, 220-222, 227-229, 234-237; theory, time preference and, 14, 36-38, 170-171, 183

International Monetary Fund (IMF) and Bretton Woods, 281, 285

International trade, 134-135, 148, 152-154, 174, 198-201, 214-215. *See also* Foreign aid; Gold movements

"Just" or "natural" price idea, 29-33

Korea, 257-260

Labor: division of, specialization, 66-68; government and, 237-238, 239-245, 256-259, 260-261; union policies, effects of, 116-129, 130-133, 135, 214-215, 241-245, 257-259; wage rates and employment,

57-58, 105-132, 132-133, 135-137, 138-139, 242, 284
Labor theory of value, 29-38, 116-118
Laissez faire, 274-275
Latin Monetary Union, 150-151
Malinvestment. *See* Inflation
Marginal utility, 40-42, 44-47, 158-159, 164-166. *See also* Value scales
Market. *See* Free market economy
Market exchange postulates, 70-71
Marxism, 19, 31-34, 38-39, 49, 109, 116-117, 175, 288
Methodology, for advancing freedom, 18-19, 21, 23-24, 133-134, 167, 276-278, 289-290
Methodology, of economics, 6-10, 13, 20, 44, 46-47, 61, 89, 172, 283
Monetary history, U.S., 175-231, 233-278; American Revolution, 176-177; 19th century, 149-151; Federal Reserve System established, 187-193; govt. securities (debt), holdings of, 194-198, 203-204, 212, 216, 226, 235-239, 246-249, 250, 270-274, 278-279, 286-287, 288; World War I through 1929, 193-231; post 1929, through World War II, to 1969, 233-274. *See also* Depressions; Federal Reserve System; Inflation
Monetary theory of the trade cycle, 141-167, 175-231 (esp. 187), 284-285
Money: cash holdings, hoardings, 147-148, 157-165, 170, 280-281; definition and role of, xii, 141-145, 153-154, 157-159, 162-167, 178, 181-182, government and, 159-161, 164-166, 231, 238,

274-278; non-neutrality of, 161-162, 164-165; theory of, 141-167, 282-283; value of, 157-159, 162, 164-165, 172. *See also* Banks/banking; Federal Reserve System; Gold standard; Inflation
Monopoly/oligopoly, antitrust laws, 94-96, 98-99, 173
National Recovery Administration (NRA), 128, 241-243
Note du Havre (May 29, 1810), 188-189
Paper gold, SDRs, 160, 174, 275, 285
Paradox of value, 31, 47
Postulates, economic: a priori, 10-13; deduced, 13-18, 42-52; market exchange, 70-71
Prices/pricing, 29-30, 33-38, 65-91, 92, 99-100, 101-102, 168, 172, 179, 222-223; law of price, 76-81, 85-86. *See also* Value; Value scales
Profit, psychic, 49-51, 54, 69-71
Profits/losses, 37, 91, 99-100, 102, 104, 111-112, 115, 124
Pump priming, 237-241
Rent control, 100
Savings: effects of, 63, 90-91, 92, 113-115, 127-128; inflation and, 290-292; labor unions and, 122-126, 135
Socialism, *See* Communism; Economic calculation; Marxism; USSR
Social Security Act, 239
Speculation: credit expansion and, 209-229, 233-92-93, 101-102. *See also* Interest rates/discounts, "manipulation" of
Stock market. *See* Speculation
Sweden, 100
Taxes: effects of, 52-53, 60, 86-88, 96, 137-138; progressive, 54-56, 61-62

USSR, 65, 96-97, 100, 155-156,
    169-170
Value, 9, 27-54, 67-70, 89, 94
Value scales, 42-46, 48-52, 70-76,
    90-91, 92-93

Value theory, history of, 29-36,
    38-42, 66-68
Velocity of circulation, 280
"Welfare" policies, 56-57, 62-63
Youth, attitudes of, 59

The Ludwig von Mises Institute

The Ludwig von Mises Institute, founded in 1982, is the research and educational center of classical liberalism, libertarian political theory, and the Austrian School of economics. Working in the intellectual tradition of Ludwig von Mises (1881-1973) and Murray N. Rothbard (1926-1995), with a vast array of publications, programs, and fellowships, the Mises Institute, with offices in Auburn, Alabama, seeks a radical shift in the intellectual climate as the foundation for a renewal of the free and prosperous commonwealth.

The Ludwig von Mises Institute
518 West Magnolia Avenue
Auburn, Alabama 36832
Mises.org